Deserters of the First World War

Deserters of the
First World War

The Home Front

ANDREA HETHERINGTON

Pen & Sword
MILITARY
AN IMPRINT OF PEN & SWORD BOOKS LTD.
YORKSHIRE - PHILADELPHIA

First published in Great Britain in 2021, and reprinted in this format in 2023 by
PEN & SWORD MILITARY
An imprint of
Pen & Sword Books Ltd
Yorkshire - Philadelphia

ISBN 978 1 52679 890 9

Typeset in Ehrhardt MT & 11.5/14
by SJmagic DESIGN SERVICES, India.

Printed in the UK on paper from a sustainable source by
CPI Group (UK) Ltd, Croydon, CR0 4YY

Pen & Sword Books Ltd incorporates the imprints of Pen & Sword Archaeology, Atlas, Aviation, Battleground, Discovery, Family History, History, Maritime, Military, Naval, Politics, Social History, Transport, True Crime, Claymore Press, Frontline Books, Praetorian Press, Seaforth Publishing and White Owl

For a complete list of Pen & Sword titles please contact

PEN & SWORD BOOKS LTD
47 Church Street, Barnsley, South Yorkshire, S70 2AS, England
E-mail: enquiries@pen-and-sword.co.uk
Website: www.pen-and-sword.co.uk

Or

PEN AND SWORD BOOKS
1950 Lawrence Rd, Havertown, PA 19083, USA
E-mail: Uspen-and-sword@casematepublishers.com
Website: www.penandswordbooks.com

Contents

Acknowledgements

There are many people to thank for their part in ensuring this book made it to publication. The manuscript was a year late, so my first thanks are due to Rupert Harding, Alison Flowers and all at Pen & Sword for their infinite patience and understanding.

I feel very lucky to have been able to take advantage of the comradeship and expertise of scholars at the University of Leeds, especially Anne Buckley, Alison Fell, Jessica Meyer, Ingrid Sharp and Claudia Sternberg. Along with Lucy Moore of the Leeds Museums Service, they have been incredibly supportive over the last few difficult years in particular and I am eternally grateful to them all. Beyond Leeds, Rachel Duffett has been a wonderfully encouraging voice during the lonely writing phase of the project.

Thanks must go to those who, sometimes unknowingly, through conversations, suggestions, questions and comments have informed the structure and content of the book. Susan Grayzel, Toby Haggith, Edward Madigan, Cyril Pearce, Tom Thorpe and Richard van Emden all gave me faith that this was a book worth writing.

Thanks, as usual, are due to the library and archive staff who have made research a joy. Leeds Central Library, The National Archives, the British Library at Boston Spa and Special Collections at the University of Leeds have treasures behind the desk as well as on the shelves.

I want to thank everyone who has given me practical support, from my family who were willing to drop everything for me when required, to friends who have given me lifts and lifted my spirits. Linda Gilhespy showed even more patience than usual and deserves a medal.

Finally, I must thank Dr Nicola Bell and Mr Kenan Deniz for their care and skill. Without their combined talents I would not be in a position to write this book or any others.

Plates

Introduction

The centenary period saw an explosion of works on many hitherto neglected topics yet the history of deserters from the British and Dominion forces remains largely unexamined. A number of books have been published about the men who were executed by the British Army for offences which may have included desertion, but the concentration on this very small number of men obscures the reality that there were many thousands of individuals who defaulted on their military obligations. Most deserters did not walk away from trenches in France and Belgium but strolled out of military camps in Britain or did not return from leave.

Most deserters were not shot at dawn but were given periods of detention of varying lengths. Unlike the British soldiers executed by their own comrades during the war, no one has campaigned for these deserters and absentees to be pardoned and their stories have remained largely hidden. Disapproval after the war meant that they were not keen to publicize their misdemeanours as they faced enough of a struggle to re-establish themselves within the civilian community without identifying themselves as deserters. The story of these men has remained untold.

Between 4 August 1914 and 31 March 1920 – the official end of the war, there were 141,115 courts martial held in respect of officers and men from the British and Dominion forces at home, with 82,423 of these being prosecutions for desertion and absence without leave.[1] By way of comparison, in the year up to September 1913 there were just under 5,000 courts martial in total in the British Army at home **and** abroad.[2] Desertion and absence was much more prevalent on the home front during the war, constituting around 58 per cent of courts martial in comparison with 26 per cent of prosecutions by the British Army abroad.[3] Persistent deserters were often sent across the Channel during the war, desertion on the front line being more difficult and dangerous than at home.

These figures considerably underestimate the numbers who did absent themselves during this period, as not every offender would have been caught and not every arrestee would have been court-martialled. Many were punished by their commanding officer directly and therefore do not appear in the official statistics, a practice that still takes place, resulting in a considerable discrepancy in the numbers of soldiers deserting when compared with those who face courts martial.[4] The names of deserters and absentees, along with their descriptions and other information taken from their enlistment forms, appeared in the *Police Gazette* every week to hasten their arrest. The 11 August 1914 edition contained eighty-one names from the Regular and Territorial armies, all of whom had gone missing from the army in July and the first three days of August 1914. The edition of the circular printed on 26 January 1915 listed 918 deserters, a massive increase in less than 6 months. Names continued to appear at a rate of around 1,000 a week during the war years, whilst the equivalent list of men who had returned or were no longer sought rarely ran to more than 100 per edition.

The official statistics show that the loss to the British Army alone from desertion during the war was 114,670 men up to January 1919, though it was claimed that many of them had re-joined the services. Though they may have re-joined, there were always others ready to walk away and the net loss to the British and Dominion forces from desertion up to the same date was 70,189. Another 20,000 men would absent themselves during 1919.[5] Had this number been killed in a particular action it would take its place in the pantheon of notorious battles alongside the Somme and Passchendaele: as it is, the huge number of deserters and absentees are barely spoken of at all. The truth is that desertion and absence were an everyday part of army life and of the experience of many thousands of British and Dominion soldiers.

From disappointment with training camps to disillusionment at the slow pace of demobilization, men deserted from all over the United Kingdom during the entirety of the war and beyond. Desertion of this magnitude required a significant amount of collusion from civilians on the home front, from family members who were complicit in helping men hide to less than scrupulous employers who would provide them with the means of existence once their army pay was cut off. Those deserters who could not sustain themselves by semi-legitimate means turned to crimes of all kinds, many utilizing the uniform they were so keen to be free from. The stationing of Dominion troops in Britain provided a more exotic breed of deserter on the home front. For some this front was very familiar whilst for others it was a land of opportunity waiting to be explored, putting soldierly duties to one side. Conscription introduced a new category of deserter as men quietly slipped away from their homes to avoid being drafted into the armed services, many finding a temporary home in Ireland where the ambiguous status of the British Army made detection more difficult, both practically and politically. Some home-front deserters would pay for their transgressions with their lives, executed by firing squad after being transported across the Channel for court-martial.

Telling deserters' stories has involved a great deal of detective work, piecing together fragments of information to trace these men's lives and motivations. Local newspapers were keen to report on the appearances of deserters before civilian courts during the war and have proved a rich research source. With any war related news at a premium, such hearings were often reported in detail. Though a court martial on the home front was technically open to the public, it was rarer for journalists to follow the case to its conclusion especially as the military hearing may take place well away from the location of the civil court appearance. Men handed over by the civilian courts as deserters were not always court-martialled and even if they were, did not necessarily find themselves convicted of desertion. The destruction of a significant amount of First World War material, accidentally in the case of service records destroyed in the Blitz, and deliberately in the case of court-martial records quietly disposed of in the years following the Second World War, makes stories difficult to follow to a conclusion. This means that the mention in this book of a man's name as a civilian court prisoner does not automatically mean that he was convicted as a deserter by a military court. The focus of this book is on deserters from the army as the vast majority of recruits served with that branch of the services. The navy often had different procedures and naval deserters often did not have to make court appearances, thereby depriving the local newspapers of reporting on their capture.

Sources purporting to be verbatim accounts from soldiers themselves often fail to include their misdemeanours. Men who wanted to leave a record of this kind were unlikely to want their misconduct recorded for posterity. The fact that some are from many years after the war also leads to potential credibility issues. The same reservation applies to the contemporary accounts given by deserters before civilian and military courts but at least these have the advantage of immediacy. Some will have undoubtedly told the courts what they thought they wanted to hear, but others clearly continued to defy authority in their court pronouncements and in their subsequent behaviour.

The reframing of all Britain's First World War soldiers as heroes has left little room for consideration of the less than heroic aspects of their service. In *Dismembering the Male*, Joanna Bourke notes that 'in war the mere fact of dying was ennobling'.[6] As part of this process the 309 soldiers shot at dawn have now been remade into martyrs who were all suffering from shell shock and were unlawfully killed. The other extreme is to consider all deserters as cowards. Neither of these positions is particularly helpful in understanding desertion as the truth is much more complex. It is impossible to know how many deserters suffered from shell shock. Not only do court-martial records not survive but the unfortunate destruction of many service records makes any study incomplete. Desertion on the home front cannot so easily be equated with cowardice – deserters came from all units, including those marked for home service only. Half of those fighting on the British side in the First World War were volunteers and official desertion figures did not increase when conscription was introduced despite the number of reluctant soldiers now in the ranks.

Joanna Bourke sees front-line desertion as a manifestation of 'malingering' – pretending to be unfit for duty – and equates this with workers seeking to take advantage of compensation payments for industrial accidents. Home-front desertion sits far more comfortably alongside industrial absenteeism, something with which the British worker has always been familiar. Failing to turn up for work has a long cultural history. Mondays were so notorious for poor attendance with men taking extra days to make up for time spent drinking over the weekend that the expression 'St Monday', sometimes known as 'Cobbler's Monday', was coined for the day in the late eighteenth century. The prevalence of these colloquialisms is an indication of the regularity of the occurrence of absenteeism in the workplace. This absenteeism went on during the war, the lack of industrial productivity as a result seen as a threat to Britain's war effort. Special Absentee Committees were formed around the country with the aim of reducing the figures by simple appeals to workers' better natures, without much success.[7] The taking of 'French leave' was an established practice amongst workers generally, not just soldiers. E.P. Thompson wrote that the factory system demanded 'a transformation of human nature . . . until the man is adapted to the discipline of the machine'.[8] Industrialized warfare meant that the British Army was one such machine and all must be moulded to its requirements. Those who could not be so shaped sometimes responded with desertion.

The proliferation of soldiers' terms for less than perfect service is telling. There were plenty of phrases to describe evasion of duty, from half-hearted performance to outright desertion, suggesting not just the frequency of such behaviour but also its cultural acceptance within the ranks. 'Coming the old soldier', 'dodging the column', 'swinging the lead' were all colloquial terms for evading duties, whilst 'doing a guy' or 'doing one's nut' meant desertion, and trying to evade the war by semi-legitimate means 'working one's ticket'.[9] Learning to be cunning was part of military life. Tolerance of slacking came from men's experience not just in the army but in wider society. Men brought with them ways of behaving that they were accustomed to in civilian life. The army was seen as an employer like any other and an authority to be outwitted. 'Shirking' was an ingrained part of army life, and absenteeism was ingrained in working life – desertion was the point at which they met.

Soldiers were obviously in a very different position to the ordinary worker, but whilst the vast majority in the army were volunteers, the underlying mentality remained the same. When working conditions were deemed unacceptable, the withdrawal of labour was still held as a right by some who were now in khaki: desertion, either alone or with others, was the exercize of that right. Soldier miners on the Western Front downed tools until they received the extra pay promised to them: soldier miners on the home front absented themselves when camp conditions became intolerable. It is notable that when J. Scott Duckers was imprisoned as a conscientious objector, he came across a number of military prisoners who would tell him with some pride that they were in custody for 'striking' when they were serving sentences for desertion and absenteeism.[10]

Deserters appearing before the courts would sometimes refer to their periods of absence as 'holidays'. There were no holidays in the army, just short periods of leave, granted irregularly and not guaranteed. Men who felt the need would absent themselves when they wanted a break. John Brophy and Eric Partridge say that men went sick to escape 'the irrationality, pettiness and the maddening repetitions of military life' and men would desert for the same reasons.[11]

The production of wartime postcards making a joke of desertion is another indication of its place within popular culture. Alongside the sentimental photographic postcards to husbands and wives and images demonizing the Hun appeared several comic cards depicting absenteeism. No scorn was heaped on the absentee – unlike the conscientious objector when he appeared in postcard form – and the crime was trivialized.

The reasons for a man's desertion were as varied as the reasons for his original enlistment. The British Army's own *Manual of Military Law* advised that a number of factors played into the decision to desert, not cowardice per se, stating that offences like desertion were often committed 'not from any want of moral character or any reluctance to serve, but from some discontent, or from association with bad companions, or from sudden and special temptation inducing the man to absent himself.'[12] Family problems, money trouble, issues within the existing battalion, conscience and criminality all play their part in our story. Whilst some making themselves absent had seen no action other than fighting in the local pub on a Saturday night, some had been to the Front and served with distinction. Others would return there after their punishment for desertion and give no further cause for complaint. Categorizing these men as 'shirkers' or 'cowards' does not come close to telling the whole story of the home-front deserter. As Robert Roberts said in his memoir of growing up in Salford during the war, 'it requires courage both to join an army and to desert it'.[13] This is not, then, a book about cowardice, but about the conflict between military law and human nature.

Chapter 1

Desertion and the Transition to War – Amnesties and King's Bad Bargains

I am willing to serve my country still, but what chance has a man got when he gives himself up to be put on a shilling a week until he pays for the kit?

Letter to the *Yorkshire Evening Post*,
11 August 1914

Desertion had always been a problem in the British Army. Traditionally recruited from the lowest classes of society and with harsh conditions and poor rates of pay, the army was not an attractive choice of career for men who could aspire to be no more than ordinary soldiers. In the years between 1868 and 1898, between 1,500 and 2,000 men were charged with desertion each year. The actual figures of desertion are likely to be much higher than this – perhaps three times as high – as many men were not caught or desertions not recorded as such.[1] In those less bureaucratic times, identification documents were not required and the most that could be done to find a deserter was to publish his details in the *Police Gazette* and visit his family periodically to see if he had returned home.

Desertion on active service was technically punishable by a death sentence, though this rarely occurred. Imprisonment or penal servitude of various lengths was the usual penalty at a court martial, and, after 1906, detention was also introduced as a less serious level of incarceration. Until the latter part of the nineteenth century deserters could also be branded and flogged.[2] Victorian recruits signed up for twelve years so arguably the most meaningful punishment for a deserter was that the service clock started at zero on his arrest. The erasure of previous service would represent a significant deterrent to those who had been in the army for some years and may explain why most deserters were those with less than two years' service.[3] A deserter could have his punishment commuted wholly or partly by being taken back into the fold for general service and potentially transferred to a different unit.[4] For soldiers who committed offences in the United Kingdom, the use of this power could mean transfer abroad in cases where there was 'a prospect of his being converted into a good soldier'.[5] A number of army reforms were informed by the need to reduce desertion figures. 'Short service' was introduced in the 1870s, though this still entailed signing up for a period of six years. Improvements in barracks facilities, deferred lump sums payable on discharge and education programmes were all introduced to keep soldiers in the army. In 1898 there were 4,107 men struck off the strength as deserters: by 1913 the number had fallen to just under 3,000.[6]

The *Manual of Military Law* (*MML*) rather unhelpfully defined desertion as 'deserting or attempting to desert His Majesty's service'. Essentially, the offence was all about the intention of the soldier. If he left his unit with no intention to return at all, or to avoid some specific duty, he would be guilty of desertion. Other aspects of the offence, like the distance he had travelled and the length of time he had been missing, were mere evidential aids to a tribunal in deciding whether a man had deserted or not. The *MML* used the example of a man found in plain clothes on a steamer for America as one where desertion would clearly be made out. Equally however, a man who did not even leave the barracks but concealed himself there until his regiment left for overseas service would be guilty of desertion though he had travelled no distance at all. The *MML* specified that a man should not be charged with desertion unless there was evidence of such intention to quit, and if there was any doubt he should be charged with the lesser offence of absence. Absence without leave was defined as:

> Such short absence, unaccompanied by disguise, concealment, or other suspicious circumstances, as occurs when a soldier does not return to his corps or duty at the proper time but on returning is able to show that he did not intend to quit the service, or to evade the performance of some service so important as to render the offence desertion.[7]

The distinction between absence and desertion was a fine one and was not applied consistently. In many cases the two terms were entirely interchangeable depending on the attitude of a man's commanding officer, the specifics of the offence, the abilities of the soldier, the make-up of a court martial and many other random considerations now lost from the records. The benefit of the doubt was to be given to the soldier, absence without leave to be preferred to desertion if there was room to do so, and room was very often found.

Men who left their original corps and enlisted in another were technically deserters, but the instructions to commanding officers in the *MML* were clear that generally such men were not to be charged with the offence of desertion unless there was evidence of this. Instead they should be charged with fraudulent enlistment, as they had lied on their attestation forms when asked about previous military service. It was also a criminal offence, punishable by the civilian courts by up to three months' imprisonment, to pose as a deserter.[8] This may on the face of it seem like a very strange thing to do, but destitute and homeless men sometimes did so to obtain a few days' accommodation and food until the army determined that they did not belong there and kicked them out again.

Once a man had been missing for twenty-one days, the army would hold a court of enquiry to establish that he was a deserter, then he would be struck off the strength and his details passed to the *Police Gazette* for publication. Once arrested the man would be taken to the local Magistrates' Court (also known as Police Courts) where he would usually be declared a deserter and handed over to the military authorities. An escort would be sent to collect him and he would then return to his regiment and await his punishment. The 'Form of Descriptive Return' (Army Form O1618) was issued to the civilian courts dealing with deserters. In addition to the usual questions about the man's name and physical characteristics, the form asked whether the man was apprehended in uniform or in plain clothes, and whether he had surrendered or was arrested. The 'fullest possible details' were to be provided to enable the army to decide what charge, if any, should be preferred and to assist at a court martial should one take place. It was incumbent on the prosecution at court martial to outline the circumstances of a man's arrest in full as this may have a bearing on whether he was convicted of desertion or absence without leave. The clerk of the civilian court at which the deserter appeared was paid 2*s.* for every descriptive return form sent to the army to encourage them to provide this information.

Soldiers arrested for desertion regularly pleaded that they were absentees, not deserters. The death penalty was not available for the offence of being absent without leave. Absentees were much less likely to have to face court-martial proceedings in the first place as the summary powers available to both a company commander and the next level up, the commanding officer, allowed for a range of punishments to be given that stopped short of imprisonment. An absentee could receive no more than twenty-eight day's detention under these powers of summary disposal with the other punishments available being Field Punishment (being tied to an object either outside for a few hours a day in the case of No. 1, or inside for No. 2), confinement to barracks (known as 'C.B.' or 'Jankers') and forfeiture of pay.[9] Short sentences of detention – less than seven days – would be served in cells at the barracks, whilst soldiers serving longer periods were shipped out to military detention facilities dotted around the country. Soldiers guilty of absence only, unlike deserters, were not liable to have their previous service wiped out. For the army volunteer signing up from August 1914 onwards for the duration of the war, this would be less of a concern but for a Regular army soldier it was very important.

Summary disposal could be applied to charges of desertion, but the offence would have to be downgraded by a superior officer to being absent without leave before this could be done.[10] It was also possible to dispense with a court martial where a signed confession to desertion or fraudulent enlistment was made and the merits of the case could be met by the exercise of these summary powers of punishment.[11] Both deserters and absentees had their pay forfeited for every day of absence, and for every day of detention, Field Punishment, imprisonment or whilst in the custody of a civilian court. They were also liable to pay for every piece of their issued kit that was missing and for the cost of an escort to collect them.

Soldiers charged with desertion or absence and dealt with by a court martial on the home front were likely to face a District Court Martial where the maximum sentence for any offence was two years' imprisonment. 'Very aggravated offences', and all offences for officers, had to go before a General Court Martial where the available range of punishments was wider, including penal servitude for a minimum of three years and the death penalty.[12] There were almost 138,000 District Court Martials at home between August 1914 and April 1920. Only 3,120 General Courts Martial were held, the vast majority of them being for officers.[13] Abroad, all ranks were dealt with at a Field General Court Martial which had the same wide powers as its domestic equivalent. Punishments for being absent on the home front in practice ranged from docking of pay to imprisonment with the need to recycle manpower as the war went on determining the approach taken. Sentences of imprisonment or detention were reviewed by senior officers and often reduced or remitted to return men to service more quickly. Offences which looked very much like desertion were turned into absence instead so that they could be dealt with more expeditiously. Theoretically, whilst the country was at war, the death penalty existed for deserters whether they had walked away from a trench in France or from a parade ground in Aldershot, as the designation of being on active service applied to both situations. In practice the death penalty was not imposed for desertions that took place on home soil except in very limited circumstances to a few unlucky men.

Given the small size of Britain's peacetime army it was imperative to secure as many recruits in as short a time as possible when war was declared in August 1914. British Army reservists, some of whom were far from home, were immediately recalled to the colours. In Canada alone there were 3,232 British Army reservists of whom 153 serving in the standing Canadian Army were allowed to remain in the Dominion. Before the end of August 1914, 2,006 reservists had embarked on passenger steamers bound for England.[14]

The recall of the reservists went hand in hand with the massive recruiting drive for new soldiers that has been well documented. Less well known are the efforts the army and navy made to take back those who had deserted the forces in years gone by. With raw recruits taking months to train up, these experienced men could be extremely valuable if they would return. However, as things stood at the beginning of August 1914 they would face prosecution for desertion, potential imprisonment and the loss of their accumulated years of service if they came back. The answer was simple – an amnesty for all deserters if they handed themselves in.

On 8 August 1914 the following notice appeared in newspapers nationwide: 'The King has been pleased to approve of pardons being granted to soldiers who were in a state of desertion on August 5 and who surrendered themselves at home before September 4 and abroad before October 4'. Posters to this effect were displayed prominently all over the country to attract the eye of as many of these men as possible.

It should be noted that this pardon only applied to soldiers at this stage, not sailors as the Admiralty took its own course and did not announce an amnesty until 11 August. The cut-off date for the naval amnesty would later be extended in an acknowledgement that many sailors had jumped ship thousands of miles from their home bases.[15]

Instructions had already been given to the courts to send soldiers who had surrendered off to their regiments armed with a free railway pass rather than have them wait for military escorts. The police were now told not to take these men to court at all but to send them to their unit in the same manner. A telegram was to be sent to the commanding officer of the depot so he knew to expect the deserter's return.[16]

With the prospect of punishment no longer hanging over them, thousands of men returned to the colours from all over the world. Their motivations were mixed – some were no doubt fired up with patriotism now the country needed them, many re-joining before the official pardon was even announced. On the day war was declared deserters were reported as turning up at barracks and police stations nationwide, some having been missing for a long period of time. The *Hull Daily Mail* reported four men at Grimsby that day handing themselves in.[17] On 5 August 1914 Fred George Strong attended Dover Police Station and declared that he was a deserter from the Royal Marines. He had left HMS *Forth* in Plymouth in July 1913 and was now living with his wife in Margate. On the declaration of war he had sent his wife back to Plymouth and walked 20 miles from Margate to Dover to surrender himself.[18] In August 1914 1,776 non-commissioned officers and men returned to the army from desertion with a further 755 re-joining in September. These were the only two months of the entire war when the numbers returning from desertion exceeded those being struck off the strength for the same offence. The figure for returning soldiers plummeted to 401 in October, indicating that the boost in the earlier numbers was heavily influenced by the amnesty.[19]

For some returnees it appears that economics rather than patriotism was their motivation and their return was not always welcomed. Thomas Green appeared before the court at London Guildhall charged with being a 'rogue and vagabond', and proffered the information that he had deserted the army in 1909 and begged to be sent to a barracks.[20] Archibald Fletcher had deserted HMS *Amphion* in 1898 after three years' service in the navy and handed himself in to the authorities at Newcastle in August 1914. Fletcher is described in the report of his surrender as being of no fixed abode, meaning that a warm berth on a ship may have suddenly become more attractive.[21] Old deserters were a problem for both branches of the armed forces, but particularly for the navy, where significant advances in technology in recent years meant that the skills of these men were now hopelessly outdated. Archibald Fletcher's plan for a life at sea was thwarted when the navy sent word that they did not want him back. He would serve, but as a soldier not a sailor, joining the Inland Waterways section of the Royal Engineers.[22] Some of those surrendering had deserted before the latest batch of recruits was even born. Alfred Turner had deserted from his barracks in 1887 and had spent twenty-seven years on the run. Patriotism now compelled him to return and he claimed in court that he wanted to go to the Front. The army rejected his generous offer.[23] The Admiralty tried to stem the flow of useless men being sent back to port by decreeing that if a deserter had been missing for more than five years, he was not to be arrested, but his details taken and sent to them for consideration. The army, meanwhile, frequently sent notification to courts that individuals arrested as deserters should simply be released as the army had no further use for them.

Some surrendering deserters were what was known in the British Army as 'King's bad bargains' A King's (or Queen's) bad bargain was 'a man who refuses to soldier' and 'a perfectly useless man kept at the Queen's expense'.[24] King's bad bargains were men who spent more time in the guard room than the barrack room, constantly being charged with offences like drunkenness, acts of violence and general insubordination. They would intersperse this with periods of desertion or fraudulent enlistment and gave no value to the army at all. In peacetime they were regularly discharged as it was recognized that they were more trouble than they were worth. Despite the fact that the country was now at war, the army often did not see the need to take these men back.

Deserters living abroad struggled to get back to Britain quickly with the impact the war had on passenger shipping. Joseph Byrne deserted from HMS *Resolution* in 1908, remaining in America where the ship was docked when he decided he had had enough of seafaring. He had established a new life with a wife and two children and a career as a chauffeur. Assured by the British Consul in New York that there was an amnesty in place, he returned to Britain in March 1915. Byrne sailed into Liverpool on the *Arabic* along with forty-eight men in a similar position, all intending to give themselves up and join the fight. The passenger list included seventy-nine British seamen who had already experienced the war, having had their boats sunk by a German battleship. The other passengers had their first brush with the Germans on the voyage home as the ship was pursued for 30 miles by a submarine off the coast of Holyhead.[25]

For deserters like Byrne who now had families to support, their entitlement to separation allowance and pensions was of paramount importance. In the Edwardian army many had left, separation allowances were only granted to those who had married 'on the strength' – i.e. with the permission of their commanding officer. Only a small percentage of recruits was allowed to marry and for those who did so without permission, supporting a family was very difficult if the man was posted abroad. Indeed, a posting abroad was a reason why some men deserted and took jobs closer to home. A week after the outbreak of war a letter appeared in the *Yorkshire Evening Post* from 'One Anxious to Serve His King and Country':

Sir – I see by your paper that the King has issued a proclamation pardoning all deserters from the Regular forces. I deserted when my regiment left England for abroad. I was a married man off the strength with one child my pay being 6s per week owing to my being a third class shot. So if I had left my wife and child what was to become of them?

I am willing to serve my country still, but what chance has a man got when he gives himself up to be put on a shilling a week until he pays for the kit? Will my wife get her proper separation allowance if I give myself up before 4 September?[26]

It was now announced that all wives were to be entitled to separation allowance and, if the worst should happen, to a pension, so long as they were married at the time a man enlisted. This still left those deserters contemplating return under the amnesty in an ambiguous position as some may not have been married during their first stint in the forces. Eventually the rules were changed so that the timing of the marriage did not preclude a woman from receiving these benefits but allowances to wives and dependents would continue to be an issue for many families.[27]

The details of the deserters' amnesty did not reach all of those who had absented themselves from the colours over the years. Horace Hobbs, Boer War veteran, deserted from the 18th Hussars at York in 1906. In August 1914 he was working as a coal hoist foreman on the Aire & Calder Navigation Canal at Goole. Hobbs had heard about the amnesty but seemed to have missed the small detail that one had to hand oneself in to the authorities to benefit from its grace. Brought before the court as a deserter, Hobbs pleaded that he would have taken advantage of the amnesty but he believed it to be law that a man could not serve under two different monarchs. He was proven wrong and was in France by November 1914.[28] Not all old deserters felt the pull of patriotism. Appearing before the court in Loughborough in August 1914 for his desertion the previous November, David Noel Page was given the usual exhortation by the magistrates that he should now do his bit for king and country. Page was unmoved, telling them 'No – I don't want to fight. I wish I'd never joined the Army.'[29]

The thousands of deserters returning under the amnesty were joined by many thousands more answering their country's call. After a short time under army discipline, some of those recruits, like David Page, would regret their decision to enlist.

Chapter 2

Training Camp Troubles

Oh why did I come to Shoreham?
Oh why did I join the Army
Oh why did I join the Coldstream Guards?
I must have been bally well barmy!

Soldier's song

Lord Kitchener's call for 100,000 men to enlist was so successful that the brakes needed to be placed on recruitment within weeks as the War Office could not cope with the influx of volunteers. September 1914 saw the highest monthly recruitment figure of the entire war, when 462,901 men enlisted. Between the declaration of war and the end of 1914 over a million men presented themselves at the recruiting offices and were accepted for duty.[1] Accommodation, uniforms and weapons had to be found at short notice to equip the New Army, and the War Office was unable to keep up with the pace of recruitment. The result was that the conditions recruits were expected to endure were unsatisfactory to say the least. Lack of warm and dry accommodation, a lack of uniforms and most demoralising, a lack of adequate food caused great dissatisfaction amongst the ranks of volunteers.[2] Men who had joined up to become soldiers found themselves dressed in civilian clothes, or in rudimentary, ill-fitting uniforms known as 'Kitchener Blues', parading with wooden rifles. The material for the blue outfits had come from cloth stockpiled by the General Post Office and the colour tended to run in the rain. Corelli Barnett describes the New Army of late 1914 and much of 1915 as 'an unarmed, ill-housed shambles'.[3] Their initial enthusiasm ebbing away, some men responded to this situation by simply leaving the makeshift camps. From 4 August 1914 to the end of September that year, there were 666 court martials on the home front. Most were for drunkenness, but there were 157 prosecutions for absence or desertion in that short period of time.[4]

The 14th and 15th Battalions of the Durham Light Infantry (DLI) had been raised in September 1914 and their ranks were full of miners. The declaration of war had badly hit the coal industry of Northumberland and County Durham as the export market disappeared overnight and many pits were on short-time working or closed altogether until further notice. Michael Martin and seventeen of his colleagues from a Durham pit marched to the recruiting office together and joined up. Martin had no idea what was in store – 'I thought we were going to get three months' holiday and it would all be over.'[5] The miners soon found themselves transported hundreds of miles south to Buckinghamshire where they were to join the camp at Halton Park, residence of Alfred de Rothschild, wealthy banker and philanthropist. The mansion at Halton was built in the style of a French chateau, though the new soldiers were to live outdoors in the extensive grounds, not in the comfort of the house itself. Two battalions of the King's Own Yorkshire Light Infantry and battalions of the West Yorkshire, Lincolnshire and Northumberland Regiments were all at Halton Park by October 1914. The DLI arrived in the area at the end of September and was temporarily placed in billets in local villages until there was accommodation at Halton. The use of civilian homes as billets was widespread as there was simply no room to house all of the men who enlisted in the early part of the war. During the winter of 1914–15, 800,000 troops were billeted on civilians in Britain.[6] At this time, many of the Durham men had no military uniforms and none of them had weapons. After a short stay in billets, the DLI joined their colleagues at Halton Park.

The *Bucks Herald* described the new camp in glowing terms: 'A more delightful spot for a camp could not be imagined, and the charming surroundings prove an inexhaustible source of wonder to the North Country men and lads who make up the various units.'[7] The sudden influx of 13,000 men into this idyllic scene changed the picture. No huts had yet been built to accommodate the soldiers, though McAlpine & Co. had the contract to do so. Labour shortages, traffic congestion and a scarcity of timber all contributed to the delays in fulfilling the accommodation requirements of the New Army. Whilst describing Halton Park as delightful, the *Bucks Herald* simultaneously reported rumours that eleven recruits had died from ptomaine poisoning with many more taken ill, and that hundreds of men had deserted from camp as a result of the conditions. The Adjutant denied that there was any truth in this, though did admit that some men were sick.

As far as the desertions went, the rumours were true to some extent, as the next article in the paper described the appearance of two of these deserters before the local court. Two miners from the DLI had been found hiding in a haystack. William Elwood from South Shields and Joseph Palmer from

Durham were brought before the court as deserters and were forthright in their complaints about conditions at Halton. Palmer said he was happy to be in police custody as he was better treated there than he had been at camp, telling the court, 'I am willing to go and fight the Germans, but I want food and we can't get it at Halton. You can call me a deserter if you like . . . Since we have been at Halton Park we have been treated like dogs.' The police at Aylesbury reported that around eighty soldiers had deserted from the camp on one day, some leaving by train. At this stage, only about twenty had been apprehended, all with the same complaints over lack of food. Three more deserters had been arrested near Leighton Buzzard where they had woken a household by knocking on the door and begging for food. They denied deserting, claiming that they had left the camp simply to try and get something to eat.

The Durham contingent were not the kind of men prepared to place themselves at the mercy of the army where pay and conditions were concerned. They were miners, accustomed to organized protest and, if necessary, strike action to remedy their grievances. They took the same approach at Halton. Michael Martin remembers the incident well:

> We went on strike and got away with it . . . We stuck it out in camp . . . we were in tents, about fourteen in a tent and no duckboards and it was mud [*sic*]. Anyway one morning I was asked what was the matter with those men and I said 'Bloody food Poisoning' and he said 'Let us go home.' So men got their kit bags and from the tents to the gate would be about 900 yards. So this red hat came and asked us where are those men going and we said 'We are going home'. 'Go and tell them to come back', but thirty-eight got to Leighton Buzzard in Bedfordshire of our battalion. I don't know how many of other battalions. Now one fellow got home to Sunderland . . .[8]

The situation was clearly being downplayed by the army. A week after the articles in the *Bucks Herald* appeared it was reported that the War Office wanted to commandeer school buildings as emergency hospitals to deal with the sickness outbreak. Commanding Officer Brigadier General Fitzgerald confirmed to Aylesbury District Council that there had been three deaths at Halton but denied that this was due to camp conditions, or that the men were short of food: Fitzgerald claimed that any sickness was due to the men's lack of camping experience.[9] Stuart Cloete, newly commissioned into the King's Own Yorkshire Light Infantry, was at Halton at this time and attributes the deaths to cerebrospinal meningitis due to overcrowding in the tents, and to men dying of cold.[10]

The deserters, meanwhile, continued to trickle back via the local Magistrates' Courts. Edward Dodgson and John Doublye Frasher were detained at High Wycombe on 23 October, whilst it was reported on 31 October 1914 that two more deserters had been arrested in Buckingham.[11] Asa Watson of Dover and Joseph Clegge of Wath on Dearne, both from the Yorks and Lancs Regiment, had run away from Halton Park after only three days. They had travelled to Leighton Buzzard where they had tried fraudulently to enlist in the Royal Bucks Hussars. Both passed a medical but their deception was soon discovered when it was noticed that they were wearing Kitchener issue New Army shirts. In court they said they were prepared to go to the Front and fight but that they were 'half starved' at Halton Park and could stay there no longer.

When the weather took a turn for the worse in November, the 'charming surroundings' of Halton Park became intolerable. Rain meant that many of the tents on the lower lying parts of the estate were completely flooded, the huts were still not built and soon men were being moved out again to be billeted on the local villages. The DLI were not able to return to Halton Park until April 1915.

The Halton Park unrest was not the 14th DLI's only instance of mass defiance of authority on British soil. In September 1915 there was a minor riot at Witley shortly before the men were to go to France. Michael Martin again describes this as a 'strike', saying that one Friday the men remaining in camp decided they were not co-operating with orders. 'Nobody gets up when we are told and nobody got up and nobody got up for the cookhouse.' Men sacked the canteen for alcohol, rolling barrels of beer through the camp. Martin was assigned orderly room duties this weekend and soon found the windows being smashed in as the rampage continued. Officers eventually came to restore order, which seems to have been done by granting everyone 48 hours' leave. Martin recalls that there were only 120 men left as others had been given leave or taken it on their own initiative before the unrest began. Those with leave passes travelled to London, where a plan was hatched to take a longer break. Martin says: 'We got to King's Cross and some men from Murton said "Nobody comes back until next Saturday" and we all stopped absent for seven days. We got back on a Saturday morning and we were in France the same day. They couldn't try us because there were too many.'[12]

Once over the Channel, discipline would not be applied so leniently. Within the year Private William Nelson of the 14th DLI would be shot for desertion.[13]

It was difficult for the military authorities to prevent men from leaving their barracks if they were determined to do so. This was especially true when, like at Halton, the offence was committed en masse. Albert Williamson was in the navy based at Chatham, and on hearing that an order had been issued forbidding him and his fellow recruits from leaving barracks at all, wrote in his diary:

> Of all Barrack rules I do not suppose there is one which is more regularly and systematically broken, for every Saturday whole train loads of Jacks unblinkingly journey up to Town. Several attempts have been made to stop the Exodus but without avail. Even armed guards at the station scooping up whole train loads of barracks breakers and a wholesale stopping of leave seems to have produced no results and now the Naval Police seem to have abandoned the attempt in wrathful despair.[14]

Most of the curfew-defying recruits from Chatham and elsewhere, determined to have a weekend's entertainment, will have returned without difficulty, but some would have undoubtedly taken the opportunity for a longer absence. Robert Graves was in charge of a detachment of reservists at Lancaster who had joined up just before the war began and who resented being in the army longer than the usual two-week training camp they were familiar with. Graves claimed that this 'rough lot of Welshmen' were constantly deserting and having to be returned to barracks by the police. Graves made sure all of the exits were guarded but was puzzled that this did not stop the desertions. He then discovered that his men were climbing through a sewer to get away.[15]

Halton Park was not unique in the inadequacy of its facilities to feed, train and accommodate troops. Soldiers nationwide were being expected to endure conditions well below expectations and unrest like that seen at Halton took place in camps from Purfleet to Preston. When the periodical *John Bull* started a regular column in July 1915 called 'Tommy's Troubles' where soldiers' grievances were aired, most of the complaints were about food and shelter in training camps. Though new to soldiering, some of these men had experience of taking collective action – miners from South Wales went so far as to hold a protest march through the town of Preston to try to improve their conditions.[16] Ian Beckett identifies two distinct waves of unrest in 1914, one when troops first arrived at their camps and were confronted with the inadequacies, into which the Halton example fits, and secondly when the bad weather hit before the hutted accommodation could be built.[17] At Halton, it was this bad weather which saw the men moved out of the tents into billets before further protest could take place. Private billets were sometimes no better, the army being more concerned with obtaining a simple space for a soldier rather than worrying too much about its quality. When Henry Stephen appeared before the magistrates at Leigh in December 1914 charged with deserting from the 3rd South Lancashire regiment, he claimed it was the state of his billet which had caused him to leave. Stephen said he had returned to his sister-in-law's house to get himself clean, as the private house in Crosby in which he was billeted was verminous and unhealthy. The clerk to the court remarked that this was not the first time a deserter had made that complaint.[18] The army recognized that billets were generally disadvantageous to maintaining discipline amongst the troops and tried to decrease their use.[19]

The poor conditions in camp can be seen by the numbers of men contracting diseases of various kinds during this period. Between August and December 1914, 101,078 men from British and Dominion troops stationed in the United Kingdom were ill enough to be admitted to hospital; 789 of them died.[20] In a population where inoculation was not yet commonplace, diseases like measles swept through the ranks. One of the more serious outbreaks was at Bedford amongst the 51st Highland Division in 1914 where a whole battalion contracted measles with eighty-five of them dying.[21] Cases of pneumonia, pleurisy and influenza were common, in addition to the self-inflicted wounds of venereal disease. The army moved quickly to compel men to be vaccinated as there was considerable opposition to the practice amongst the rank and file. For the police trying to track down deserters, vaccination marks on a man in civilian clothing would soon become a telltale sign that he had recently been in the military.

For the early deserters, the poor conditions were undoubtedly a trigger as we have seen with the troops at Halton. Downing tools when conditions were not adequate was a practice ingrained in the miners and other trade unionists and the fact that the army was now their employer changed nothing. Neil Maclean, Labour MP and a former engineer, claimed in Parliament after the war that the new soldiers' 'whole outlook upon life was dominated by the outlook they had gained in the workshops' and that they did not easily adapt to military discipline.[22] Added to a lack of both weapons and uniforms, the situation may have led to a feeling amongst these new recruits that they were simply playing at soldiers, with an accompanying attitude to discipline. Michael Martin said he was expecting a 'holiday' and the seriousness of deserting may not have been appreciated by the volunteers. George Coppard's comrades in the Royal West Surrey Regiment had no fear over taking extra days on leave without permission prior to their deployment overseas in 1915. A rumour persisted that a soldier's record was wiped clean when he was sent abroad, resulting in Coppard and a number of his mates overstaying their leave. They had calculated that the punishment of seven days of 'jankers' was worth the sacrifice. Coppard records that so many men took 'French leave' that 'there were more defaulters than work to keep them busy'.[23]

There were certainly enough deserters and absentees to keep the civilian police busy. The Metropolitan Police Commissioner wrote to the War Office in early December 1914 to ask if it was possible to send deserters straight back to their units without the need for a court appearance, thereby adopting the same procedure as for the pardoned deserters in August. The War Office refused. In a letter dated 11 December 1914, they underlined that any desertion or absenteeism now was 'practically desertion on active service, which cannot be properly dealt with except by Court Martial'.[24] The War Office believed that absentees could not be trusted to make their own way back to barracks. The deterrent effect of a public appearance before a magistrates' court may also have been considered, these proceedings often being the only part of an alleged deserter's case that was reported in the newspapers. Local newspapers were vital to the life of many communities and enjoyed considerably larger circulations proportionally than the national newspapers in working class areas. For some recruits, being declared a deserter in such a public arena may well have brought a degree of embarrassment to themselves and their families. The police, stretched as they were in performing their ordinary peacetime duties under the extra pressure of war, wanted to rid themselves of the responsibility for processing deserters in this laborious manner. It was not until 1917 that the War Office relaxed the rules slightly, agreeing that a deserter or absentee **surrendering** to the police could be returned directly to the military: if he was **arrested**, then the usual rules applied and he must go to the local court first.[25]

The views of the police at the top of the organization often differ from those at the sharp end, and there were undoubtedly many police officers who were more than happy to spend their time chasing deserters due to the reward money on offer. When a deserter was brought before the civilian courts, the magistrates were able to grant a sum of money to the arresting officer ranging from 5s. to 20s. depending on 'the degree of trouble taken and the intelligence shown in effecting the arrest or in establishing the man's identity'.[26] Where the wanted man surrendered himself to the police, no reward money was meant to be given at all.[27] This money was for the individual officer concerned and it was his to keep. The army paid this sum, though it was in their power to decline to do so if they thought that the bounty should not have been offered or was excessive. *John Bull* was indignant on the routine grant of this sum to police officers who arrested men who may have committed no more serious an offence than overstay their leave by a day. Describing the payment as 'blood-money', the paper said that the process of arresting 'technical deserters' was 'undignified, and a sad waste of time'.[28]

Police pay was not high and did not rise at the same rate during the war as in other sectors. By late 1917 a police officer at the top end of the scale had seen his wages increase by 20 per cent to 48*s*. a week; labourers in the engineering industry were now earning 48*s*. 9*d*. a week having seen an increase of 113 per cent.[29] Arresting deserters was a handy income boost for a wartime police officer. Detective Drake of Halifax was one of many officers improving his pay in this way. When he brought deserter Horace Eastwood to court it was remarked that this was the third award of 10*s*. he had received in as many days. The *Yorkshire Evening Post* described Detective Drake as 'A man to be feared by deserters'.[30]

By the spring of 1915, the Army Council had concerns over the number of deserters and absentees at large on the home front. Men were now being granted leave from the front line and some were not returning. The ties of military comradeship and the threat of discipline lost some of their power when men returned to home and hearth, even temporarily. A man who would have never turned his back on his mates on the front line found it far easier to do so once he was at home. No positive act was required, just a failure to act. Sometimes a little extra encouragement was needed to make sure men returned to their barracks. The Revd Andrew Clark lived in Great Leighs in Essex and kept a diary throughout the war. He wrote that after his leave, local soldier Harry Hull was transported by pony and trap to Chelmsford train station accompanied by his brother and a friend with another friend cycling alongside 'to make sure of him'.[31]

There was a particular problem with men from the British Expeditionary Force who had been sent home wounded or sick and had absconded during their recovery rather than be sent back to the trenches. This would continue to be an issue throughout the war, especially when the manpower shortage resulted in the reclassification of men initially deemed unfit to return to the ranks. Writing in 1920 Ernest Thurtle reflected:

It is not because of the fact that a man had been wounded that he was reluctant to go back . . . The wound, however, had been instrumental in bringing the soldier back, for a period, to normal life and a normal outlook. He had been into the reality of this thing called war and was now fully alive to its horror . . .[32]

Charles Wilson, later to be named the 1st Baron Moran, was a major in the Royal Army Medical Corps during the war, and described this process as 'a subtle undermining of his will' that may cause a man to try to stay home or even to desert: 'The wounded soldier has just visualized danger in a new and very personal way. It has been brought home to him as never before that he is not a spectator but a bit of the target.'[33] Lord Moran was clear in his book *The Anatomy of Courage* that the range of options a man may then use to stay away from the front line 'may be indefensible but it is not cowardice'.[34]

The military experience of these men was invaluable and whilst many thousands of New Army volunteers were still in training, it was imperative that these old soldiers be available for active service as soon as possible. The police were given special instructions in how to deal with these cases. It would have been distasteful to arrest a man who had already shed blood in defence of his country if he was simply taking a few more days to recover, so the police were told simply to trace these men and make enquiries as to their reasons for absence.[35] If the man had no good excuse he should be told to rejoin his unit immediately and be issued with a travel warrant if necessary, a report being sent to his commanding officer. If the man claimed to still be unfit, and in the eyes of the police officer attending, this claim was unfounded, he was to be sent to the nearest military hospital for further examination. Only if specific instructions were received from his commanding officer that the man was to be arrested should this be done.

An Army Order was simultaneously issued to tighten up the procedure as it related to deserters generally, 'especially those who are trained soldiers'.[36] A more detailed form (Army Form B124) was to be sent by a missing man's commanding officer to the recruitment officer at the location where he enlisted and to the area in which his family lived. A physical description of the recruit alongside his basic details were now included along with any other information which may assist in his detection. This form would be the basis of the entry in the *Police Gazette*, copies of which would be sent to every recruiting officer to help identify fraudulent enlisters. A distinction was made between deserters and absentees, with the latter being told to return to their units and given travel warrants to do so whilst deserters were to be immediately arrested and placed before the local court.

The strain on the police began to tell. By July 1915 the Chief Constable of Manchester was writing to the War Office complaining that his force was receiving 200 'telephonic, telegraphic and written' enquiries a day from the military authorities about missing soldiers in his area and had had to set up a special unit to deal with the issue. Chief Constable Peacock was also concerned that some of this information was not necessarily accurate, leaving the police open to expensive civil suits by those falsely detained at the behest of the army.[37] In typical War Office style, the Chief Constable's request for a blanket indemnity to cover police costs in such cases was refused, though individual applications would be considered.

The police were certainly carrying most of the burden of tracing and arresting deserters in the first years of the war. The Military Police Corps was disorganized and numerically small, with limited powers to deal with deserters. On 4 August 1914 Redcaps numbered a mere 401 and were based only in areas where troops were stationed. Industrial cities like Sheffield had no Military Policemen at all meaning that deserters flocked there confident in avoiding detection but also hopeful of obtaining lucrative employment in munitions. Sheffield did not see its first Military Policemen until January 1917. After the introduction of conscription things became more organized, Military Policemen now co-operating more closely with their civilian counterparts to round up deserters and also travelling to areas where they previously had no presence. The huge increase in the number of men in khaki saw a corresponding increase in the number of Military Policemen: by August 1918 there were 13,414 in the ranks, with 4,286 of these men being stationed on the home front. Detecting and detaining deserters was a full-time job.[38]

Chapter 3

The Restless, the Feckless and the Brave

Could it be that they attested merely to get two shillings and sixpence?
George Coppard,
With a Machine Gun to Cambrai

After the war army psychiatrist Major E.N. Woodbury was asked to study desertion in the US forces as part of a wider investigation of the causes of military crimes.[1] A sample of over 1,000 courts martial for desertion between March 1919 and March 1920 led Woodbury to identify four main categories of motivation, recorded as those:

a) Connected with the character of the offender
b) Connected with the service itself
c) Connected with family matters
d) Connected with matters outside the army

Within these general categories Woodbury listed the most frequently cited reasons for desertion, which included dissatisfaction with the general environment, immaturity and entanglements with women amongst other factors. He concluded that 'mental deficiency or weakness, including criminal tendencies' was the biggest cause of desertion, whilst drink and drugs were the main causes of men going absent without leave. Of course, the reasons a man gave for his desertion before a court martial may not have been entirely true, though thirty-five men in Woodbury's sample did confess that cowardice was their motivation. Woodbury concluded that in general desertion occurred when the 'pull outward' from the services exceeded the 'pull inward'. Bullying, for example, would be a pull outward, whilst shame at being considered a deserter would be a pull inward. External factors like the ease of obtaining alternative employment or the tolerance for deserters amongst the civilian population also had an influence. The emphasis placed by the British Army on teaching regimental history and traditions to new soldiers was an attempt at manufacturing a pull inward, creating a bond to the ethos and discipline of the corps that would discourage men from desertion and disobedience. How effective this would be for men who had no intentions of being soldiers beyond the duration of the war is questionable, even more so for the reluctantly conscripted. As Alan Thomas, a young officer in the Royal West Kents, wrote of the 'civilians in uniform' under his command, 'What could they have cared for belonging to the "finest" company? . . . All they wanted was to win the war and go back home as soon as possible.'[2]

As already noted, failure to meet soldiers' basic needs in terms of food, clothing and shelter could result in mass desertions, and Woodbury stressed the importance of attending to these practicalities. In order to reduce desertion rates further he advocated an examination of potential recruits to try to eliminate those who possessed characteristics that would make them more liable to desert, i.e. criminals, gamblers, 'chronic wanderers', drug and drink addicts and those in debt. In 1919 in Britain a committee under the direction of Lord Southborough was convened to investigate the phenomenon of shell shock and made a similar recommendation about the need for more careful screening of recruits.[3] Some men, it was now accepted, were just not suited to the military. Many of those historically welcomed into the ranks of the British Army displayed the undesirable characteristics listed by Woodbury. The British forces were accustomed to knocking off the rough edges of miscreants and turning them into fighting men. Where this process failed, desertion was one response available to the unhappy recruit. During the Second World War, British Army psychiatrist Lieutenant Colonel J.C. Penton studied a much smaller sample of deserters than Woodbury but came to not dissimilar conclusions. Penton said that domestic troubles, training issues, transfers from one unit to another, 'in fact, any circumstance which may upset the emotional relations of the man towards the unit in which he is serving' could result in desertion.[4]

Though most of the deserters in this study fit into categories identified by the psychiatrists above, one kind of deserter appearing in the first year of the war was arguably quite different. Stories began to emerge of men who had deserted their original units to re-enlist in other regiments to reach the Front more quickly. Some were stationed abroad whilst others were new recruits or Territorials frustrated at the lack of progress in their deployment. On 16 May 1915 Private Thomas Hardy of the Queen's Royal West Surrey Regiment was killed in action at Festubert. 'Thomas Hardy' was not a humble Tommy but a Captain with an impeccable military pedigree, serving under a false name. Captain Hugh Sale Smart was with the 15th Khyber Rifles in India when war broke out. His father was a Colonel in the Indian Army, and Hugh was a former pupil of Clifton College in Bristol, Douglas Haig's alma mater. After attending Sandhurst Smart received his commission and was posted to India in 1907. In December 1914 he came back to England, ostensibly on a month's leave to visit his parents in Tring in Hertfordshire. When he did not return as scheduled his Indian Army superiors guessed, correctly, that he had deserted to fight in France. Though enquiries were made in England and elsewhere, Hugh Smart could not be traced. By the time he was officially struck off the strength as a deserter, he was dead.[5]

Captain Hugh Smart had become Private Thomas Hardy. His new battalion had been recalled from service in South Africa to go to the Western Front. This no doubt made it easier for Hugh Smart, with his extensive Indian service and tanned face, to fit in. Interviewed by journalists after his death, some of Smart's new colleagues suspected he had served in the army previously at a higher rank, his knowledge of drill and insistence on saluting being clues to his real identity: his nickname in the new battalion was 'The Colonel'.[6] Shortly before the Battle of Festubert, Smart confessed his real identity to his Company Sergeant Major Frederick Barter and swore him to secrecy. Barter won the Victoria Cross that day for his part in capturing over 100 German prisoners and 500 precious yards of trench, but a posthumous recommendation for the same honour for Hardy/Smart was refused. The true story of the death of Captain Smart only reached the newspapers in August 1915, when the King revoked the earlier striking off and a notice was placed in the *London Gazette* to this effect.[7] Rather than be criticized for the extra work he had caused his parent unit and for fraudulently enlisting, Smart was lauded as a hero.

Hugh Smart was one of thousands of men who enlisted under a false name whilst already in the armed forces, though a new name was often unnecessary given the limited abilities of the army to cross-check applications. Arthur Bonney left the 10th London Regiment having been told that it would stay a home-service unit. He posted his uniform back to the battalion and, under the same name, joined the South Wales Borderers instead. Bonney fought at Gallipoli and in France and though his crime was detected whilst he was in Egypt, he was never punished.[8] Under peacetime conditions deserters would not be prosecuted if they had given three years' good service in the corps in which they had fraudulently enlisted but in wartime this did not apply. If a recruit was doing well in his new regiment, punishments were often light. Horace Calvert joined the 6th West Yorkshire Regiment when he was 15 years old but deserted after nine months, ironically because he felt that discipline in his battalion was too lax. He was determined to join the Grenadier Guards, having seen photographs of a smart soldier in a Guards' uniform at his billet in Gainsborough. After a short time with the Guards he was found to be a deserter and, declining to return to his original regiment, was punished by being confined to barracks for fourteen days.[9] Sympathy for the impatient deserter was sometimes shown by the civilian judiciary. When Henry Brooks, deserter from the Royal Welch Fusiliers, appeared at Old Street Police Court in September 1916 he was recovering from wounds suffered whilst serving on the Somme with the Manchester Regiment. Brooks had reportedly left the Royal Welch to get to the Front more quickly. When the magistrate was told that his original battalion wanted him back for punishment, he refused to comply, instead adjourning the case *sine die*, essentially dismissing it. Brooks was free to go and limped out of court.[10]

Anxiety to get to the Front led some men to falsely declare themselves as deserters in the belief that they would be sent straight to a regiment with no questions asked. James Butterworth tried to enlist in July 1915 but was rejected due to defective eyesight. His response was to get drunk and present himself at the local police station declaring that he was a deserter from the Scottish Rifles. This was found to be false and instead he was charged with disorderly conduct. Not to be thwarted, Butterworth managed to join the army a month later, serving in the Labour Corps. He didn't find army life to his liking, deserting shortly afterwards and being in trouble regularly for absence until his discharge in February 1919.[11]

There was undoubtedly an element of rewriting history by some of those who were caught after fraudulently enlisting. Framing their desertion as a brave attempt to join the fray more quickly could obscure the real reasons for their untimely departure. When William Carruthers claimed to have left his Canadian regiment to join his former British unit for this very reason, the prosecutor at his court martial poured scorn on the suggestion: had Carruthers successfully re-enlisted in the Royal Garrison Artillery he would be less, not more likely to go to the Front imminently.[12] Press reports of the impatient deserters were generally positive. The *Western Mail* went so far as to declare in November 1914 that, in contrast to the 'hundreds' of soldiers deserting the German Army, the only desertions on the British side were from Territorials trying to get to the Front.[13] The reality was that 1,322 men had been struck off the strength of the British Army as deserters in the month of October 1914 alone.[14] The general attitude of the press is demonstrated by the headlines that announced the story of two Liverpudlian Territorials who managed to conceal themselves on a troop ship going to France in October 1914. The stowaways were admired for their spirit, their actions declared to be 'The Right Kind of Desertion'.[15]

The wrong kind of desertion was much more common and the confusion of wartime coupled with the need to have a constant stream of men available for active service allowed fraudulent enlisters to have quite a run of success. It was an easy task to pretend to be someone you were not. No proof of identification was required to enlist, with a man's word being taken at face value for most of the answers on the attestation form. It was not usual for a man to be in possession of his birth certificate, so the document was never required for enlistment. Birth and marriage certificates did have to be produced by war widows claiming pensions, though the army had needed no such proof of identity to send their husbands to their deaths.

George Coppard enlisted on 27 August 1914 at Mitcham Road Barracks in Croydon and was put on a train to Guildford with his fellow recruits. Between enlistment and roll call there were already absentees. Coppard was incredulous, asking, 'Could it be that they attested merely to get two shillings and sixpence?'[16] Some men were indeed satisfied with their enlistment pay and immediately made themselves scarce, whilst some waited until they had been issued with uniforms and equipment that could be sold on. The Thames Police Court was told that one defendant appearing before them was part of a gang of fifteen men who went around together, enlisting and deserting en masse, selling the army's property each time.[17] In Belfast in February 1915 a group of four deserters appeared who were said to be working in concert, enlisting, disappearing then enlisting again in new regiments. William Garrigan aka William Stewart aka William Loughran, Frederick O'Neill aka James Smith aka John McCusker, Thomas Kane aka Thomas Kennedy and Patrick McCabe aka Patrick Crowley had joined an array of regiments since war was declared. The gang were arrested having enlisted in the 5th Royal Irish Rifles the day after enlisting and deserting from the 7th Leinster Regiment. Suspicion was aroused by the fact that they were selling kit from the Leinsters as soon as they were issued with Royal Irish Rifles uniforms.[18] Henry Tufft reportedly managed to join and desert three different regiments between August and October 1914. Within a week of war being declared he joined the Royal Horse Artillery in Birmingham and, issued with two days' pay, didn't turn up at Woolwich as directed. A month later Tufft enlisted in the Worcestershire Regiment under a false name, was given a further allowance and again disappeared. Two weeks later he enlisted in his own name in the Army Service Corps, received more money and was ordered to report to Salisbury Plain. Unsurprisingly, he never arrived. He was eventually arrested after a police constable in Sutton Coldfield asked to see the army discharge papers Tufft claimed to possess and instead received a punch in the face.[19]

A determined deserter could turn the War Office administration into knots that proved difficult to unravel. When Alfred Long was convicted of stealing a trunk in London in September 1918 his remarkable career was exposed. Long, a childhood absconder from a Barnardo's home, was a serial deserter. He was treated in a Chelsea hospital for gas poisoning as a Private from the Royal Field Artillery and by August 1916 was a deserter from both the RFA and the Army Service Corps. After his arrest he managed to evade his escorts and was next heard of as a patient in Netley Hospital. On his recovery he was sent to Southampton to await a draft to the Front but escaped on three further occasions. Long seemed to regard hospitals as better places to spend the war than trenches, leaving whenever his cover story wore thin. He next surfaced at Thornton Heath Hospital, requiring treatment for a gunshot wound and claiming to be a Corporal in the Cambridgeshire Regiment. A month after his arrival at Thornton Heath, he was in the Ipswich Military Hospital in a Norfolk Regiment uniform. His next port of call was the Norfolk and Norwich Hospital where he stole money from fellow wounded soldiers before absconding. Turning up at King's College Hospital in London as a Dragoon Guard, he was finally arrested and was given six months' imprisonment at his court martial. By the time he appeared in court for the theft of the trunk in September 1918 he was dressed as a Corporal from the Royal Warwickshire Regiment, complete with three wound stripes and ribbons for the Military and Mons Medals. The court heard that Long had told so many lies that the War Office had no idea who he really was.[20]

Swapping fraudulently between different branches of the armed forces was one option for men who found that their original choice of corps did not suit them. After the war a number of cases came to light of men who had left the army to serve in the navy, or vice versa. *John Bull* printed a letter from an army to navy deserter in September 1918. Wounded at Festubert in 1915, he returned home to find that his wife had been given notice of his death and he was unable to access his army pay. Struggling financially, he swapped uniforms and joined the navy instead. Speaking from experience he declared that there must be 'hundreds of cases not dissimilar to mine'.[21] Many of these men had good records in their new unit. The same could not be said of Charles John Thurston, who joined the army in 1913 straight from the Bedfordshire Reformatory. By the time war was declared he had deserted from two different regiments and served under two different names, his own and 'Charles George'. He was at the Battle of the Aisne with the Northamptonshire Regiment where he suffered shrapnel wounds and was sent back to hospital in England in November 1914. After a period of detention served for absconding from hospital, Thurston was released in early April 1915 to return to duty. The Northamptonshire Regiment did not see him again until July 1917. Charles Thurston had become Charles George again and decided he would try his luck in the navy. He liked the navy no better and deserted from Chatham several times during the next two years. In June 1917 the navy decreed he should be discharged. He was lucky in the timing of his expulsion; two months later the barracks at Chatham were targeted by Gotha bombers and 136 navy personnel died in the raid. Returning home to Bethnal Green, Thurston was finally arrested as an army deserter. He was sentenced to twelve months' imprisonment, but the majority of this term was remitted and he was transferred to the Labour Corps to go abroad with the next draft. Thurston went to France at the end of August 1917 and was there until January 1919, the transfer abroad having the desired consequence of making desertion more difficult. The effect of discounting all previous service when a deserter was apprehended can be seen in action with Charles Thurston: by the time of his discharge he had been in the army for six years yet had accrued only 1 year and 220 days of service.[22]

The navy was more circumspect in weeding out unsuitable men from the service whilst the army dragged serial deserters back to barracks time after time. Harry C. Vaughan, travelling showman, had deserted seven times by December 1915.[23] Thomas Hawker of the 14th Middlesex Regiment disappeared from his regiment on twelve occasions between September 1914 and February 1916. The magistrate at the North London Police Court where Hawker appeared told him, 'You are a disgrace to the uniform you are wearing. You are costing too much money and it is a pity you cannot be whipped.'[24] When James Veevers appeared before the court in Rochdale in July 1915, he proudly proclaimed that his army career had seen him serve with three different regiments. His assertion of patriotism was somewhat undermined by information from the prosecutor that he had deserted from them all. Veevers had been discharged from two regiments due to his frequent desertion and criminal offending on the home front and but had found a home in the Middlesex Regiment. He had initially made good progress, being promoted from Private to Sergeant, only to fall to the bottom of the ladder again thanks to his periods of absence without leave. Veevers was eventually sent to France in late December 1915 but his pattern of unauthorized absences and criminality continued. Despite his regular stays in various custodial establishments, both military and civilian, he was not discharged until May 1920.[25]

The evils of alcohol were cited in many cases of absence. George Stott, aka George Mulpetre, from Middlesbrough appeared before that town's court in November 1914 charged with desertion from both the Scots Guards and the DLI, lasting only five days in the latter corps. Alcoholism was his problem and it must have been a big issue as the army washed their hands of him immediately.[26] Joseph Sheils presented himself at the local constabulary barracks in Trim, County Meath in November 1914 declaring himself a deserter from the 2nd Royal Irish Rifles. Sheils was in civilian clothing and had traded in his army boots for a pair of slippers. He could not remember what had happened to the rest of his kit and blamed the drink for leading him astray after a short three months in the army. Sheils presented such a pathetic figure at the subsequent court hearing that the magistrates doubted he was a soldier.[27] Drinking was deeply ingrained in soldier's culture but was also a big part of many civilian working men's lives. Alcohol was as important a factor in absenteeism in civilian life as it was in the military, and absenteeism in industry was a major impediment to the war effort. Reports published in 1915 were clear that overindulgence in alcohol was having a marked effect on levels of absence in industry. The percentage of men missing at one colliery in the Yorkshire coalfield was as high as 30 per cent.[28] A similar pattern was reported amongst shipyard workers on the Clyde and the north-east coast where 35 per cent of the working week for riveters was lost due to absenteeism. The report concluded 'The evidence is really overwhelming that the main cause of this alarming loss of time is the "lure of drink"'.[29] Woodbury later cited prohibition as being one of the measures he would recommend to the US armed forces to reduce the figures of desertion and absence.[30]

Men sometimes deserted thanks to the pull outwards of families at home, often due to some temporary difficulty but occasionally with a view to staying there permanently. As already noted, there was often a delay for a wife in the receipt of separation allowance once her husband had joined up and men sometimes quoted this as a reason for their desertion. Of course, once a man was declared a deserter the payment of separation allowance to his wife would stop anyway, making such 'strikes' counterproductive. As the magistrate told Alfred Wasby's wife when she claimed this was the reason for his desertion, he had absconded twice in a month so it was little wonder she could not get her money.[31] Fred William Gray's wife was confined to the workhouse thanks to her lack of separation allowance, causing him to desert the Inland Waterways Department of the Royal Engineers to take care of her.[32] For Boaz Gurr it was his wife's failure to go into the workhouse that prompted him to desert. Gurr was found working on a farm in Laughton, East Sussex in September 1915 when he should have been with the Royal Garrison Artillery in Dover. He told the police that he had left his unit when he heard his wife had reneged on her promise to enter the workhouse whilst he was away and had instead 'gone on the road'. He deserted to go and find her and must have had a good long search as he had been missing since November 1914. Gurr replaced farm labour with hard labour when he appeared before the court martial and was given a year's imprisonment with this additional punishment.[33]

Family illness was another reason for desertion. Ernest Greenslade absconded from Deptford in November 1914 on hearing that his wife and three children were sick. At his court martial, Greenslade handed in a written statement of mitigation, claiming he had deserted on 'the impulse of the moment' and that but for the illnesses he would have been 'only too pleased' to have gone to the Front. Greenslade had only four months of service and begged for another opportunity to prove himself: he was given eighteen months' imprisonment. He could consider himself lucky as his desertion was the night before his unit were leaving for the Front, a circumstance which would see other soldiers face the death penalty.[34] Thomas Rule was a Regular soldier who deserted from the Middlesex Regiment in December 1914 after hearing that his daughter was gravely ill. By the time he returned to the family home, 13-year-old Jessie was dead. Rule then tried to get permission from his commanding officer to remain at home for the funeral but was arrested before the ceremony took place. Appearing at Highgate Police Court, Rule was told there was not time for him to attend the funeral, but his final pitiful plea just to be able to see his daughter one last time was granted by the sympathetic bench who allowed him to be released to a plain clothes policeman for the sad visit.[35]

Happier family occasions were sometimes cited as reasons by arrestees appearing before the court. James Knight of the Worcestershire Regiment had asked for leave from his commanding officer so that he could get married. When this was refused, Knight left anyway, cycling from Malden, Surrey to his home in Dudley in the West Midlands.[36] James Duncan begged the court that he be allowed to marry his sweetheart before being handed back to the military. The Provost sportingly granted his wish and the couple were married in the less than romantic surroundings of the Kirkcaldy Police Office.[37] Magistrates also decreed that John Carter of Holloway could be married before being returned to the Royal Artillery as a deserter. The honeymoon was short: the couple were parted again at the church door. The romantic story did not have a happy ending. By March 1915 Carter had been discharged as medically unfit and was now charged with being drunk and disorderly having launched a beer bottle at his dear wife's head, causing a wound requiring seven stitches.[38]

Deserter Herbert Caulder returned to the bosom of his family in October 1918 and got more than he bargained for when father-in-law William Buss shot him. Buss may have been enraged by the fact that when Caulder turned up looking for wife Cissie he had been missing for fifteen months. He had failed to return to his unit in France after the expiry of his leave in August 1917 and wherever he had been, it certainly wasn't in the company of his wife as she had written to his regiment several times asking for information on his whereabouts. The police arrested Caulder at the hospital in Kingston upon Thames where he was recovering from his injuries. At his subsequent trial for the shooting, Buss claimed that his son-in-law had produced a revolver and threatened him first. He had then acted entirely in self-defence and had merely 'winged' Caulder. This defence was somewhat undermined by the fact that Caulder had fifty shotgun pellets in his back. Buss was convicted but sentenced to a mere two days in custody. By the time of the trial Caulder had been sentenced to five years' penal servitude at a court martial in France.[39]

Men charged with desertion were very often anxious to assert their status as absentees. It was far more palatable to be seen as someone who had simply taken a few extra days away from duty than as someone who was abandoning their duties completely at a time of national crisis. Prospective groom James Knight was indignant at the thought of this imputation on his character telling the court, 'I would rather be shot than be a deserter'.[40] Leaving the ranks on the home front was not only more straightforward logistically, it must have been easier psychologically. Distanced from the mission at hand and performing instead routine tasks which must have seemed far removed from fighting the Germans, it must have been far simpler to reconcile a few days or weeks of 'French leave' with a patriotic conscience.

Woodbury said that a lack of understanding of military discipline was a factor in desertion rates, and there must be an extent to which this underlies many cases of absence amongst volunteers and, subsequently, conscripts.[41] One of the reasons later advanced in support of a post-war amnesty for military offenders was that volunteers and conscripts had no experience or understanding of army orders. In post-war debates, several Members of Parliament pointed out the unusual ethos of the New Army. William Adamson, Labour MP and former miner, said that 'its outlook was civilian and its conception of freedom and right was civilian'.[42] Civilians confronting the intransigence of the British Army for the first time were often in for a shock. When grocer's salesman Andy Hardie of the Cameron Highlanders wasted a day of his leave waiting for a boat at Boulogne, he and his three companions from his battalion assumed that their return date was now also a day later. The civilians turned soldiers were dismayed to find themselves placed under arrest as deserters when they reported to return to France and taken across the Channel in custody.[43] Hardie was killed in action three months later on the Somme. Norman Collins recorded the shock of military discipline on an officer cadet reduced to the ranks and given fourteen days in prison for refusing to tidy under a lance corporal's bed: 'Hard luck for a chap who hasn't been under military discipline before.'[44] Even men who had some military experience in the Territorials found that there was a big difference between weekend soldiering in peacetime and being part of an army at war. K.W. Mitchison writes that Territorials were not subject to the same rigours as the Regular army soldier and that the part-time soldiers' behaviour was more casual as a result. He cites the example of a route march being interrupted by several of the company nipping out of the line to call in at a local shop, behaviour which could not be tolerated now the country was on a war footing.[45] The lists of Territorials printed in the *Police Gazette* as deserters grew ever longer as the war continued.

Many new soldiers saw little wrong with going home to see friends and family whether or not they had a valid leave pass. Desertion figures always showed a spike each January as men failed to return from Christmas leave, or took their own unauthorized festive break. Henry J.J. Parish deserted from the 4th Northamptonshire Regiment and at court said, 'I wanted a holiday. They would not grant me one so I took French leave.'[46] John Waterhouse and George Nelson were refused leave to visit their families having been warned for a draft to the Front. Taking matters into their own hands, the pair hired a bicycle near their camp in Bedford and planned to take it in turns to cycle all the way to Yorkshire. They almost made it but police seeing them in Chesterfield became suspicious and detained them. The duo also used the term 'French leave' to characterize their desertion.[47] Boxer Gus Platts absented himself from the Sheffield City Battalion when he was refused permission to leave camp for two pre-arranged bouts, one with a Sergeant from the Manchester Regiment. In front of a crowd of 3,000 people he fought and beat his opponent and was arrested outside the venue as he got into a taxi.[48] Platts was not the only Sheffield based boxer to walk away from the army that spring – lightweight Edwin James Alger, known in boxing circles as 'Young Brum' as he was originally from Birmingham, also appeared in court as a deserter from the East Yorkshire Regiment. Alger was sentenced to six months' hard labour which was then commuted to seven days' detention.[49] Both continued to box whilst in uniform, Alger sending back reports from France to the newspapers at home about inter regimental boxing tournaments. Both men were able to resume their careers after the war, Platts becoming British and European middleweight champion in 1921.

Perhaps the most inventive reason for desertion, literally, was that proffered by Robert John Prowse when he appeared before the magistrates at Bristol in 1917. Prowse told the court that he had deserted in order to complete an invention he was working on that would increase the country's vegetable crop output by 25 per cent. His 'electric culture' system was 'practically perfect' when he was detained and he needed but a short time period to finish it. The magistrates advised him to tell the army all about it when he got back to barracks.[50]

Some of the reasons given by deserters for their departure were trivial – John Florey didn't return to his unit because he had lost his military overcoat and feared being punished for it.[51] Frank May left the ranks to collect a clean shirt from his mother.[52] Edward Stanley Scott absconded in despair at the amount of bad language he heard in his barracks.[53] Guy Chapman, serving as an officer in the Royal Fusiliers, said that many of the men under his command were 'like children, moving in a haze of their own dreams, unconnected with practical things'.[54] Lord Moran also wrote of soldiers as being like children.[55] This attitude was reported in the pre-war army too: John Baynes wrote that the average British soldier in the ranks had remained a child by nature and frequently acted irresponsibly. Baynes cited the example of a soldier who would make his way up the ranks then engage in drunken antics that saw him dumped back at the bottom of the ladder, from which point he would start the whole journey again.[56]

Whilst soldiers were being characterized as having the outlook of children, some of them were children. Several underage recruits appeared before the courts as deserters when army service became too much for them: Edward Stanley Scott, so upset by swearing, was only 17 years old. To serve abroad a man had to be 19 years old, leading many eager youngsters to lie on their enlistment papers, often encouraged by recruiting sergeants. It is estimated that as many as 250,000 boys served in the British Army during the conflict.[57] Some of them were shockingly young. Joseph Onslow from Poplar was only 15 years old when he stood in the dock at the Old Street Children's Court as a deserter. He had run away from home and joined the King's Royal Rifles but had deserted and returned to London because 'army work was too hard and he did not want to go back'.[58] Onslow had claimed to be 19 when he enlisted. He was 5ft 3in tall. George E. King was reported to be 14 when he joined up, though he had at least enlisted in a Bantam regiment to cover his lack of height. He had deserted because he wanted to join a different regiment.[59] Henry Spencer deserted after a week in uniform because he had been ordered to transfer out of his regiment of choice. The 15-year-old had gone back to his job in a mill instead.[60]

When these boys appeared before the court they were routinely handed back to the army, the magistrates perhaps being under the impression that they would be immediately discharged. The court told Joseph Onslow that it was likely he would be released by the army, but this did not happen for nearly eleven months. In the meantime, Onslow continued to misbehave, breaking out of barracks, refusing to obey orders and causing disturbances every few weeks. He was sent to France with his regiment and it was not until the end of April 1916 that he was confirmed as being underage and he was discharged at the beginning of May.[61] John Arthur Mewes was 16 when the Aberdeen Sherriff's Court detained him as a deserter. Though the case had been adjourned for enquiries and Mewes handed to the Salvation Army in the meantime, the ultimate outcome was that he was sent back to his unit. He was punished for his desertion before being discharged in September as underage.[62]

By 1917 women could be deserters too. The Women's Army Auxiliary Corps (WAAC) was established in July 1917 with the aim of freeing up more men for the Front by having women perform their duties. Between 40,000 and 50,000 women signed up and often performed in khaki the tasks they were accustomed to doing in civilian life – cooking, cleaning, laundry and clerical work, for example. WAAC deserters were liable to have their details published in the *Police Gazette* but once apprehended the women were to be asked to return back to their units and if they agreed, simply sent on their way, making the journey at their own expense. Only if they refused to go back to military service were they brought before the civilian courts.[63] A WAAC deserter was to be charged under Regulation 42c of the Defence of the Realm Regulations, not under the Army Act, allowing fines to be imposed by a civilian court.

This reflects the ambiguous status of the WAAC, who despite their uniforms were to be treated in some ways as civilian employees of the army, not as soldiers.[64]

Just like the men who deserted, women had a range of motivations for leaving the military. Two soldiers' widows, Millicent Cross and Leah Lemmon, joined the WAAC after struggling to live on their widow's pensions. They deserted from camp in Aldershot, claiming that they did not fully appreciate what they were signing up for. The pair had found jobs in a munitions factory in Tinsley, near Sheffield when they were arrested. Neither woman wanted to go back to the WAAC but they were not given a choice, being fined 20s. and then handed over to the authorities.[65] Mary Waugh and Mary Jane Savage appeared to struggle with military discipline and walked away from camp at Morfa in North Wales, appearing before the Liverpool Police Court in May 1918. Mary Jane Savage, 4ft 11in of defiance, complained that discipline was too harsh – 'You get C.B. if you smile' and that it would take 'fixed bayonets' to make her return. The Liverpool bench fined them both £1 and sent them back to Wales.[66]

Sisters Edith and Constance Jackson deserted to bring attention to the deplorable way they had been treated by their superiors. Accommodated in the Gateshead workhouse, they were given dirty beds which previously belonged to scabies sufferers, a fact admitted by the establishment's administrator. Prior to that they had been housed in a filthy hovel in Sheffield which had been unoccupied for nine years, where they were given nothing but bread, jam and water.[67] The sisters were determined to be brought before the court so that publicity could be given to the plight of their comrades. Edith and Constance claimed that the other nine WAACs in their company would have deserted too but they did not have the means. The sisters certainly did have the means, being described in the press as 'two well-known young Goole ladies'.[68] They were treated quite differently to the working class WAAC absconders, being found not guilty of the charge of desertion because the Goole magistrates decided they had a valid reason for leaving. The fact that their father was the former head of Goole Council must have significantly enhanced their chances of acquittal.

Whatever the reasons for a man or woman's desertion, some were determined not to return and went to great lengths to avoid arrest. Desperate measures adopted by some deserters could have tragic consequences. Deserters met their deaths in a variety of ways. Travelling back to barracks by train seemed too good an opportunity to miss for some, as if they managed to jump from the carriage the train would be miles away before the escorts could stop it and search for them. Leaping from a moving train was incredibly dangerous and some were not lucky enough to land in one piece. Edward Brady was being brought back under armed guard to his regiment at Reading when he threw himself out of the train, landing hard and dying in hospital without regaining consciousness.[69] John Wallace of Wigan tried a more subtle ruse, climbing out of the train window and making it look as though he had jumped, instead lying on top of the carriage. Unfortunately, the train went under a low bridge at Bulkington and Wallace's head was smashed to a pulp on the brickwork.[70] Benjamin Cook was arrested at Guy's Hospital, where he was visiting his sick wife, a few months after his desertion. The police allowed him to go and say goodbye to her, but he instead jumped out of a window and climbed down a drainpipe. He lost his grip and died from injuries sustained in the fall.[71] Some deserters were in such despair that they deliberately harmed themselves. James Briley went to the fort at Chatham to surrender as a deserter from the King's Royal Rifle Corps in September 1914 and on the same day, stabbed himself with his bayonet, dying in hospital.[72] James Brown of the Royal Field Artillery was on the platform at Newport railway station with his escort when he stabbed himself in the neck and face in an apparent suicide attempt. Brown's poor wife witnessed the bloody scene as she had come to the station to see him off.[73] Thomas Weeden and his wife, Minnie, were so distraught at his first taste of army life after his conscription in 1917 that they gassed themselves, their 7-year-old son and their dog at their newsagent's shop in Croydon. Weeden had spent just three days with the Army Service Corps but was determined not to go back under any circumstances. His appeals to the Military Service Tribunal for exemption had been unsuccessful and the Weedens had agreed on their next plan of action. The couple thoughtfully left notices on the doors warning entrants not to bring a naked flame into the living areas of the shop. They were found dead in each other's arms. Driver Weeden's rolled up uniform was located inside the shop and returned to the army depot by a family member.[74]

Those seeking to arrest deserters were often in danger themselves if they encountered a particularly determined escapee. It was common for the arrest of a deserter to involve a fist fight of some kind, either with the wanted man or his family and friends, but on some occasions the violence was much more serious. Inspector Moore of the Hyde police in Cheshire got more than he bargained for when he casually strolled past a firm of accountants in the town in September 1916. Deserter Robert Jenkinson Taylor was in the office at the time and believed that the officer was coming to arrest him. Taylor produced a revolver and went out onto the street, firing several shots at the Inspector during a prolonged chase along the canal tow path. Taylor was a fantasist with serious mental health issues who had deserted both the Royal Navy and the Royal Field Artillery and claimed in court to have served in the French Foreign Legion and as a Mountie in Canada. The Chief Constable of Hyde testified that he had known Taylor's very respectable family for over a decade and that the prisoner had never had a job in his life. He was cleared of attempted murder, being convicted simply of shooting with intent to resist arrest and sentenced to twelve months' imprisonment with hard labour. Despite his problems, the army retained his services until August 1919 when he was discharged due to 'delusional insanity'. Tellingly, in 1921 he appeared before the court again for an unprovoked assault on a police officer he thought was laughing at him.[75] Whilst Inspector Moore escaped injury, an officer attempting to arrest William George Jepson as a deserter in 1918 was not so lucky. Jepson shot at two officers on a steamer travelling between Ireland and Scotland, missing with his attempt to shoot the first in the head, but managing to hit the second in the leg. When the steamer docked in Glasgow Jepson was detained and was eventually sentenced to three years' penal servitude.[76]

It was not unheard of for men evading their military service to disguise themselves as women to thwart their capture. In October 1915 a police detective asked the name of a woman he saw in the marketplace in Dover. Unconvinced that she really was 'Ethel Smith', he followed her back to her boarding house where he asked permission to search her room. Nothing incriminating was found save for a small safety razor and lather brush. 'Ethel Smith' was 19-year-old William Mason, a recruit from the King's Liverpool Regiment who was currently absent without leave from his base at Canterbury. Rifleman Mason had absconded to Dover and disposed of his uniform, registering at the boarding house as a woman. He appeared before the court on the charge of being a deserter and was handed over to the army, eventually receiving a few day's detention for being absent without leave. Mason's story did not have a happy ending – he committed suicide in camp in Aldershot in July 1916. Mason had suffered prolonged bullying over his earlier escape, though this was trivialized as 'ragging' by the army at the inquest.[77]

At least by the time Mason appeared before the court he had been allowed to change into uniform. When Frederick Wright was brought before the Highgate Magistrates in similar circumstances in June 1916 he appeared there in women's clothing. Wright, a deserter from the Royal Fusiliers, stood in the dock in female attire, wearing 'a long, braided navy-blue coat with college cap and veil and white kid gloves'. He was an object of ridicule in court and forced to remove his hat and wig by the presiding magistrate. Wright had tried to persuade the detective arresting him that he was a woman called Katherine Woodhouse. A plain gold ring, some cosmetics and breast padding were found at his lodgings along with a photograph of a male music hall artiste dressed as a woman. Wright was a conscript who had failed in his attempts to avoid military service. A butler in a smart London household, he had tried to persuade his employer's private doctor that he was suffering from a heart condition but was unsuccessful. In despair, he attempted suicide by taking an overdose and was prosecuted for that offence in March 1916. The court on that occasion had bound him over and instructed the police to march him to the recruiting office. When granted a leave pass from his regiment he immediately changed into women's clothing and became Katherine Woodhouse, allegedly telling the police that he intended to maintain this identity until the war was over. Cruelly, he was kept in women's clothing for a few days on remand before the court made a final decision. On determining that he should be handed back to the army the magistrate told the police to allow him to change into khaki before he went with the escort.[78] Charles Morbin also appeared in court in women's clothing, having to be carried into the dock because he had collapsed. He had deserted from the Army Service Corps and was found hiding under the bed in a house in Fulham in 1917. Morbin told the court that he was only wearing women's clothing because his uniform was being cleaned.[79]

Though William Mason's arrest was reported nationwide, nothing much was made of his femininity by the press, the only reference being that he spoke in a 'soft voice'. He had also been allowed to change back into his uniform before his court appearance. By way of contrast, Frederick Wright's every female feature was emphasized and his appearances in court were a source of hilarity. Charles Morbin's weakness was highlighted, though identified as mental rather than physical by a doctor who said he was simply 'in a funk'. The portrayal of Wright and Morbin was not dissimilar to popular representations of conscientious objectors who were often deliberately feminized in cartoon representations and in press reports.[80] Wright and Morbin may have been more harshly treated than Mason because conscription had now come into force. William Mason was a volunteer, not a conscript, whilst Wright had to be literally dragged into the army.

Whilst many recruits would not have understood the methodology of deserters like Mason and Wright, they did understand desertion. Soldiers had sympathy for those who clearly were not suited for the army, men understanding this better than their superiors in some instances. Some men might be a liability on the front line so their comrades did not necessarily resent their departure. Frank Crozier's memoir recalled the attitude of his men to a deserter he called 'Crockett' (actually a private by the name of Crozier) who was shot for his crime, saying he was never branded as a coward by his soldier comrades and was just 'poor Crockett'.[81] Max Plowman, serving as a Second Lieutenant in the Yorkshire Regiment, wrote of life in the army as being 'The endless hideous life of the automaton' and understood desertion as an attempt to impose some agency of one's own.[82] The assault on individuality by the military was relentless and deliberate. Lord Moran wrote that the citizen soldier needed to learn that the army was right even when it was obviously wrong, because 'in this life the individual shrinks to nothing, he has no longer the right to an opinion, only the regiment matters'.[83] This was a difficult process for many. Jack Lawson MP, later Baron Lawson, served in the Royal Field Artillery during the war and told Parliament in 1919, 'I know how very difficult indeed it was, with the best will and the best intentions, to fit oneself into the organisation and to move in the mass after one had been used to moving and thinking for oneself.'[84] Escorts often showed a great deal of empathy towards those they were sent to collect, sometimes leading to the prisoner 'escaping', often after all had shared an evening's drinking. Thomas Gillies thwarted his arrest as a deserter by getting drunk with the escort and running away.[85] Henry Brooks, the deserter released by the sympathetic judge, had been apprehended as a deserter from the Royal Welch before his fraudulent enlistment into the Manchester Regiment but had escaped from his military escorts.[86] Thomas Rule's return to the Middlesex Regiment after his daughter's death was delayed when the original escort sent to retrieve him also deserted.[87]

Huge numbers of men have entries on their conduct records for absence or desertion, the court martial statistics only telling part of the story. Heroes were just as likely to make themselves scarce as any other soldier when it suited them. William Mariner won the Victoria Cross for his bravery with the King's Royal Rifle Corps in France in May 1915, yet also appeared before the court as a deserter. Mariner received his medal at Buckingham Palace in August but overstayed his leave and was still in the United Kingdom in October 1915. He told the court that he had been 'doing some recruiting' with Jack Johnson, heavyweight champion of the world. They must have made a rare double act as

Mariner was only 5ft 4in tall.[88] Thomas Alfred 'Todger' Jones of the Cheshire Regiment already had misconduct on his record when he won the Victoria Cross in 1916 for single-handedly capturing over 100 German prisoners. Jones was given twenty-eight days' Field Punishment No. 1 for overstaying his leave to England.[89] William Carruthers, mocked for his claim that he deserted to get to the Front more quickly, went on to prove his mettle, working his way up to Lance Sergeant and winning the Military Medal at Vimy Ridge in 1917, a battle in which he also lost a leg.[90]

John Bull, positioning itself as the voice of the Tommy, consistently showed a tolerant attitude to those who had deserted from the ranks having actually served, its wrath being reserved for 'shirkers' (including conscientious objectors) who did not serve at all, and for war profiteers. The paper displayed an appreciation of the strains men were under and the domestic problems they may have. Articles not infrequently protested against the punishment of men who had overstayed their leave by a day or two and the paper campaigned against death sentences for British soldiers. *John Bull* advocated pardons for deserters who had left the colours due to some temporary difficulty but were willing to return. One correspondent claimed to know at least twenty men in this position who would go back immediately if they knew they would not be punished for their desertion.[91] The paper suggested on several occasions that the King should issue a pardon to all deserters and absentees, but no further amnesties would be granted in wartime.[92] Sympathy for deserters was sometimes tinged with envy. F.A. Voigt, a schoolmaster when he was conscripted in 1916, fantasized about desertion, writing, 'From time to time I felt a wild desire to run away and enjoy a few days of freedom, but the realisation of the futility of such a wish always brought on a fit of such black despair that I tried not to think about it at all.'[93]

Resistance to the military machine took courage of a kind that Voigt did not possess.

Chapter 4

Arrested in Britain, Shot at Dawn

If I am not too severely dealt with I will try to do my best in the future.

Private John Lewis,
5th Dorsetshire Regiment, 1917

In February 1925 Sir Laming Worthington-Evans told Parliament that no executions for desertion had taken place on British soil during the war.[1] Whilst this was true, the distinction was a fine one. Men arrested in a state of desertion in Britain whilst their regiments were at the Front were at risk of execution and in some cases did suffer that fate. When these men were caught they were treated as front-line deserters from active service, being returned to their regiments in France and Belgium for the court martial and sometimes sentenced to death. For the lucky ones, this sentence was commuted to a period of imprisonment instead, but for some it was subsequently carried out. A week after his initial assertion, Worthington-Evans, under pressure from Ernest Thurtle, was forced to admit knowledge of two such cases where men were executed, but claimed it would be too time consuming to see if there had been others in the same position.[2] The two cases were those of Privates Jennings and Lewis, considered later in this chapter. Julian Putkowski and Julian Sykes identify fourteen home-front deserters who were shot at dawn.[3] Further investigation reveals that six of these men were arrested in the United Kingdom having failed to return from leave, whilst five had managed to cross the Channel by their own methods after deserting their battalions. Two deserted on British soil on their way to the Front, and one appears to have been sent home by the army so that he could be identified.[4]

The overwhelming majority of deserters from the front line were sentenced to imprisonment and even those sentenced to death did not always suffer that fate. Amongst British and Dominion forces during the war, 3,080 death sentences were imposed by courts martial but only 346 of these were carried out, the rest being remitted by the relevant military authority into prison sentences or suspended death sentences.[5] The destruction of court-martial records for non-death penalty cases and the paucity of service records which remain make it difficult to ascertain why some men would be spared whilst others were shot. An examination of the workings of the British Army's disciplinary system is necessary to try to find the answers.

Field General Courts Martial (FGCM) dealt with 'capital' cases at the Front, i.e. those where the death penalty was one of the available punishments. A panel of three officers heard the evidence, decided on guilt or innocence and recommended a sentence. This sentence would not be confirmed until passed up the chain of command. The officer in charge of a man's unit would have the opportunity to pass comment before the case went to brigade headquarters for their views. After a check by the Adjutant General to make sure any death sentence imposed was legally valid, the Commander-in-Chief would be asked to confirm the decision. The officers reviewing the sentence as it went upwards through the administration would be asked to address three questions:

1) Does the man have anything to recommend him as a soldier?
2) What is the current state of discipline in the battalion?
3) Was this a case of deliberate desertion?

The last question seems superfluous, as by this stage a man had been convicted of desertion, by definition, a deliberate act. There are conflicting accounts of what documentation was actually forwarded to the final decision maker: Anthony Babington, writing as a civilian, claims that the notes made by the President of the FGCM were sent, but Frank Crozier, who served as a Brigadier General, says they were not. The inclusion of this last question would suggest that either the full papers were not sent, or the Commander-in-Chief was not going to read them, preferring to rely on the precis given by his officers further down the line.[6] There was no appeal available against the original decision, so this chain of promulgation was a man's only chance to have his sentence overturned. Gerard Oram has described the top brass who were looking at these sentences as 'dangerously remote' from the ordinary soldier but the flow of information up the chain from a man's commanding officer was an attempt to address this issue, though it is questionable how effective this was.[7]

Junior officers on the adjudication panels undoubtedly felt under pressure to maintain discipline in the eyes of more senior colleagues. It was for this reason that the junior officers were asked to give their verdicts first, to rebut any suggestion of undue influence from the more senior men.[8] Guy Chapman wrote of his experience at a court martial where he and his inexperienced colleague wanted to impose the death penalty for what was a fairly minor offence until talked out of it by the more senior officer.[9] FGCMs may have also been more willing to impose the death penalty in the knowledge that the case had other levels to travel through before a man would actually face a firing squad. The irony was, as Anthony Babington says, that a reviewing officer may take the view that the tribunal imposing a death sentence had been given every opportunity to look at all of the facts and see the man himself, and in those circumstances decline to contradict their decision.[10] Accused men routinely went without legal assistance at court martial fearing that the utilization of a 'prisoner's friend' would count against them.[11] Officers acting as prisoner's friends were only available from 1916 onwards and were not usually legally qualified. It was not until 1917 that officers with legal training were sent to advise at courts martial on the front line. Some solicitor soldiers did the profession no credit in a number of cases, failing to put forward any kind of active defence on behalf of their clients. When Private Arthur Briggs was charged with desertion after overstaying his leave by four months in 1918, he had as his prisoner's friend an officer who was a solicitor in civilian life. It is difficult to see what meaningful assistance was given as the officer did not cross-examine any witnesses or address the court and failed to bring forward any positive evidence of his client's character. Briggs was convicted and eventually executed.[12]

Harsh punishments were specifically encouraged in the *Manual of Military Law* in units where there was a perceived issue with discipline, the individual circumstances of the offender being deemed unimportant. Notes from the *MML* were issued to officers taking part in courts martial and the message was clear:

When there is a general prevalence of offences or of offences of some particular class, an example may be necessary, and a severe punishment may justly be awarded in respect of an offence which would otherwise receive a more lenient punishment. In such cases the punishment for the offence must be regarded in reference to the effect to be produced on the military body to which the offender belongs, rather than in reference to the act of the individual himself.[13]

As Brigadier General H.C. Lowther wrote in his notes on a case coming before him, the man should be executed 'not to punish the man for having deserted, but in order that men may not desert'.[14] Private J.E. Bolton's Battalion Commander strongly recommended that the death sentence imposed on him by the FGCM should be carried out 'as the want of realization as to what amounts to desertion as a military offence is very marked in the Battalion and this case is one in which the example of full punishment should be beneficial to the Regiment'.[15] Driver James Swaine was shot despite having a clean service record because it was said that cases of overstaying leave were 'very common' in the 39th Royal Field Artillery.[16]

Stephen Graham, who enlisted as a Private in the Scots Guards though his civilian social status was akin to those with commissions, outlined the army's position as he saw it, saying that if a deserter was shot 'every man knows what is likely to be his fate if he fails at his post. He knows also that the army has absolute power over him, and that it is not the least use rebelling or mutinying or endeavouring in any way to oppose his puny strength to its complete power.'[17] The individual was at the mercy of the military machine.

The shooting of a deserter was designed to provide an example to the rest of the troops, to display the ultimate authority of the army and to ensure that those who may have behaved in a similar way thought twice about their actions. The example was displayed firstly in the public announcement of the sentence. At the execution itself, troops lucky enough to have escaped firing squad duty were sometimes forced to watch the gruesome proceedings. For the shooting of Private J.E. Bolton the instructions from Brigade Headquarters to the officer commanding the 1st Cheshire Regiment were very clear; 'The Divisional Commander wishes one platoon from each company of your Battalion to be present at the execution.'[18] Executions were further burned into the memory by the reading out of the sentences on parade.

Concerned at the numbers of men committing offences in France that incurred sentences removing them from the front line, in March 1915 Parliament passed the Army (Suspension of Sentences) Act 1915. This allowed the army greater leeway in dealing with offences committed by soldiers abroad, giving them the power to suspend sentences and review the position three months later. This gave a man time to regain his reputation on the battlefield and potentially put the crime behind him, as the army had the power to remit the sentence completely if he had behaved well. If not, the sentence could be immediately imposed or further suspended for another review. The Act only applied to men on active service overseas, so the suspension of a sentence was not available for deserters on the home front. However, the deserters discussed in this chapter were treated by the army as though they were on active service abroad, so were eligible for the application of the Act despite the location of their arrest. Huntly Gordon, serving as a teenage 2nd Lieutenant in the Royal Field Artillery, recorded in his diary the case of a man who showed bravery extreme enough at Rifle Farm near Passchendaele to be recommended for the Victoria Cross in September 1917. The honour was downgraded to a Distinguished Conduct Medal because at the time of his selfless heroics the man was under a sentence of suspended imprisonment for 'indefinitely overstaying his leave'. As part of his reward the suspended sentence was quashed.[19]

Sir John French, Commander-in-Chief of the British Expeditionary Force in 1915, said that the suspension of sentences was: 'designed to take away the desire of men to commit military offences whilst at the same time to provide the machinery for affording sympathetic treatment to men convicted of offences of extreme gravity from a military point of view, due often to exhaustion or temporary loss of nerve.' This was not a new idea: commutation of sentences had a history in the British Army, as we have seen, with men often transferred to new units or to service abroad with a view to making a fresh start. After the war it was claimed that between 50,000 and 100,000 men had been dealt with under the 1915 legislation.[20]

The existence of this power no doubt saved many from paying the ultimate price for their misbehaviour. It equally put some men back in the firing line who really should not have been there. Philip Brocklesby, as a junior officer on a court-martial panel, found a man guilty of desertion who had been missing for two days. Though he had some sympathy for the soldier, he felt that he was not much use to the battalion as a fighting man and would be better off out of the front line. Brocklesby calculated that if he gave him a harsh sentence he would be returned home, so announced that he should get five years' penal servitude – a sentence to be served back in England. When the sentence was promulgated, those reviewing it had commuted it to two years' hard labour, which was immediately suspended, the prisoner to remain with his battalion in France.[21]

In fact, the suspension of sentences provisions stipulated that no man was to be committed to prison without the approval of the higher military authority, and there was a presumption that a sentence should be suspended unless there was some good and sufficient cause as to why this should not happen. Looking at the desertion figures for the summer of 1915 it is to be wondered if the new provisions did not actually help to increase the numbers of men deserting. Soldiers becoming aware of the new rules may have felt more confident of the odds of escaping significant punishment for a first-time offence. Brocklesby claimed that there was one man in his platoon who had been sentenced to death three times, only to see the sentences commuted or suspended.[22]

Some spared in this way certainly did not take the hint – ninety-one of the soldiers executed were already under a suspended sentence of some kind, thirty-eight of them previously sentenced to death for desertion.[23] Of the fourteen cases considered here, five men had bad disciplinary records, including suspended sentences of imprisonment, and two, Joseph Edward Bolton and William Jones, were already under a suspended death sentence for desertion.[24] It is hard to argue that these men had not been given fair warning as to what was likely to happen should they desert again. Daniel Gibson of the 12th Royal Scots was given the most direct of opportunities to redeem himself. Arrested in June 1918 for overstaying his leave, Gibson was back in the ranks awaiting court martial as his battalion were due to take part in an attack. He was told in no uncertain terms that if he did well in the forthcoming engagement it would count in his favour before the tribunal. Faced with this chance to prove himself a valuable soldier, Gibson again deserted.[25]

Whilst the sentence on home-front deserters may seem harsh, it is at least in line with what they may have faced had they been arrested on the French side of the Channel. These deserters could not be given special treatment simply because they had been more successful in their escape efforts than men who were found wandering in France and Belgium. A significant number of other men who were executed for desertion were arrested at ports in France, the inference being that their next step would have been back to Britain and freedom.[26] For those who had overstayed their leave, however, the imposition of the death sentence at first glance seems extreme even by the standards of the day.

One example was Lance Corporal Peter Sands, a Regular soldier from West Belfast serving with the 1st Battalion Royal Irish Rifles. At the end of February 1915 after four months in France he was granted four days' leave. This was not much time to travel to Belfast and back to see his wife and child, but any leave was precious. Peter Sands was away for four months, not four days, eventually being arrested at his home address in July 1915. When returned to France for the court martial, he claimed he had stayed at home because he lost his travel warrant and when he reported to the army in Belfast in March no one would provide him with a new one.[27] He denied that he was a deserter and claimed to have worn his uniform throughout his stay in Belfast. Of course, the fact he remained in khaki would probably have made it less likely he would be detected in a city which was then a hive of military activity. He was, not surprisingly, found guilty of desertion. Sands had been a good soldier up until this point and received a glowing character reference from his battalion, but this did not save him. Douglas Haig, then commanding the First Army, confirmed the sentence, calling it 'a bad case'. Sands was executed on 15 September 1915. The experiences of his battalion in the four months he was missing must have been a major factor in the decision to carry out the death sentence. A week after Sands' anticipated return from leave, the 1st Royal Irish Rifles took part in the Battle of Neuve Chapelle, during which their commanding officer received fatal wounds. Two months later the battalion were in action at Aubers Ridge, fighting their way into the German trenches only to be marooned with no support, eventually withdrawing and suffering heavy losses. The British ranks suffered 11,000 casualties in the battle on this date, with the 1st Royal Irish Rifles losing 467 officers and men, once again including their commanding officer. The date of this battle was specifically mentioned during Sands' court martial, the image of the missing lance corporal sitting at home in Belfast whilst his comrades went through these experiences weighing heavily on the tribunal.[28]

Gerard Oram believes that Irish soldiers like Peter Sands were specially selected for execution to use as examples to maintain discipline in regiments where revolt may have been more feared given the political situation in Ireland.[29] Sands' nationality may have been less important in the decision to execute him than the general picture of army discipline in 1915. Peter Sands had his court martial at a very unfortunate time. The early months of 1915 saw a concern amongst the top brass of the army over the state of discipline, with reports of widespread drunkenness and desertion. A bad winter had left the troops in Belgium living in very unpleasant conditions and a swift end to the war was now a distant dream. General Smith-Dorrien, commanding the Second Army, reportedly stated in January 1915 that the only means of combating the rise in desertion was to execute some of the offenders.[30] Fourteen men were shot in January and February 1915 with no appreciable effect on the desertion figures. This harsh attitude can be seen in the notes attached to the file of William Turpie. When Turpie's case of absconding across the Channel appeared at FGCM that summer he was tried alongside two men from the Middlesex Regiment who had lost touch with their company for just a few days. Privates Chapman and Gibbs were given penal servitude, not the firing squad and when the sentences were sent up for promulgation, 2nd Corps Headquarters were unhappy – they wanted all three privates shot. Chapman and Gibbs escaped with their lives but Turpie was executed on 1 July 1915.[31]

Concern had also been expressed in 1915 on the home front about the frequency with which soldiers overstayed their leave. When Oswald Llewellyn's father was prosecuted for concealing his deserter son, the Chief Constable for Merthyr told the court that the case was of 'considerable importance' because of 'the large number of soldiers on leave who absented themselves from their regiments'.[32] The figures were certainly worrying. The average number of men struck off the strength for desertion each month during 1915 was 3,778, the high point coming in August 1915 when 4,830 men disappeared. The net loss to the army from desertion during the year between October 1914 and the end of September 1915 was just under 32,000 men – the worst year of the war by far. This only includes men who were missing long enough to be struck off the strength, so, as usual, is likely to be an underestimate of the numbers of those who actually left the ranks.[33]

Some overstayers may well have been intending to return after a lengthier rest at home than their leave pass allowed, though others had clearly decided their army careers were over, despite their protestations to the contrary at court martial. J.E. Bolton was found working at Balls Corn Mills in Ince, Lancashire, under the surname Cunningham, three months after he should have returned to his regiment. William Watts had, by his own admission, signed up to work on a merchant ship docked in London, though he was found in his hometown of Liverpool. William Turpie was wearing civilian clothing when arrested in Dover and claimed to be in the merchant marine. The apparent resumption of civilian life undoubtedly increased the chances of all three men being shot.[34]

For others it was the length of their absence which led the court martial to conclude that they were not intending to return. John Jennings and Griffith Lewis of the South Lancashire Regiment had deserted together in October 1915 and were not apprehended until May 1916. They had not even left Britain before they absented themselves. The pair were with their battalion at the Union Jack Club in London but were missing a few hours later when the time came to leave for France. Acting on a tip-off almost seven months later the police arrested them at an address in Tilbury Court, London. Both were old soldiers – Jennings was a recalled reservist whilst Lewis had re-enlisted before the declaration of war. Both were officers' servants, and both had already been to the Front so knew exactly what awaited them. Neither could demonstrate good disciplinary records. Both handed in written statements to the FGCM that were identical in almost every respect. They claimed to have been told they could leave the Club if they were back for a certain time, so had gone elsewhere to have a drink. Returning before the relevant time they fell asleep and missed the battalion's departure. The only difference in their accounts was the location of their snoozing – Jennings claimed to simply be asleep in a chair at the club, whilst Lewis accepted he was in a cupboard, though claimed this was for comfort, not concealment. Thereafter, they had been too embarrassed to surrender. The officers in the chain of promulgation made a point of noting the similarity in their statements, interpreting it as evidence of a conspiracy. The officer in command of the 75th Brigade said they should be shot because, 'There was apparently collusion between the men as to the best manner in which the offence could be committed and as to how they could conceal themselves afterwards.'[35] Not every officer was happy with the circumstances in which Lewis and Jennings found themselves. Lieutenant Colonel Colton, Commanding Officer of the 2nd South Lancashire Regiment, pointed out in both cases that, 'Had this man been tried by Court Martial at Home, it is possible that he would not have been condemned to death.' As we have seen, it is **certain** that if they had been tried at home they would not have faced the death penalty. As Stephen Graham recalled, after being warned for a stint overseas 'there are always one or two who imagine they can escape the hand of Fate by resorting to various tricks to avoid it at the last moment, by reporting sick, committing a crime, trying to square someone, or bolting home until the draft has gone'.[36] Lewis and Jennings were the only two such men who were executed.

Understandably none of the home runners admitted that they were intending to stay away from the ranks permanently. Some cited family problems as the catalyst for their desertion, both William Watts and Daniel Gibson claiming that they had overstayed due to discovering that their wives were having extra-marital affairs. Arthur Briggs married the mother of his child in Sunderland during his leave, and when she was dismissed from her job, leaving her homeless, was not prepared to return to the Front until she was settled. Mrs Briggs found work in munitions in Scotland, where Arthur was arrested in civilian clothes having been missing for four months. None of these stories cut any ice with the FGCM or the confirming officers, falling into the category of 'individual circumstances' deemed unimportant by the *Manual of Military Law*.[37]

The idea that executions would provide a lasting example to the deserter's battalion is difficult to accept. Stephen Graham recalls that the execution of a man for cowardice in his battalion did have an immediate galvanizing effect on the man's company, who felt the sting of being associated with shirking and vowed to redeem their honour in the next action. This attitude was taken by the men even though they did not agree with the sentence imposed on their comrade.[38] How long this effect would last is another matter entirely. Given the lengthy casualty lists and changes in the compositions of units, could it really be the case that an execution of a man in 1915 could prevent a recruit who had never met him from deserting two years later? On the other hand, the army were in a difficult position with these men. After spring 1915 the existence of suspended sentences arguably had the potential to undermine discipline. If men believed that they were not, to all intents and purposes, going to endure any significant punishment for indiscretions the temptation to abscond would be greater. Against that background, it could be argued that an occasional execution was even more necessary than before. Though on the face of it, if men overstaying their leave were less culpable than those who escaped from France, it was arguably more important to make an example of them. Not every man would have the audacity to desert the front line and smuggle himself aboard a ship at the Channel ports or even think about such an action; surely every man who had ever been on leave wished on some level that he did not have to return to France. Leave was a very precious thing and the scarcity of it was acknowledged as a problem for morale at the Front. Failure to severely punish men like Peter Sands would potentially open the floodgates for men to overstay on a regular basis and raised the spectre of the army being forced to cancel leave altogether for the duration of the war. If one accepts that the death penalty was a punishment which the army should have at its disposal in a time of war, one can recognize the need to apply it in the case of the overstayers.

Any discussion of the cases of deserters who were shot at dawn inevitably raises the issue of shell shock. The idea that these men were suffering from shell shock was a key element of the Shot at Dawn campaign, coalescing around the case of Harry Farr in which there was clear evidence of this. The cases of the home runners considered here are much less clear cut even though several claimed to be suffering from symptoms which had become synonymous with shell shock. The most frequent symptom cited by the fourteen men considered in this chapter was memory loss, which was a major feature of the odd story of Private John Lewis. Lewis disappeared from a work party at the end of September 1916 with a comrade called William Anderson. The rest of the group all became casualties thereafter, save for the two deserters and the officer in charge. Anderson was not at large for long, being arrested by the Military Police in France in October. Lewis, meanwhile, was nowhere to be found.[39]

In October, a strange young man appeared in the town of Puchevilliers. On being questioned by the Town Major he claimed that he was 'Tom Jones of Barking', a civilian who had made his way to France before the war and been unable to return home. The main flaw in his argument was that he was in British Army uniform, but he claimed that this was an accumulation of mismatched pieces he had picked up along the way so he could cadge food and accommodation. Unable to confirm his true identity, the Military Police eventually sent 'Tom Jones' back to England under armed guard and he was charged with the offence of wearing military uniform without authority. He appeared at Folkestone Police Court in December 1916 in the name of Thomas William Jones, sticking to his story of having been a civilian in France. His downfall came when a week's remand for further enquiries revealed him to be a deserter, his identity confirmed by his sister, Joanna Lewis, who had previously been told by the War Office that her brother was missing.[40] Had she realized what was about to happen she may well have kept quiet.

Private John Lewis of the 5th Dorsetshire Regiment was now taken back across the Channel for his court martial. For some reason which is not immediately apparent, he went through two trials for the same offence. At his first trial he confirmed much of the evidence given about what took place in Puchevilliers, though claimed to have no memory of leaving the trenches at all. By the time of the second court martial he claimed to have no recollection of being in the Dorset Regiment, of being at Puchevilliers or of being in the army at all. He said he did not know he was a soldier until his brother told him so when he was back in England. He pleaded with the court, 'If I am not too severely dealt with I will try to do my best in the future.'[41] No detailed medical enquiries seem to have been made and the soldier was clearly considered to be faking his memory loss. Brigadier General Pedley, commanding the 34th Infantry Brigade, made much of the fact that Lewis had consistently lied during his two months in Puchevilliers, not revealing his identity until back in England when confronted by his own family.

In the meantime, his comrade in desertion, William Anderson, had made matters worse both for himself and his pal. Having been apprehended in October, Anderson had run off again in early January 1917, this time making it all the way across the Channel. Anderson, like Lewis, was from Barking and was arrested there at the end of that month. He had a poor disciplinary record with several convictions for absence and he now ran out of luck. He was convicted and sentenced to death, being executed on 31 March 1917. The same sentence was passed on John Lewis a week later. One of the commenting officers attempted to save Lewis's life, though not because he felt the man was suffering from shell shock. Major General A.B. Ritchie, commanding the 11th Division, felt that the good discipline of the Dorsetshire Regiment did not need the example of an execution. Certainly once Anderson had been shot, he felt that the point had been made and there was no need to shoot Lewis too.[42]

Amnesia of varying degrees was also cited by other deserters. William Turpie claimed to not remember what had happened to him once he stepped out of line to defecate whilst suffering from dysentery in Belgium. Turpie said that he had suffered bouts of memory loss following an accident whilst working as an engine cleaner at King's Cross Station some years earlier. He did, however, remember precisely how he had managed to escape across the Channel once he was in Boulogne, talking the British Consul into giving him a pass for a leave boat and getting civilian clothes from a sailor.[43] George Hunter also claimed his behaviour was due to an industrial accident, in his case a blow on the head whilst working at Pease's Iron Works in Middlesbrough that left him with 'a wandering mind'. Hunter served with the 2nd Battalion of the DLI, had been convicted of absence on twelve occasions on the home front and had a poor record once in France. He had deliberately blown off his little finger and a suspended sentence of one year's imprisonment with hard labour was hanging over him at the time he failed to return from leave. Hunter specifically mentioned having 'got a shock' during a bombardment and said he had been 'suffering from debility for a long time'. His commanding officer, Lieutenant Colonel Irvin, wrote, 'I consider that he is not of normal mental development' and suggested that before the decision to execute him was promulgated Hunter should be examined by a mental health specialist. This did not happen because Irvin also expressed the opinion that Hunter was of no worth to the battalion: 'As a fighting man this man is perfectly useless – he is very nervous and has no control over himself.'[44] As far as those higher up were concerned, it was the second part of Lieutenant Colonel Irvin's statement which carried the most weight. Hunter was seen as a King's bad bargain so of no utility and not worth wasting any more time over.

Two of the home-runner cases did merit further investigation as far as the army were concerned, though it is difficult to see why they would warrant this when Hunter's case did not. Charles Bladen had not simply overstayed his leave but had escaped across the Channel in December 1915 with no authorisation at all. He too claimed that he was not in his right mind when doing so and said that friends had told him he had 'gone dotty'. 'Dotty' or not, Bladen had made concerted attempts not to be returned to France, escaping from rest camp in Southampton after his initial arrest in February 1916. He gave a false name and number when stopped by the police in the capital but was detained and placed in the Tower of London. He found the guard room of the 11th Yorks and Lancs Regiment less of a challenge than the Tower and escaped the very next evening. A day later Bladen again gave false details on arrest but his true identity was discovered and he was finally returned to France. Surprisingly, the order came that he was to be mentally examined before the ultimate sentence of his court martial was confirmed. Bladen spent four days under observation by a Medical Board, but they detected nothing other than a 'a certain want of intelligence'.[45] In the case of William Watts, detailed investigations were made, possibly because his case fell more easily into the ideas of mental illness with which the top brass were familiar, namely hereditary madness. Watts claimed to be suffering from a mental disorder passed on to him by his father, who died in Rainhill Asylum. Looking at the scant consideration other soldiers' cases were given it is surprising to find the lengths to which the army went to investigate Watts' claims. Enquiries took place with the Watts family in Liverpool and it was confirmed that his father had been confined to the asylum suffering from 'religious mania'. Watts had a sister who appeared not to have inherited this insanity gene, being described as 'an intelligent woman for the class she belongs to, which is the low labouring class of dock workers'. Watts was a Regular soldier and neither his commanding officer from the 1st Loyal North Lancashire Battalion nor the Brigadier General of the 2nd Infantry Brigade wanted him shot. Discipline in the battalion was said to be good and their one previous execution for desertion had taken place after Watts had already deserted, depriving him of the example it set. However, Watts was a determined deserter, his intention to go to sea as a civilian and his escape from the guard room at Southampton after his initial arrest demonstrating this beyond much doubt. This and his poor disciplinary record spoke much more loudly to the General commanding the First Army and Watts was executed in May 1916.[46]

It is impossible at this juncture to definitively diagnose these men. No one would argue that a stint on the Western Front was likely to improve one's mental health but that does not mean that these men were suffering from an illness that explained and excused their desertion by the standards of the time. No thorough medical examination of the men shot at dawn generally took place and it was not until questions were asked in Parliament about their mental state that measures were eventually introduced, from March 1918 onwards, to have such men examined by a Medical Board that contained an expert in neurology.[47] Whilst it is undoubtedly true that some of the soldiers executed for desertion were suffering from shell shock, it can also not be denied that there were a number of malingerers who would feign symptoms in the hope that it would save them from the ultimate penalty. It was certainly the view of the army administration that a great deal of 'scrimshanking' of this kind took place.[48] Initial treatment plans for shell shock followed those in place for serious wounds in that the man would be evacuated to Britain and treated in hospital there until deemed fit to return to the front line. This gave greater encouragement to fakers wanting to go home. Later in the war it was decided that the best course of treatment was removal from the front line temporarily and for a short distance, removing the promise of a berth back to Britain. It is noteworthy that the symptom consistently complained of in our cases was memory loss. With medical officers primed to weed out malingerers by methods fair and foul, memory loss was the easiest symptom to fake and the hardest to disprove.

By 1916 the term 'shell shock' was being widely used on the home front and the battlefield for all kinds of emotional disturbance suffered by soldiers. It was also being used as an excuse for all kinds of misconduct on both sides of the Channel. Lord Moran wrote that when the term was coined the number of men reporting sick with no physical wounds increased. He claimed that shell shock was 'giving fear a respectable name'.[49] There certainly appeared to be no shame attached to the term back in Britain, as from 1916 onwards shell shock was used as defence or mitigation in a wide range of cases before the civilian courts. Offences of desertion, being drunk and disorderly, threatening the police with a revolver, attempting to procure a 16- year-old girl for immoral purposes and the perennial officer's offence, passing bad cheques, all saw defendants plead shell shock, some of whom had never crossed the Channel. As a defence before a jury it was often successful: in the case of Thomas Maynard, before the court for bigamy in February 1918, the assembled spectators burst into a round of applause when he was acquitted.[50] By 1919 the police were clearly tiring of the regularity with which it was put forward – Superintendent Fairclough, faced with a man using the defence before the Bury Magistrates in August 1919, wearily announced, 'That game is played out'.[51] Played out or not, it later saw a schoolmaster acquitted of involvement in the Luton Peace Day riots of 1919.[52] One of the key recommendations of the Southborough Committee convened after the war to examine the army's response to shell shock was that the term should no longer be used as it had become completely devalued. As far as some army administrators were concerned, including several Medical Officers, the term 'shell shock' was simply the medicalization of cowardice. Others felt that it was a condition to which the less able had a predisposition – Frederick Mott treated shell-shocked men at the Maudsley Hospital in London and claimed that the vast majority had family histories of mental illness of some kind. The thinking of eugenicists like Mott informed the investigations carried out in the William Watts case. Charles Myers, originator of the term 'shell shock', found that the centre he set up to deal with sufferers in France was actually full of men who could be termed King's bad bargains, sent there by units keen to get rid of them, regardless of the nature of their ailment.

An examination of the files that survive would suggest that the length of a man's absence, the experiences of his battalion during that time and any sign that he was intending to stay away permanently would impact upon the chances of his being shot for desertion. But there was a completely arbitrary element to military discipline too and not every case meeting this description would result in an execution. Several examples were reported in the press. Tom Hillier of the 2nd Dorset Regiment claimed to have made his way home from Salonika to Somerset.[53] Private 17983 Byrne of the 2nd Royal Inniskilling Fusiliers was arrested at the train station in Dover and confessed that he had managed to sneak home on a leave boat without authority.[54] J. Scott Duckers, conscientious objector, found himself in prison with a man who claimed to have escaped across the Channel and was now serving a custodial sentence for desertion. The man had made his own way back from France twice, the first time fraudulently re-enlisting and the second time leaving the army altogether to work in a munitions factory. He told Duckers how his Channel crossings had been achieved, saying that a man simply had to make his way to a Channel port, then pretend to have missed a newly departed leave boat. He should then go to the British Consul and claim to have been robbed of his paperwork, seeking a further pass to board a boat bound for Britain. The Consul would have no facilities to detain the man whilst enquiries were made, so would just write him a pass and have done with it. He may have suspicion that the man was a deserter but as the prisoner told Duckers, ''E can think wot 'e likes but 'e don't know nothink.' This seems to have been the procedure adopted by William Turpie in his escape across the Channel.[55] An issue of the *Police Gazette* chosen at random, for May 1916, lists thirty-four men in the pages of deserters and absentees who have deserted from the ranks of the BEF by overstaying leave or making their own way across the Channel. None of them were executed for the offence.[56]

One of the most extraordinary stories of deserters making it home is that of the Ship brothers of Chelsea. Charles and Harry Ship were with the 13th (Kensington) Battalion of the London Regiment, a Territorial battalion sent to France in early November 1914. Territorials could not be forced to serve abroad at this time, though were under great pressure to volunteer to do so.[57] K.W. Mitchison writes that there was a widespread belief amongst Territorials at the start of the war that they would be reserved for home service, and even if sent abroad, would not be in the front line. Both beliefs proved to be false.[58] The Kensingtons were part of the 25th Brigade, the same as Peter Sands' Irish Rifles and fought alongside them in 1915 at Neuve Chapelle and Aubers Ridge. The Ship brothers did not take part, having already deserted the ranks.

On 26 December 1914 Charles and Harry Ship were seen walking away from their billets in a French village.[59] Their unit was due to relieve their comrades that evening, half of the battalion having been in billets whilst the rest were in the front-line trenches (and witnessed the Christmas Truce). Major Parnell, the Ships' commanding officer, said that he had last seen the two that morning but that when they did not reappear later in the day he reported them as deserters. Fellow soldiers said they had seen the brothers leave their billets at 8am and had presumed that they were going to buy bread. When they did not return their comrades wondered if they had drowned in the fast-flowing river that ran alongside the path to the village. Despite Major Parnell's certainty that they had deserted, the brothers' names originally appeared on a War Office list of the missing. It was not until October 1916, twenty-two months after the Ships were last seen, that statements were taken from others in the battalion as to the circumstances of their disappearance. The War Office then declared that they could officially be considered as deserters from 26 December 1914.

Nothing further was seemingly heard of the Ship brothers until late February 1917 when the police arrested a man at a Salvation Army shelter off Edgeware Road in London. The man said he was Jack Smith and that he was an absentee from the Royal Fusiliers: he was really Charles Ship, deserter from the 13th London Regiment. To confirm the identification, Ship's parents were brought to the police station and were delighted to see him, having believed him to be dead. His mother had been receiving a pension on that basis for both of her sons. Ship told the magistrates at his subsequent court hearing that he had made no contact with his parents since his return to England as he knew his father would make him go back to the army.[60] He gave no information at court about the means of his escape from France or where he had been in the intervening two years. Ship claimed that brother Harry had been killed during their escape.

Charles Ship's court martial did not take place until June 1917 in France. Presumably, it was difficult to trace and assemble witnesses to the desertion so long after the event, especially given the upheaval to the 13th London Regiment in the intervening period. Ship's case was, on the face of it, worse than some of the examples outlined here of deserters who were shot: he had deserted from billets just behind the lines, knowing he was going into the trenches that night, had managed to cross the Channel unlawfully and had been missing for more than two years. His comrades had been through terrible fighting in the time he had been away and there was no doubt that he had no intention of returning to active service. At his court martial Ship was found guilty of desertion and sentenced to death. On promulgation a month later the sentence was commuted to five years' imprisonment which was immediately suspended. He returned to the ranks and served for the rest of the war until his demobilization in 1919.[61] Three other men on the same page of the courts-martial ledger for that month were given death sentences for desertion which were then suspended – Frederick Loader, R.M. Davies and E. Keeling. Loader and Davies didn't respond to this warning and both were shot for further desertion before the year was out.

The postscript to Charles Ship's story is that his version of events was untrue: brother Harry was not dead, surviving the war and being demobilized in March 1919. Harry's whereabouts after his desertion are difficult to trace, though it seems likely that he re-enlisted, possibly with the 6th Essex Regiment. *The National Roll of the Great War* has an entry for H.W. Ship, outlining his military achievements with the 6th Essex Regiment, including involvement in the Battle of Neuve Chapelle.[62] This does not accord with what we know of Harry Ship's record with the 13th London Regiment, or indeed of the record of the 6th Essex Regiment, which never saw action on the Western Front. *The National Roll* was compiled from information supplied by soldiers themselves, or by family members, not from official sources. The soldier's address noted at the bottom of the fanciful entry is 32 Meek Street, King's Road, Chelsea – an address also used by Charles Ship as his discharge address and by Harry Ship on his marriage in January 1919. Though the initial medal roll prepared for the Kensingtons in 1921 states that Harry Ship was not entitled to medals and was still in a state of desertion, there is a note that his name appeared elsewhere in the roll and that he did eventually receive his medals. Both brothers were clearly keen to promote their military service – not only had Harry greatly exaggerated his experiences for *The National Roll*, but when Charles applied for his medals he insisted on having a clasp on his 1914 Star because he had been under fire abroad before he deserted.

One conclusion to be drawn from an examination of the home deserters' files is that it was the sheer arbitrary nature of the application of the ultimate punishment which acted as the real aid to military discipline. Andrew Godefroy, in his study of the twenty-five Canadian servicemen who were executed, states that the men were 'victims of time, place and circumstance' rather than of any firm and settled policy and this is undoubtedly holds true for the British soldiers too.[63] Direct comparisons between those shot for desertion and those convicted of the offence who received lesser punishments is now impossible due to the destruction of the bulk of the British court-martial records. Indeed, the inability to carry out any meaningful comparative exercise was one of the reasons why all 309 soldiers shot at dawn for military offences were eventually pardoned in 2006. It was also the reason repeatedly given by the Ministry of Defence for resisting any pardons in the first place.[64] In February 1920 there were still 176 soldiers serving terms of imprisonment for desertion. These were described as 'bad cases' where 'men had left their units for a considerable time and hidden away in villages behind the firing line'. It remains a mystery as to why these men did not share the fate of Peter Sands and his fellow home-front deserters.[65] Lord Moran's assessment of capital courts martial as 'rough decisions' is correct, the verdicts playing on his conscience after the war 'because they were not decisions at all but only guesses with a bullet behind one of them'.[66]

Chapter 5

Safe Harbour

He is my only son. Would you have not done the same?
Thomas McDonald to Detective Inspector
Knowles, March 1915

From August 1914 until the end of the war, newspapers were full of cases of friends and family concealing deserters. Section 153 of the Army Act 1881 made it an offence to persuade a soldier to desert or to assist him in the act of desertion or conceal him thereafter. The offence carried imprisonment, with or without hard labour, for up to six months and the courts were not slow in imposing harsh sentences.

Many deserters ran no further than their home addresses and simply hoped they would not be detected. Coal cellars, outhouses and attics nationwide now served new functions as boltholes when the police knocked on the door. Serial deserter James Veevers was invariably arrested at his family home in Hardman Street in Rochdale. This was in spite of the fact that his wife, Florrie, had taken him to court for deserting her and their children several times and eventually obtained a legal separation in March 1915.[1] Robert Roberts writes that his local newspaper never showed less than a dozen names a week of men being arrested for desertion and recalls one man being pulled out of a coal hole in South Street in Salford.[2] Hiding places could be ingenious and sometimes dangerous. One intrepid deserter in Liverpool hid up a kitchen chimney and when pulled down by the visiting police inspector, claimed to be a chimney sweep.[3] Police in Glasgow searching the house of a Mrs Vaughan initially found nothing but became suspicious when she remained seated on a large chest throughout their visit. Eventually moving her from her perch they found the hapless deserter Patrick Boyle stuffed into the chest, half suffocated.[4] William Trenfield of Gloucester was found in a cupboard which had been papered over to look like a regular wall. Furniture had been piled in front of the cupboard and it was only by knocking on the walls that the arresting officer realized the area was hollow and found Trenfield hiding inside.[5]

By returning home, deserters put their immediate family at risk of prosecution and imprisonment. Assisting a deserter had always been an offence under successive Army Acts, but there was an imperative to prosecute once war was declared. The police sometimes used their discretion, both to prosecute or not and over which offence to charge. Obstructing a police constable would sometimes be preferred – a less serious alternative to the offence under the Army Act, giving a court wider scope in sentencing. G.H. Herbert, the Chief Constable of Barnsley, told the court in December 1915 that he received a great number of telegrams seeking the arrest of deserters and that the police often carried out this duty without taking court proceedings against those in whose houses the men are found.[6]

In order to be prosecuted for assisting a deserter, it seems that a wife had to do more than simply allow her fugitive husband to live with her. Florrie Veevers, for example, appears never to have been taken to court for harbouring husband James. *The Justice of the Peace*, the official publication for magistrates and their clerks, declared in 1917 that unless a wife played 'an active part' in her husband's concealment, 'she would probably be regarded as not even technically guilty'.[7] A wife would have difficulty in barring a man's access to his own home. The writer cited burning a man's uniform as an example of playing an active role, and the cases reported in the newspapers in detail often involve some positive action by the wife in aiding the husband's desertion such as obstructing the police to allow her man time to escape from another exit. Whether magistrates around the country took the same view as the *The Justice of the Peace* writer is uncertain.

Many of those appearing before the court for harbouring deserters in the first year of the war undoubtedly did not fully appreciate the seriousness of their offence. Whilst military service was still voluntary, desertion may have been seen in a different light by those welcoming soldiers home. Most families in civilian life would be unfamiliar with the harshness of army discipline and would have little basis on which to challenge a relative who said he had a valid reason for being at home. Others no doubt knew exactly what was going on and were happy to give a man a hiding place from the military, even for a short period of time. The enlistment of a husband, son or brother in the armed forces was not always well received by his family, so his return, authorized or not, may have been welcomed regardless of the potential consequences. Ken Weller notes the tradition of resistance to authority in working class communities at this time, citing social acceptance of the 'moonlight flit' from the landlord and resistance to bailiffs as examples of this.[8] The concealment of deserters fits into this culture. There was a healthy distrust of the police in working class areas, even amongst the outwardly respectable. Robert Roberts notes that the rule in Salford was that 'one spoke to a "rozzer" when one had to and told him the minimum'.[9] Major Woodbury's study of US desertion rates concluded that education of the public about the seriousness of the offence of desertion was necessary to reduce the numbers of men absenting themselves.[10]

As one of the first Women's Police Volunteers, Mary S. Allen was asked to assist the army in keeping order at Belton Camp near Grantham. She describes the raids on houses in the area looking for deserters:

> Women answering the sharp military knock on their doors would assume an air of shocked and surprised indignation, vehemently denying that any men so much as crossed their thresholds, while dimly discernible in the background, huddled in some corner, would be overcoats, unmistakenly masculine and military. Myriads of nephews and first cousins sprang up and were claimed by women or girls with angelic faces of injured innocence.[11]

Sympathy in many parts of the country was very firmly on the side of the deserter. In February 1915 four navy deserters being returned to the docks in Montrose were freed when a mob of women and children attacked the escorts, allowing the deserters to escape.[12] The general public in Sheffield were said to be always on the side of the soldier, no matter the reason for his arrest.[13]

The high desertion figures in the summer of 1915 led the authorities to announce a clamp down on harbourers.[14] In August 1915 notices were printed in newspapers from Edinburgh to Portsmouth making the position perfectly clear:

HARBOURING DESERTERS

Civilians are warned that persuasion, assisting, concealing or the harbouring of deserters from H.M. Army is an offence of great seriousness. The section of the Army Act applicable to this states that any person who in the United Kingdom or elsewhere by any means whatsoever

> (1) procures or persuades any soldier to desert, or attempts to procure or persuade any soldier to desert: or (2) knowing that a soldier is about to desert, aids or assists him in deserting; or (3) knowing any soldier to be a deserter, conceals such soldier, or aids or assists him in concealing himself, or aids or assists in his rescue, shall be liable on summary conviction to be imprisoned, with or without hard labour, for a term not exceeding six months.[15]

Magistrates sentencing harbourers began to make comments in court clearly designed for publication to make sure the message hit home. During the hearing of the case against Mary McCall and Johanna Mullin from Collyhurst in Manchester the police claimed that they had great trouble tracking down absentees because they were being shielded by women. To show the extent of the problem, the police stated that thirty men had been arrested as deserters in the same area in just a few days. The women were sent to jail for a month, the bench announcing that they were being imprisoned 'as a warning to other women who might do this sort of thing'.[16] Upon sending shopkeepers Mr and Mrs Wallace of Ardwick to prison for seven days for concealing a deserter the Stipendiary Magistrate for Manchester made a pronouncement that this was no trifling offence – the *Manchester Evening News* printed his words in bold letters in its report of proceedings: '**Let it be understood by the public that at the present time this is an extremely serious matter and cannot be passed over**'.[17] By November, Portadown Petty Sessions had decided to make an example of women concealing deserters. Eliza Kingsley was sentenced to two months in prison for concealing her husband, Robert, and at the same court sitting Margaret Faloon was gaoled for a month for concealing James Judge. The police told the court 'this thing of concealing deserters was taking hold and the women all over the town were encouraging their husbands to reman away from the Army and become deserters'. The prison sentences were 'to teach people that they were not to encourage soldiers to desert'.[18] In Barnsley the Chief Constable asked the magistrates to make an announcement that the practice of harbouring deserters must stop.[19]

The Army Act gave no alternatives to imprisonment for those convicted of assisting deserters. With conscription looming, this was potentially problematic, raising the spectre of thousands of civilians of previously good character filling the prisons if the letter of the law was applied. In February 1916 the Home Office wrote informally to the War Office asking them to consider an amendment to the Act to give the courts wider discretion in sentencing. The motivation for this request was not sympathy for those accused of such crimes, but fear that where magistrates had to impose prison sentences they may err on the side of leniency and acquit defendants completely. There was a different concern about those who would harbour conscientious objectors – noted as 'unconscientious objectors' in the letter – because it was felt that such politically motivated individuals would 'imitate the suffragettes' with hunger strikes whilst in prison, providing further propaganda for their cause. The War Office was unsympathetic to the request, replying, 'A person who deliberately harbours a <u>deserter</u> in war time is guilty of a serious offence, and deserves a severe punishment.'[20]

Despite the views of the War Office magistrates all over the country were **not** automatically imprisoning those convicted of harbouring deserters: fines and, in appropriate cases, bind overs were also being imposed as alternatives. Looking at the pages of *The Justice of the Peace* this appears to be partly due to a misunderstanding of the magistrates' powers. Throughout the war years there was a recurring question in the 'Practical Points' section of the publication as to whether magistrates had the power to fine those charged with assisting deserters. On occasions the question was answered in the positive, citing the Justices' inherent powers under the Summary Jurisdiction Act 1879 to fine anyone facing an imprisonable charge. In other issues the same question would be answered negatively, which was probably the correct legal position, as the Act specifically excluded the exercise of this power for offences arising from Acts concerned with the military. The President of the Justices Clerk's Society made a speech in August 1916 in which he reiterated that there was no power to fine those convicted of concealing deserters. This did not stop the question arising in the pages of *The Justice of the Peace* on several occasions in 1917 and it did not stop magistrates using fines rather than prison sentences in cases that attracted their sympathy.[21] The power to bind someone over to keep the peace is one of the magistrates' oldest powers and courts used it in circumstances they felt merited no punishment.[22] In fact, the 1917 article already quoted from *The Justice of the Peace* envisaged this as the worst punishment a wife would face for concealing her husband, claiming that 'it would be difficult to find a court which would do more than bind her over . . .'.[23] Unfortunately this was not true, and wives all over the country had been imprisoned for the offence of assisting a deserter by the time this article appeared. Technically, an offence was not committed by someone sheltering a mere absentee. *The Justice of the Peace* debated the topic in 1917 and came to the conclusion that unless a man was shown to be a deserter, no offence was committed by harbouring him.[24] Margaret Faloon successfully appealed her conviction for concealing James Judge on the grounds that he was an absentee, not a deserter.[25] The War Office spotted the anomaly and in June 1918 plugged this loophole with Regulation 43B of the Defence of the Realm Act specifically applying to those sheltering or encouraging absentees. This offence carried a fine to a maximum of £25.

The pressure faced by parents asked to help their deserter sons was recognized by the courts, with sentencing reflecting this in many cases.

Parents often escaped prison in circumstances where wives may not. Thomas McDonald appeared before the court in Bradford in April 1915 charged with concealing his son, Private James McDonald. James had been to the Front and suffered a bullet wound to the lung but had recovered and was now deemed to be fit again for active service. Rather than return to his unit, he had deserted. After being arrested he escaped from the escort sent to fetch him and hid at his father's house. James had told his father he was not going back to the Front because 'it was not fighting, it was murder'. The Stipendiary Magistrate said he had sympathy for Mr McDonald and bound him over to be of good behaviour for six months.[26] The parents of 17-year-old sailor Michael Evans believed that their son had drowned on HMS *Invincible*. The ship had been sunk during the Battle of Jutland with the loss of all but six crew members, but Michael was not on board at the time, having deserted shortly before *Invincible* left port. Whilst his parents were at the door of their house showing the police their telegram of condolence from the King, Michael was concealing himself under a bed, where he was found wearing nothing but his shirt. His mother apologized to the court for her actions, explaining that Michael was the third of her sons in the armed forces, one already having been killed whilst serving with the Northumberland Fusiliers. Mr and Mrs Evans were fined a lenient 10*s*. each by a sympathetic bench.[27]

The police also occasionally exercised their discretion in the cases of parents. Joseph Woods from Ballyoran in Ireland had been reported as killed in June 1915. His grieving mother had her letter of condolence framed on the mantelpiece of her home alongside his photograph. Joseph Woods had not been killed, and, in fact, had not even made it to the Front. He had transferred from his original corps to the Leicester Regiment and had then deserted and eventually made his way home. In such circumstances it is not surprising that his mother had allowed him to stay and had denied knowledge of his whereabouts when the police came knocking.[28] Though the *Dundee People's Journal* claimed that the story was 'an excellent basis for a war comedy', Mrs Woods did not find it funny. She told the paper, 'I could not describe to you the experiences of the past fortnight. Only those who have gone through the same would understand . . . The only thing that has made it bearable is the knowledge that my son still lived.'[29] The police did understand and did not charge Mrs Woods with an offence.

Ellen and James Terry of Sellindge in Kent concealed a deserter in their house for nearly sixteen months. This soldier, however, was not their own flesh and blood, but a Canadian called Francis Herbert Neary. Neary was from Halifax,

Nova Scotia and had been serving with the 85th Battalion of the Canadian Infantry before deserting in 1916. The Terrys looked after 24–year- old Neary because he allegedly bore a striking resemblance to their own son. Stanley Terry was 21 years old when he was killed in France in March 1916 whilst serving with the East Kent Regiment. During the time Francis Neary was missing from the Canadian Expeditionary Force he had been working as a steam-engine driver, presumably alongside James Terry as that was his protector's profession. The village of Sellindge was small and one might presume that Neary would stand out. However, Canadians were commonplace in Kent at the time, the district seeing an influx of approximately 40,000 such troops in 1916, large numbers of them housed at camps in Sandling, just 3 miles from Sellindge. Ellen Terry was in poor health, suffering an epileptic fit in the court room and proceedings were eventually dismissed against the couple.[30] Neary was sentenced to two years' imprisonment at his court martial, serving eight months before the balance of his sentence was remitted and he was returned to active service. He declined to give evidence on his own behalf, so the story of how he came to be living with the Terrys remains untold.[31] Francis Neary was killed in France on 6 November 1918. Coincidentally, at the same time Ellen Terry of Sellindge was hiding her surrogate son from the authorities, her famous namesake the actress Ellen Terry was appearing in cinemas nationwide in a film called *Her Greatest Performance*. The plot of the film involved Terry playing a mother trying to save her son from being falsely imprisoned.

One parent who was not shown any sympathy by the court was Robert James Roberts of Sale. His son, a Gunner from the Royal Field Artillery, had already appeared before the local court as a deserter and was remanded to await an escort. Gunner Roberts had left his bandolier at his parent's address and the escort took him back there to get it before the trip to Aldershot for his court martial. Robert Roberts came home, apparently under the influence of drink, and threw the escort out of his house, threatening to shoot the soldiers. By the time a police inspector arrived to assist the escort, Gunner Roberts was gone and was still at large when his father appeared before the magistrates three weeks later. Robert Roberts denied the charge, claiming he was unaware at the time that his son was a deserter. He was convicted of an offence under the Army Act and sentenced to two months' imprisonment. Robert Roberts was stated to be a retired bank manager and the case was widely reported in both local and national newspapers: the imprisonment of a hitherto respectable middle-class man for harbouring a deserter sent the message that no one would be spared the full force of the law for this offence. Roberts' class and financial position did come to his rescue in the fact that the court granted him bail on the surrender of £500 with a further surety in the same amount whilst he pursued an appeal.[32] The result of the appeal went unreported.

Magistrates took a very dim view of women concealing deserters at home whilst their husbands were away fighting and when they got the opportunity, punished them accordingly. Hannah Penrose of Truro was having an affair with another man whilst her husband, a naval reservist, was in the Dardanelles. Her lover was a deserter and was found in bed with her when the police attended. He himself was married with two children. These indignities could not be tolerated and she was sent to prison for two months. Hannah had four children but this did not help her: it was said in court that two of the children would be looked after by an aunt, the baby she could take to prison and the remaining child could go into the workhouse.[33] The house of 19-year-old Lena Herron from East Rainton was allegedly a haven for soldiers. When a deserter was found there and Lena was prosecuted, the court was told that she had already been warned by the police as she frequently had soldiers and other women at the house.[34] Whilst she was entertaining deserters Lena Herron's husband was said to be missing at the Front. She was sentenced to a month's imprisonment with hard labour.

Further punishment could follow for these women, as improper behaviour by a soldier's wife could result in the suspension or removal of her separation allowance. Maria Reay of Hartlepool was said to be drinking in public houses where she met a deserter who she took into her own home whilst her husband was fighting for his country. After coming to her house to retrieve the man's uniform, the police wanted to see her 'ring paper' (colloquialism for the separation allowance book) specifically so that details could be passed to the body responsible for the administration of allowances.[35] Winifred Shepherd paid a heavy price for helping a deserter whilst her husband was at the Front. Though simply fined by the Gateshead bench, she had her separation allowance removed and her three children taken into care.[36]

Billeting arrangements forged bonds which were sometimes later exploited by deserters. Charlie Webster had been billeted on Ada Hart in the village of Kirby-le-Soken earlier in the war and returned there having run off from his regiment in November 1916. A keen-eared policeman heard a man's voice in the house and found Private Webster hiding there. Ada's own husband was at the Front and the article specifically mentioned the amount she was receiving in separation allowance. She was given six weeks' imprisonment and her children were sent to the workhouse.[37] As the war continued and more households were left without their male breadwinner, billeting became more of a problem as it was felt that it was undesirable to place soldiers in houses occupied by the wives of absent soldiers and sailors. The possibility that a soldier would desert or break up the home by forming a relationship with the wife left behind had certainly been considered by the military authorities.

On the rare occasion a soldier's wife did not go to prison for harbouring a deserter who was not her husband, it was often specifically stated by the court that it was only for her husband's sake that she was spared. When Alice Maud Smith appeared before the Barnstaple Police Court she was contrite and tearful, saying she had only allowed the deserter to stay for his mother's sake. Alice's husband was serving on the front line but there was no evidence placed before the court to suggest that her relationship with the deserter was improper. In binding her over, the bench specifically remarked that it was her husband's service which saved her from a harsher punishment.[38]

The suspension of a man's pay on desertion also included the separation allowance paid to his family, meaning that they were automatically punished for his offence whether they had assisted in its commission or not. Harshly, the suspension of allowances for dependents of deserters also applied to a man's children. This was not the position when allowances and pensions were removed from soldier's wives for their own misbehaviour, when any allowances paid to the children continued. The suspension was calculated to shame deserters into surrendering to ease the financial burden on the family, though it did not always have the desired effect. Clara Thorpe (née Binns) remembers that her father showed no concern over the position his family were in once he deserted from the East Yorkshire Regiment: 'He didn't think about mum or us, just himself.' Robert Binns left the army to go to sea instead, working on former cruise liners transporting US troops to Europe. His wife not only had the indignity of the army periodically raiding the house to arrest him but was forced to borrow from her parents and sell her belongings to survive. Mrs Binns eventually left East Hull in embarrassment, moving to an old house in another area of the city. A neighbour bought all of her furniture except the sideboard.[39]

The Doyle family of Kilkenny faced even more severe consequences. Mary Doyle had been receiving 27*s*. 9*d*. a week for herself and her three children until her husband, a soldier with the Royal Irish Fusiliers, deserted in July 1918. Mary struggled on, moving in with her mother to cut costs, but was still not able to provide for the family adequately: two adults and three children were now living on 19*s.* a week made up of her mother's separation allowance from three sons in the army. Mary was eventually taken to court by the National Society for the Prevention of Cruelty to Children in February 1919 where an order was sought to commit the children to industrial schools. Though they recognized she 'was more sinned against than sinning', Mary's refusal to go into a workhouse with daughters Anne (10), Mary (7) and Martin (4) incurred their displeasure. Mary sobbed in court, begging the magistrates to leave her with her little boy at least and declared she would rather spend the rest of her life in gaol than go into the workhouse with the children. The magistrates had a great deal of sympathy for Mary Doyle but were eventually persuaded to commit the two girls to an industrial school.[40]

John Bull decried the practice of stopping separation allowances and provided women in these circumstances with financial assistance from their own fund, given that charitable agencies were loath to assist wives of errant soldiers. Reporting that an increasing number of husbands 'have forgotten they are soldiers', by February 1916 *John Bull's* fund could not stand the financial strain of supporting their families and announced that they could no longer help save in exceptional circumstances.[41]

Whilst wives were being refused any assistance, the police officers who arrested their deserter husbands could count on the customary financial reward from the court. The wife of serial deserter Henry Tufft was herself admonished during his court appearance in October 1914, being berated by the Chairman of the Bench for threatening legal action against the local war relief agencies. The Chairman told Mrs Tufft that no charity would assist and it would be better for her and her children to go into the workhouse. The constable who apprehended Tufft was given 'the usual fee of 15s' for so doing. At least one of the Tufft family did go into the workhouse: Henry's 3-year-old daughter Florence Tufft died there at the end of November 1914.[42]

Wives concealing their own husbands faced the prospect of appearing before the courts for fraud if they were still in receipt of separation allowance. The army administration could not keep up with the number of deserters and the amount of paperwork involved, often failing to send notification to the correct department to put a stop on the separation allowance. This happened frequently enough for the practice to be noted post-war as responsible for deficiencies in the Army Appropriation Account.[43] For some women, the fact that the Post Office suddenly had no money to give them was indeed their first indication that their husband was in a state of desertion: others were well aware that he had deserted because he was back in the family home. A wife continuing to draw the allowance in these circumstances was asking for trouble. Criminal statistics for 1917 show that the Director of Public Prosecutions instituted charges in over 200 cases of the fraudulent receipt of separation allowance.[44]

Despite the fact that the men concerned often benefitted from the fraud as much as the wives, the deserter's wife often found herself the sole occupant of the dock. Annie Vauden was sent to prison for a month for drawing £8 in separation allowance during the period of her husband's desertion. Though she claimed he had made threats towards her and refused her requests for him to return to the army, the bench in the Manchester Police Court showed her no mercy. Mr Vauden was not at court to verify her story, having been court-martialled and given twelve months with hard labour for his desertion.[45] Margaret Close faced trial by jury in Belfast for fraudulently claiming £18 in separation allowance. She had claimed she did not know her husband was a deserter and could not read and write, but the fact that he was actually living with her for most of his period of desertion hardly helped her case. Margaret told the court that it was her husband who forced her to draw the allowance and had spent most of it on drink. The jury found her guilty of the fraud, but recommended mercy. Margaret had two sons at the Front and nine children altogether, including a baby who she held in her arms at the hearing. The police did Margaret Close a favour in bringing forward evidence of what could be seen as her good character, telling the judge that she was a thrifty housewife who looked after her children well and sent them to school. The judge followed the jury's recommendation, discharging her with no further penalty.[46]

Catherine Fitzpatrick was fully aware that her husband had deserted but when she appeared before Bootle Magistrates for continuing to draw her separation allowance blamed the War Office for not stopping the monies. Mr Fitzpatrick had enlisted in October 1914 but disappeared from the ranks just two weeks later, returning home and signing up to go to sea on a commercial ship. Catherine cashed a cheque from the shipping company for advance wages and collected her separation allowance until June 1915, even applying for and receiving an extra allowance for the birth of a new child. By the time the fraud was discovered she had received over £24 in total. The prosecutor said that frauds of this kind were being carried out all over the country to an appalling extent. The fact that she had already spent time in custody on remand and appeared in the dock with the baby in her arms led the magistrates to show some leniency, fining rather than imprisoning her.[47]

As casualties mounted and conscription arrived, it seems that some communities may have become less tolerant of deserters in their midst. It was all very well having a local man cheekily coming home for a few days or weeks rather than being in barracks, but quite a different matter if his place in the front line was having to be taken by one of your own family. Anonymous letters and more direct tip-offs to the police from neighbours, friends and even other family members were now more frequently reported in the press. In September 1916, Mabel Lockridge appeared before the court in Leeds charged with concealing two deserters. Her neighbours reported her to the police and, in fact, caused quite a demonstration outside the house on Craven Street where the men had been staying for three weeks.[48] An anonymous letter betrayed the presence of absentee Thomas Orchard at the house of his cousin, Flora Lees, in Gloucester.[49]

Changes in the habits of a household were often a tell-tale sign that there was someone new on the premises. Gunner Young of the Royal Field Artillery had taken every precaution when deserting and returning home to Enfield, lying low and not leaving the house at all. Unfortunately, he could not do without his home comforts and was arrested after the police noticed that his wife was going to the local pub and buying extra amounts of beer to take away.[50] Food shortages and the introduction of rationing in late 1917 made it even easier for the sharp eyed to spot that there was a change in domestic arrangements. This also increased the burden on a deserter's family if they did harbour him as there would be no ration card for the extra member of the household. Mary Morby's concealment of her deserter son in Nottingham was detected when she started to order two extra loaves a day from the baker. When the police investigated and searched the house, Private Morby was found locked in a box upstairs.[51]

Women with husbands serving abroad were now angry to see other soldiers dodging their duties and acted accordingly. Mary Thomson or Davidson, from Aberdeen had a husband in the army, by March 1918 a prisoner of war in Germany. She also had two deserters from the Gordon Highlanders staying at her house. Another local woman with a husband serving at the Front contacted the police, believing it was 'a great shame' that these able-bodied men were at Thomson's house when they should have been in the firing line. Mary Thomson/Davidson went to prison for thirty days, Sheriff Dudley Stuart warning that this sentence was lenient, and that others coming before him could expect more.[52]

Sometimes women gave up their own deserter husbands to the police, especially if they had not deserted to be back at the family home. In one of the oddest harbouring cases of the war, the wife of Private Walter Yelin shouted for police assistance when she saw her husband getting off a train at Belsize Park when he should have been with his regiment. She had not seen him for seventeen months. Yelin was in the company of a man called Romanoff Omar, a colourful character, described in the press reports as 'a Brahmin' and by the police as 'a kind of American crank'. Omar used the alias 'Brother Ramavanda' and the court heard that he claimed to possess mystical powers including the ability to tame wild tigers, which must have come in useful in Belsize Park! Omar had allegedly concealed Yelin and spread the rumour that the soldier had thrown himself in the Thames, leaving his clothes by Cleopatra's Needle. Omar later appeared before the court for harbouring the West Surrey Regiment deserter and pleaded not guilty. He relied upon his religion as part of his defence, claiming that he was not allowed to refuse anyone who was seeking sanctuary. Omar claimed that he helped Yelin because the deserter was both a conscientious objector and unfit for military service. Omar was correct on the latter point as Yelin was discharged from the army a month after his arrest thanks to an eye condition which could have led to blindness. Omar was convicted and fined £50.[53]

The majority of home front deserters were accommodated by family and friends regardless of the consequences. For families who had endured the worry of having a man abroad on active service, it is easy to see why they would provide sanctuary if he came home. If a man had returned wounded or after erroneous reports of his death had been received, the offence is even easier to understand. As Thomas McDonald asked the police officer who came to his door in Bradford, 'He is my only son, would you have not done the same?'[54]

Chapter 6

Alternative Employment

BOOT REPAIRING – Wanted immediately, 30 good all-round Men as MANAGERS or WORKMEN: ineligible: benchmen's wages raised 33 per cent and finishers 15 per cent since war commenced: splendid situations to suitable applicants. – Apply Johnson, 110 Devonshire St, Sheffield.

Sheffield Daily Telegraph,
3 November 1916

For a deserter cut off from his army pay, a new source of income had to be found if he was to remain successfully at large. In some cases it was the lure of higher civilian wages that caused a man to desert in the first place, army pay being less than generous even considering the additional allowances paid to his family. If enlisting in August 1914 was a strategy to maintain employment during a trade depression, then leaving the ranks once more lucrative employment was available can be seen in a similar light. Ken Weller notes that in 1914 there were a vast number of casual workers in Britain who were paid hourly or seasonally and some may have joined up for the promise of regular pay and food.[1] Many of those same men may have not fully appreciated the difference between regular employment and the British Army. The transition from casual worker to soldier may have been too much for some and undoubtedly fuelled the figures of desertion and absenteeism. An analysis of deserters reported in the *Police Gazette* shows that 'labourer' was by the far the most frequently noted civilian occupation. Of 1,302 deserters listed on 11 January 1916, for example, 321 were listed as 'labourers'.[2] This, of course, reflects the fact that this class of men was traditionally more willing to enlist, but even after conscription when it may be imagined that a broader range of occupations would be contained within the deserters' ranks, the bias towards labourers in the lists remained similar. It can be argued that in leaving the army to take up other work men were simply displaying the same attitude to the military that they did to any other kind of employment – staying as long as it suited them but leaving when conditions changed or when better work was available, sometimes planning to return on the same basis when that work was at an end.

After the glorious summer of 1914, the war did not remove the need to bring in the harvest. September was hop-picking season in Kent and traditionally hundreds of working class families from London and beyond would migrate to the region temporarily to do this work. It was reported in *The Field* in 1914 that the war had made no real difference to the numbers of pickers and that vacancies had been easily filled.[3] Soldiers left barracks to go to Kent and take part in the harvest themselves or to visit their families who were employed on the hop farms. Faversham Police Court dealt with a group of deserters who had left the 3rd Battalion of the Buffs Regiment in Dover and come to the hop fields to pick up a few days' work. James Richard Matthews was the first of the men to be arrested as they all sat in a pub in Selling in their uniforms. When asked to produce leave passes to the investigating police constable, two of the men ran off. The respite was short and Privates Stephen Burnett and William Vincent were picked up a few days later hiding under a bed in a hop-pickers' hut in Fairbrook. Showing an admirable grasp of military law, when warned by the magistrate that they were deserters in a time of war and liable to be shot, one of the men retorted, 'We are not deserters yet.' They were eventually punished as absentees, receiving short sentences of detention.[4]

Employment for some was seen as a necessary interlude, not a career, with single men in particular taking work on a short-term basis and moving on once they had earned some money or were tired of the job. Transferring the same attitude to the army was asking for trouble. Max Plowman describes a man from his unit who faced a court martial for desertion. The man was a miner in civilian life and, 'In this occupation he had always plenty of money, and drunken bouts between spells of work had become a habit with him which he could not break'.[5] Miners worked on short-term contracts before the war and often moved from pit to pit at certain times of year. The fact that Plowman's Private had walked away from the ranks was no reflection on his bravery, simply his working practice. The Revd Andrew Clark recorded in his diary in September 1917 that three deserters had recently handed themselves in at the military camp established near his village of Great Leighs in Essex. The men had been gone for four months, taking civilian work (presumably in agriculture) and 'jolly well enjoying themselves'. When the work was over and they ran out of money, they wandered back into camp.[6]

Given the huge numbers now in the army still undergoing training and not ready for the Western Front, a decision was made to allow some of those men to be temporarily redeployed as agricultural workers. Farmers could apply for assistance through their local Labour Exchange and would be sent soldiers to ensure continuity of food supplies on the home front. This release system operated periodically throughout the war and resulted in a significant amount of absenteeism. Farmers would sometimes ask for specific individuals to be sent to them as they were friends, family members or former employees, many of them outstaying their allotted period on the land. Other new recruits made unofficial arrangements of their own, walking away from training camps to farms all over the country. It was a long-standing working class tradition for men to exchange their regular employment for a month of harvesting and the war did not stop this.[7]

To ensure sufficient levels of manpower in other key areas as the war progressed, men were sometimes transferred from the army specifically to work in munitions, or, in the case of miners, to return to the pits. This muddied the waters for those seeking to apprehend deserters as it must have made it easier for a fugitive to conceal himself amongst those who had been directed to this employment by the military. From 1916 onwards the army sometimes chose this route for those it felt were troublesome, including some men who were persistent deserters. Oswald Llewellyn of the South Wales Borderers was one of them. Having seen his father prosecuted for harbouring him in 1915, Oswald deserted again shortly after his release from military detention. He was again sentenced to a short period of imprisonment but by January 1916 the army had taken the view he was better used elsewhere. Llewellyn was directed to undertake munitions work at Stewarts and Lloyds Ltd in Glasgow.[8]

For those who were tired of the army there was plenty of work available at home. The expansion in munitions production that saw large numbers of women enter the workplace also provided employment for men. Wage levels were significantly higher than army pay. In shipbuilding, munitions and transport in 1915 wages were 'uniformly high' with sums of £5 or £6 a week common, and skilled mechanics reportedly able to earn as much as 15 pounds a week.[9] At the same time an ordinary private in the infantry was earning basic pay of just 1*s*. and 1*d*. per day, an extraordinary disparity. It is little wonder that men deserted to take advantage of these wages and, should their consciences be troubled at all by their actions, they could always console themselves with the fact that they were still engaged on work of national importance.

James Ryder, the deserter housed by Maria Reay in Hartlepool, had originally found employment at the Central Marine Engineering Works in the town. Maria then dyed Ryder's uniform trousers black and he obtained a job at the Zinc Works near Seaton Carew with her husband's National Insurance card as identification.[10] George Farrow of the 6th Battalion of the Rifle Brigade had a long run, deserting in 1915 and spending the next two years working in a munitions factory in Great Yarmouth. He was sentenced to serve those missing two years in prison when he was court-martialled in May 1918.[11]

Munitions work also attracted Henry Rigg, who was both a deserter and a bigamist. Rigg, originally from Bolton, joined the Loyal North Lancashire Regiment after deserting from the Royal Field Artillery in June 1915. Punished summarily for fraudulent enlistment he found he liked his new regiment no better and deserted again in May 1916, leaving his wife and three children penniless. Riggs dumped his uniform in a toilet in Liverpool and it was assumed he had gone to sea, though he had only travelled as far as Wrexham. There he found work in a munitions factory and met a war widow called Hettie Esther Morgan who was raising two children alone. Hettie married her beau, a man she knew as James Robert Roberts, in December 1916. Eight months later he was arrested as a deserter in his real name and his bigamy revealed. Riggs was sentenced to six months in prison for the offence and was handed over to the army thereafter.[12]

Mining was a popular choice of employment amongst deserters for obvious reasons – no one other than a fellow miner was going to see you at work and there were large numbers of men in the pits who were technically still soldiers. There were also a lot of miners deserting: after labourer, the most commonly mentioned occupation amongst those whose names were circulated via the *Police Gazette* was that of miner.[13] Deserters James Fawcett and Henry Wood were arrested in West Stanley, County Durham in June 1915 at the house of Fawcett's fiancée. Both men had been working at Burnhope Colliery under false names since their desertion from the 15th Battalion of the DLI. Fawcett's prospective father-in-law had helped them get work and provided them with civilian clothes and was prosecuted for his actions. Both soldiers were convicted of desertion and received eighteen months' imprisonment with hard labour when returned to Halton Camp.[14] Thomas Alton was a footballer who had played for several teams around Yorkshire and Derbyshire before the war. He found army life not to his taste and deserted, getting a job at Hardwicke Colliery. Alton had been missing for seventeen months when he finally appeared before the Chesterfield bench as a deserter in August 1917.[15]

Comparatively well paid and traditionally reliant on casual labour, dock work was particularly attractive to deserters. Charles Williams deserted from the 3rd Battalion of the King's Liverpool Regiment to work on the Merseyside docks. The job was rendered even more lucrative for his family because his wife was still drawing her separation allowance.[16] At the other end of the country, Leonard Angus Rix deserted from the Essex Regiment in November 1916 going back to his home address and taking a job as a dock labourer. When apprehended in South Woodford, he was charged with being a deserter and both he and his wife were charged with fraud, having had £45 from the military to which they were not entitled.[17]

Harry McShane, who would become an important figure in the history of Socialism in Scotland, went further than the docks after his desertion, going away to sea. Leaving the Royal Engineers, McShane returned to Glasgow and initially obtained shore-based work but had to leave several jobs because he was recognized by workmates. As a skilled engineer McShane found it easy to find employment on ships, signing up with the Eagle Oil Transport Company and completing three voyages from Glasgow to Texas under his real name. McShane claimed that the company were so short of men that the sight of his apprenticeship certificate was enough to have him taken on, regardless of any other considerations. Returning to Glasgow, McShane managed to pick up short-term work, though was careful not to look for employment in the city centre where he was too well known and the police were very active in their search for deserters. Amazingly, he even appeared before a Munitions Tribunal to try and get a leaving certificate to allow him to move from one workshop to another. Though his application was refused, he was not detected as a deserter.[18]

As the war went on, the number of former soldiers in the community who had been legitimately discharged increased, allowing further scope for deception on the part of those who had left the army illegally. Arthur John Piddock aka Ernest Hill was one of many deserters who had re-entered civilian life in the guise of discharged soldiers. Piddock/Hill had obtained employment at Cammell Lairds in Sheffield claiming to have been legitimately discharged from the army. Not satisfied with the wages munitions work could bring, he had devised a scam whereby he sold raffle tickets purportedly on behalf of poor Private Tom Davies who had been blinded at the Front. So convincing was he that the printer doing the tickets even gave him extra for free. To add to his authenticity, Piddock wore DCM and Mons Star medal ribbons. Of course, there was no raffle and Piddock's prize for the deception was three months' imprisonment with hard labour.[19]

The Defence of the Realm Act regulations required employers to keep proper lists of their employees, to notify the authorities if a man left their employment and to take all reasonable steps to check that a man was exempt from military service before offering him a job. An updated list of employees of military age was to be provided to the local recruiting office each month so that they could check any suspicious entries. Failure to comply with these regulations constituted a criminal offence. After the introduction of conscription, job advertisements routinely carried the word 'ineligible' in their listings, meaning the positions were only open to men who were ineligible for military service for one reason or another. The prospective employee was under an obligation to provide all information, certificates and passes necessary to allow their employer to comply with the regulations.[20] This made it more important for deserters to try and obtain some kind of documentation to fool an employer into taking them on, further fuelling the burgeoning market in forgeries and the trafficking of certificates. Employers were taking the risk of employing men without documentation because they were so short of labour that it proved difficult to run a business.

Farmers appear to have either been particularly easy to fool or particularly desperate for workers as the number of prosecutions of agricultural employers was high. Farmers traditionally employed 'tramp' workers who would sleep in barns for the short period of time they were working on the farm and this practice seems to have continued during the war. No doubt many farmers knowingly employed deserters. At his trial in 1917 for failing to follow the necessary regulations, Richard Charles Bull, a farmer from Fyfield in Oxfordshire, said in his defence that he was paying 'Jack Bishop' – in reality a deserter called Walter Gotobed – 18s. a week and providing him with food in exchange for his labour, and if he had known he was a deserter he would have paid him much less! The soldier, an illiterate 5ft 1in tall cowman in civilian life, would receive a year's detention for his desertion.[21] William Hughes of the Royal Welch Fusiliers was reported to have been working on farms all over the country after his desertion in the spring of 1916, with none of the farmers giving him away.[22] When farmer Dobson Smith of Doncaster was found to be employing a deserter in September 1918, his list of employees had not been updated for over a year. Smith denied knowing the man was a deserter but told the court he would not have employed him but for the fact he was so short of labour.[23] Farmers like Smith appear to have been mostly the subject of financial penalties rather than sentences of imprisonment. The magistrates who were now punishing employers for taking on deserters were often the same men who sat on the Military Tribunals and refused applications for exemptions from both workers and employers. This may explain the fairly lenient sentences which appear to have been given out: magistrates could not say they had not been warned about labour shortages.

This leniency was not extended to all employers and in August 1918 two businessmen were sent to prison for having deserters amongst their workers. Both were tailors, both were Jewish and both were from the East End of London. Morris Koppitt was sent to prison for five months by Thames Police Court for employing deserters at St George in the East.[24] A few days later, Jack Isaacs of Sidney Street, Stepney, appeared before the same court charged with employing two deserters at his factory. Isaacs initially told the police that the men were exempt from service but later confessed that he knew they had absconded from the army. He was sentenced to three months' imprisonment and a £10 fine.[25] This disparity in sentencing can partly be explained by the area in which Koppitt and Isaacs lived. The East End of London was widely portrayed throughout the war in newspapers and in the House of Commons as the crucible of deception, shirking and impropriety. An area which had attracted thousands of Jewish refugees from Eastern Europe, the disparaging of the East End was undoubtedly antisemitic in origin. The imprisonment of a couple of Jewish tailors for offences that were only attracting fines in the case of English-born farmers must be seen in this context.

The need for documentation in order to obtain legitimate employment no doubt steered many deserters to work of a less respectable nature. One time-honoured way for soldiers to make money was prostitution. Soldiers were notorious for their willingness to earn a little extra in this manner and the practice was almost encouraged within certain battalions.[26] London was a hive of sexual activity of all kinds with Piccadilly Circus, Marble Arch, Hyde Park, Trafalgar Square, Waterloo Road and the area around Victoria Station all notorious pick-up locations. The war intensified this with thousands of troops stationed in and around the capital or passing through on a fleeting basis. Most of the soldiers engaged in prostitution only engaged in homosexual acts for reward, not only cash but also presents and treats from regular customers. Edward Casey's wartime memoir records his meetings with 'queens' in London and Dublin from whom he takes money and meals in return for his company.[27] Scorn was reserved mostly for those buying these services rather than the sellers. Clients were given unpleasant nicknames amongst the soldiers, milked financially for all they were worth and sometimes threatened with blackmail or subjected to violence.

Homosexual acts were illegal in both civil and military life. The *Manual of Military Law* stated that any acts of gross indecency with another male person were punishable by two years' imprisonment.[28] Anal sex itself was more seriously punished, the sentence ranging from ten years to life imprisonment. Officers would be cashiered out of the service in disgrace. There were 13 courts martial of officers on the home front for indecency between August 1914 and March 1920, and 114 of men, the disparity suggesting that officers were very much given the benefit of the doubt.[29] The threat of exposing officers for committing indecent acts was sometimes used by soldier prostitutes to extort more money from these clients.

In April 1917 an unusual court martial attracted the attention of the newspapers when deserter Frederick Charles Carter appeared for blackmailing Captain Henry Huggett. Captain Huggett had joined the Royal Fusiliers in 1911 and had seen action at Gallipoli where he had lost an eye. Private Carter had been serving with the London Regiment but had deserted six months earlier and was hanging around London in uniform, frequenting YMCA huts and other locations to pick up food and money. He also appears to have been frequenting notorious gay cruising areas for another kind of pick-up entirely. Carter and fellow deserter Private Robert Smith met Captain Huggett in the West End late one night and ended up at his flat. Carter said that Huggett had made indecent suggestions to the pair and he had asked for money by way of compensation. Huggett, himself under arrest for indecency at the time of Carter's court martial, protested that he was giving simple hospitality to a couple of stranded soldiers when he was suddenly blackmailed. Officers were not meant to fraternize with the lower ranks in any way and Huggett's decision to invite the pair to his flat was described in court as 'an act of grave impropriety'.[30] The prosecutor, Sir Archibald Bodkin, later to become Director of Public Prosecutions, identified Carter and Smith's offences as part of a trend taking place in London at that time. Bodkin remarked that there were 'people in the crowded parts of London who were hunting in couples in order that after one had picked up some officer and pretended to accompany him the other might follow until a compromising situation had arisen'.[31] Carter was convicted of blackmail, received three years' penal servitude and was dismissed from the army with ignominy. Huggett was acquitted of any indecency and continued his military career.[32]

When there were prosecutions for indecency in the civilian courts soldiers were often presented as naïve and easily corrupted by predatory older homosexuals, meaning that customers were routinely more harshly punished than the prostitutes themselves.[33] The case of a deserter called Robert Anderson, described by one newspaper as 'a smart, well set up soldier', exemplifies this.[34] Anderson joined the Scots Guards in May 1914 and served two spells in France. His disciplinary record was patchy and he deserted from Wellington Barracks, Westminster in December 1917, thereafter becoming part of a demi-monde centered around Piccadilly Circus. He had taken his uniform with him when he deserted – an essential part of a soldier prostitute's kit – and like Privates Carter and Smith, was hanging around the YMCA huts. Though in court Anderson denied he was a prostitute, he admitted he was living on money given to him by acquaintances he met in the streets. One such acquaintance was Cecil Samter and the two men stayed in hotels, dined in fashionable restaurants and frequented Turkish baths together. Anderson's eventual arrest as a deserter took place at his own wedding (to the wonderfully named Mabel Whale) in June 1918 and he convinced himself that Samter had betrayed him. His revenge was to report Samter for indecency. Cecil Samter was arrested and charged in August 1918. Anderson's story was that Samter had approached him in Piccadilly Circus and encouraged him not to go back to barracks. The two had gone to the Regent Palace Hotel and Anderson claimed to be so drunk he conveniently could not remember what took place. Samter told him that they had committed indecency and blackmailed Anderson to keep meeting or he would report him as a deserter. He also gave him 20*s*. Anderson continued to see Samter, taking advantage of his hospitality and his money. Cecil Samter was not the only customer to be prosecuted – Albert 'Bertie' Stopford, aged 58, was also accused of gross indecency with the deserter. Stopford was once a fashionable milliner and dressmaker and was well known in high society. He became a British government informant in Russia, where he had close links with the royal family, helping them smuggle out jewels at the time of the Revolution. Stopford took Anderson to hotels and performed indecent acts, paying him £2 a week for the privilege, the deserter making a total of £50 from the older man.

Anderson was produced from the detention barracks at Wandsworth to give evidence against his clients. The army had convicted him of absence without leave, not desertion, and sentenced him to six months' imprisonment. Ironically, the fact that he had not settled himself into society by discarding his uniform and taking up regular employment would have worked in his favour. He had not faced prosecution for indecency. Cecil Samter and Albert Stopford would pay dearly for their encounters with Robert Anderson, both being convicted and sent to prison, Samter eventually receiving nine months' imprisonment with hard labour at the Old Bailey.[35] Stopford was also sent to Wormwood Scrubs and left England for good on his release in 1919.

Albert Stopford and Cecil Samter may well have been victims of a backlash against homosexuality triggered by what became known as the Billing case. Noel Pemberton-Billing, entrepreneur and sometime MP for Hertford, published a magazine called the *Imperialist* (to be renamed the *Vigilante*). In 1918 an article in the magazine claimed that 47,000 high-ranking individuals in Britain had their names in a so called 'Black Book' of sexual deviants and were being blackmailed by the Germans to undermine the war effort. When Billing was prosecuted for libel he claimed justification as his defence – i.e. that the allegations were true. The case attracted a huge amount of publicity and, incredibly, Billing was acquitted by the jury. Two months later, Cecil Samter and Albert Stopford made their appearances at the Old Bailey. According to the evidence of Robert Anderson, Stopford had cited the Billing case as a reason for the two to temporarily stop their assignations.[36]

Engaging in homosexual activity was illegal by the laws of the time, but some deserters made their living from acts that will always be against the law.

Chapter 7

Scamps in Khaki

For stealing £35 5s 0d. from a mess at Blandford Camp, 24th ult. – ALFRED CLEASER, age 28, ht. 5ft. 7 ½., c.dk,h.dk.brown,e. brown,cleanshaven;dress:khaki uniform, marines badge on cap. Is a deserter from the Divisional Engineers, Royal Naval Division, Blandford, where he was acting as band sergeant. Warrant issued. Information to Supt. Beck, Blandford.

Police Gazette, 16 September 1916

For some deserters, resorting to criminality of various kinds was the only way to keep themselves fed and clothed. The fact of a man's desertion could be inferred, according to the *Manual of Military Law*, by the commission of a 'heinous offence' and there were plenty of offences being committed by absent soldiers.[1] The front page of the *Police Gazette* featured 'Apprehensions sought' – notices containing descriptions of crimes and the perpetrators around the country. As the war went on many of these cases involved men in uniform, a significant number of them being deserters on the run trying to make ends meet.

In 1914, 381 men convicted by the criminal courts of England and Wales were recipients of the Royal Prerogative of Mercy, exercised by the Lord Chancellor, to allow them to join, or re-join, the military.[2] Many more who had criminal records enlisted voluntarily. Robert Holmes, a probation officer in Sheffield, wrote in 1915 that 1,267 men who he had met through their appearance in the Police Court had answered the nation's call and joined various branches of the armed services.[3] Criminals could be patriots too: one man, fearing rejection due to his previous offending, stole a bicycle specifically to travel to a recruiting station where he was not known, whilst another paid a man to serve his prison sentence so he could enlist.[4] Some enlisted to avoid arrest for their criminal offending: Denis Winter recalls his father serving with Bertie Warrant, who had joined up in June 1915 because he had just robbed the Hackney Empire. Warrant had been discharged with ignominy in his first period of service as a teenager due to his multiple desertions, but was a diligent soldier this time, winning the Military Medal and leaving the army as a wounded hero.[5]

By 1916 the drop in the convict population in Britain allowed the prison authorities to give both Dartmoor and Wakefield prisons over to the Home Office to house conscientious objectors carrying out non-combatant work. The decrease in the number of criminals in prison was matched by the increase of their number in the armed forces after the introduction of conscription. *The Justice of the Peace* commented in 1916 that the criminal classes often made good soldiers. 'Headstrong and dissatisfied with their lot in life, they find a new opening and new interests.'[6] Whilst some, like Bertie Warrant, served in an exemplary manner, some used their status as soldiers to find new opportunities to commit crime.

George Orwell wrote that a soldier's attitude to life was essentially a lawless one.[7] The lines between right and wrong were blurred if it was a matter of making life more comfortable for oneself or one's immediate comrades, especially on the front line. George Coppard says that this was something recruits learned along the way, remembering that 'it was an important part of my army training to learn how to be fly and cunning'.[8] Herman Mannheim went as far as to suggest that the attitudes developed by men during military service may have contributed to rising crime levels between the wars. Mannheim wrote that the Tommy's practice of scrounging things resulted in a general erosion of respect for government property.[9]

A deserter's first crime was sometimes to steal from the military prior to making good their escape. The *Police Gazette* contained a number of reports during the war of men like Alfred Cleaser, wanted in September 1916 for the theft of £25 from the mess at Blandford Camp. 'Cleaser' may have been a pseudonym as no one of that name was ever apprehended but a bandmaster from Blandford called Albert Victor Davis was later convicted of stealing from the Camp.[10]

Described as 'Scamps in Khaki' in a newspaper headline, deserters Harry Chapman and James Charlton travelled around the Ely area in 1915 with forged leave passes bought in the barracks canteen for 2½d., tricking gullible civilians into giving them money. The pair claimed that they had lost their railway passes and needed the cash for train fares to re-join their regiment, specifically targeting those they felt may be more trusting including a minister of religion and a number of widowed ladies. One woman had actually borrowed money in order to help. The court seemed to find their crimes amusing and laughter often broke out during the hearing. To concentrate the minds of the magistrates on the seriousness of their behaviour, the police prosecutor had to remind the court that these 'scamps' had deserted after being warned for the Front.[11] Simple deceptions like this were commonplace in the early months of the war, with soldiers claiming accidental separation from their regiments, or pretending to be collecting monies on behalf of charities. Private W.A. Thomas from 3rd Battalion Cornish Light Infantry was arrested in Stratford where he was shaking cigar boxes, purportedly for the Prince of Wales Fund and the Red Cross. Thomas was in truth a deserter from his battalion at Falmouth and was spending the proceeds of his collection in public houses.[12] Two Royal Irish Fusiliers appearing in court in Lurgan had a more specific purpose, claiming to be collecting on behalf of the Ulster Volunteer Force to buy a motor car for use at the Front. W.J. Kettle aka Cadden and David Thompson were deserters and the cash was going straight into their pockets. The court decreed that all monies found on the two on their arrest was to be given to the Prince of Wales Fund.[13] At a time when war related charities of all kinds were constantly springing up, these frauds were easy to perpetrate, playing as they did on the patriotism of the general populace.

Wounded soldiers began to be seen in the streets of Britain and previously unknown places like Mons and Hill 60 became part of everyday conversation. This gave fraudsters ample opportunity to exploit the sympathy of the public. By April 1915 the *Manchester Guardian* was claiming that bogus wounded soldiers were 'a crying nuisance just now' with cases reported daily of men claiming handouts who had never been to the Front at all and were often deserters. The paper made the point that poor treatment of veterans by past governments had resulted in men tramping the streets after their discharge and looking for charity. People had become accustomed to seeing men in this situation before the outbreak of the war, so were less likely to question their sob stories now.[14] When deserter Arthur Cunningham appeared before Willesden Police Court in June 1915 charged with operating a wounded soldier fraud he was in possession of a considerable amount of money, telling the court 'you only have to sit in Hyde Park and tell the tale and it flows in'.[15] In fact, a uniform was to some degree just a new tool for career criminals to utilize in committing offences. Those sentencing Frank Francis aka Samuel Frank Bentley for deceptions in Norwich in the autumn of 1914 took the view that he had only enlisted in order to get his hands on a uniform, spending just five days in barracks before he deserted. In a nod to the low regard in which the army was held in peacetime, the judge remarked that in this time of national crisis people would have 'regard to his Majesty's uniform and trust those wearing it more than they perhaps would under ordinary circumstances'.[16]

Thomas Jackson aka Tomlinson had the misfortune to stumble across two detectives who knew him as he was limping around Manchester with the aid of a stick. With a bandaged arm for extra effect, he claimed to have been shot at Hill 60. When examined he had no injuries at all and was exposed as a deserter from the 4th Welsh Fusiliers.[17] Donald M'Kinnon arrived home at Campbelltown on crutches with a swathe of bandages round his head, also claiming to have been wounded at Hill 60. Local police were aware that he had previously been sentenced to a term of military imprisonment for desertion so went to speak to him. At this point M'Kinnon made a remarkable recovery, throwing his crutches to the ground and making for the open road. After a lengthy chase he was caught and taken before the court as a deserter.[18]

After the first use of poison gas on the Western Front in April 1915, the use of bandages and crutches was no longer required to fake a war wound, and a number of fraudsters thereafter claimed to have been victims of German gas. A uniform was not even necessary to perpetrate the 'wounded soldier' fraud. Fred Norman turned up at Houghton Colliery in June 1915, claiming to have worked there previously and asking for his job back. He said he had been discharged from the army on account of wounds received at Neuve Chapelle and that his wife and children were starving as his disability pension had not yet come through. As a result of this tall tale, he was offered a job at the colliery and given a 10s. advance on his wages – he was never seen at the pit again. Norman went to the treasurer of the local distress fund with the same story and was given another 15s. which he was to repay when he received his pension. Fred Norman was a serial deserter of both the army and his family. He deserted both the 3rd Manchester Regiment and his wife in 1913 and the Northumberland Fusiliers on two occasions in 1914. Part of his story was correct – he had served in France and had been wounded – but the rest was a lie. He had failed to report back to his unit once fit and was arrested for similar frauds in February 1915. This latest spree came after he had fraudulently enlisted in the Royal Garrison Artillery and again deserted.[19]

Not all deserters committing crime were career criminals. Some were ordinarily law-abiding men who resorted to stealing simply as a means of existing once their army pay was cut off. Thomas Williams, for example, was living in a barn and feeding himself by burgling shops in Oakdale. He had overstayed his leave and been too ashamed to return thereafter. His wife and children were left without any allowance and his wife was forced to go out to work. Williams was also reportedly further shamed when he found out that his latest food haul had been stolen from a shop owned by a widow.[20]

Recruits training in 1914. Wooden rifles and Kitchener Blues. (Author's own collection)

Postcard from camp. The poor conditions of 1914 were a source of humour but made life miserable for new recruits. (Author's own collection)

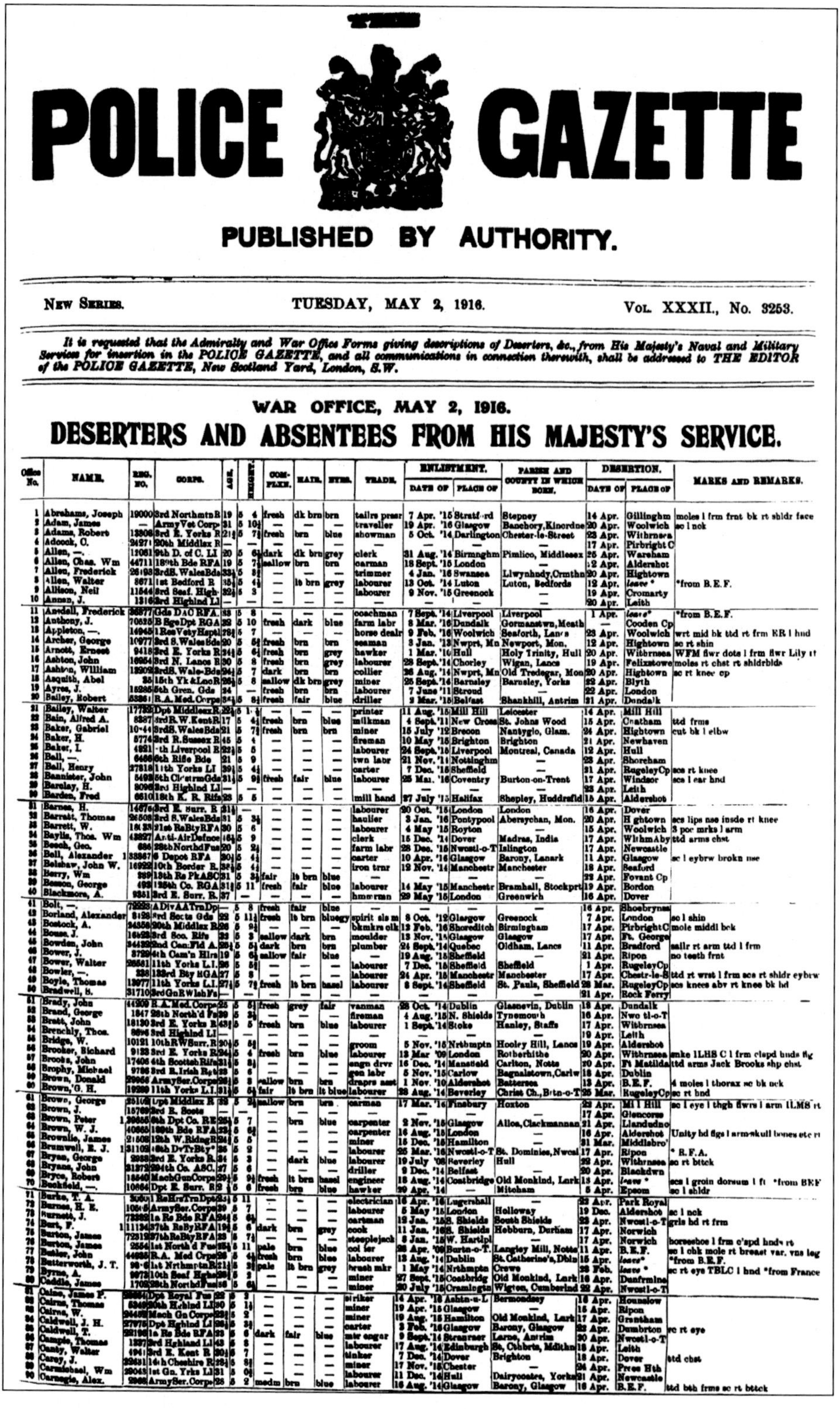

POLICE GAZETTE

PUBLISHED BY AUTHORITY.

New Series.   TUESDAY, MAY 2, 1916.   Vol. XXXII., No. 3253.

It is requested that the Admiralty and War Office Forms giving descriptions of Deserters, &c., from His Majesty's Naval and Military Services for insertion in the POLICE GAZETTE, and all communications in connection therewith, shall be addressed to THE EDITOR of the POLICE GAZETTE, New Scotland Yard, London, S.W.

WAR OFFICE, MAY 2, 1916.

DESERTERS AND ABSENTEES FROM HIS MAJESTY'S SERVICE.

Office No.	NAME.	REG. NO.	CORPS.	AGE.	HEIGHT.	COM-PLEX.	HAIR.	EYES.	TRADE.	ENLISTMENT. DATE OF	ENLISTMENT. PLACE OF	PARISH AND COUNTY IN WHICH BORN.	DESERTION. DATE OF	DESERTION. PLACE OF	MARKS AND REMARKS.
1	Abrahams, Joseph	19000	3rd Northmtn B	19	5 4	fresh	dk brn	brn	tailrs presr	7 Apr. '15	Stratf-rd	Stepney	14 Apr.	Gillingham	moles l frm frnt bk rt shldr face
2	Adam, James	—	Army Vet Corp	31	5 10½	—	—	—	traveller	19 Apr. '16	Glasgow	Banchory,Kincrdne	20 Apr.	Woolwich	sc l nck
3	Adcock, C.	13000	3rd E. Yorks R	21	5 7½	fresh	brn	—	showman	5 Oct. '14	Darlington	Chester-le-Street	22 Apr.	Withrnsea	
4	Adcock, C.	24271	30th Middlsx R	—	—	—	—	—	—	—	—	—	17 Apr.	Pirbright C	
5	Allen, —	11063	9th D. of C. LI	20	5	5½dark	dk brn	grey	clerk	31 Aug. '14	Birmngham	Pimlico, Middlesex	25 Apr.	Wareham	
6	Allen, Chas. Wm	44711	18th Bde RFA	19	5	7½	allow	brn	brn	carman	18 Sept. '15	London	—	3 Apr.	Aldershot	
7	Allen, Frederick	26493	3rdS. WalesBds	33	5	8½	—	—	collier	4 Jan. '16	Swansea	Llwynhwdy,Crmthn	20 Apr.	Hightown	
8	Allen, Walter	5671	1st Bedford R	18	5	4½	—	lb brn	grey	labourer	13 Oct. '14	Luton	Luton, Bedfords	19 Apr.	Hightown	
9	Allison, Neil	11544	3rd Seaf. High	20	5	5	—	—	—	labourer	9 Nov. '15	Greenock	—	19 Apr.	Cromarty	*from B.E.F.
10	Annan, J.	1316	3rd Highlnd LI	—	—	—	—	—	—	—	—	—	20 Apr.	Leith	
11	Asdall, Frederick	32877	Gds DAC RFA	23	5 8	—	—	—	coachman	7 Sept. '14	Liverpool	Liverpool	1 Apr.	*leave*	*from B.E.F.
12	Anthony, J.	70835	B BgeDpt RGA	32	5 10	fresh	dark	blue	farm labr	8 Mar. '16	Dundalk	Gormanstwn,Meath	—	Cooden Cp	
13	Appleton, —	14945	1 ResVety Hspl	29	5 7	—	—	—	horse dealr	6 Feb. '16	Woolwich	Seaforth, Lancs	23 Apr.	Woolwich	wrt mdl bk ttd rt frm ER l hnd
14	Archer, George	10977	3rd S. Wales Bds	20	5	5½ fresh	brn	—	seaman	3 Jan. '15	Newprt, Mn	Newport, Mon.	13 Apr.	Hightown	sc rt shin
15	Arnott, Ernest	9418	3rd E. Yorks R	24	5	6½ fresh	brn	grey	hawker	1 Mar. '16	Hull	Holy Trinity, Hull	20 Apr.	Withrnsea	WFM flwr dots l frm flwr Lily rt
16	Ashton, John	16004	3rd N. Lancs R	30	5	8 fresh	brn	grey	labourer	28 Sept. '14	Chorley	Wigan, Lancs	18 Apr.	Felixstowe	moles rt chst rt shldrblds
17	Ashton, William	1200	3rdS. Wals-Bds	30	5	5 fresh	brn	grey	collier	26 Aug. '14	Nwprt, Mn	Old Tredegar, Mon	20 Apr.	Hightown	sc rt knee cp
18	Asquith, Abel	85	15th Yk-Lnes R	23	5	8	allow	dk brn	grey	miner	28 Sept. '14	Barnsley	Barnsley, Yorks	20 Apr.	Blyth	
19	Ayres, J.	16285	6th Gren. Gds	24	—	—	fresh	brn	—	labourer	7 June '11	Stroud	—	22 Apr.	London	
20	Bailey, Robert	—	R.A. Med. Corps	24	5	5½ fresh	fair	blue	driller	3 Mar. '15	Belfast	Shankhill, Antrim	21 Apr.	Leith	
21	Bailey, Walter	17782	Dpt Middlesx R	25	5	1	—	—	printer	1 Aug. '15	Mill Hill	Leicester	14 Apr.	Mill Hill	
22	Bain, Alfred A.	8327	3rd R.W. Kent R	17	5	4½ fresh	brn	brn	milkman	4 Sept. '15	New Cross	St. Johns Wood	15 Apr.	Chatham	ttd frms
23	Baker, Gabriel	10444	3rdS. WalesBds	22	5	7½ fresh	brn	brn	miner	15 July '12	Brecon	Nantyglo, Glam.	24 Apr.	Hightown	cut bk l elbw
24	Baker, H.	6774	3rd R.Sussex R	45	5	4	—	—	fireman	10 May '15	Brighton	Brighton	21 Apr.	Newhaven	
25	Baker, I.	4821	-th Liverpool R	22	5	5	—	—	labourer	24 Sept. '14	Liverpool	Montreal, Canada	12 Apr.	Hull	
26	Ball, —	6466	6th Rifle Bde	21	5	9	—	—	twn labr	21 Nov. '14	Nottingham	—	19 Apr.	Shoreham	
27	Ball, Henry	27818	11th Yorks LI	25	5	4½	—	—	carter	7 Dec. '15	Sheffield	—	21 Apr.	RageleyCp	sc rt knee
28	Bannister, John	5495	5th Cl-strmGds	21	5	9½ fresh	fair	blue	labourer	25 Mai. '16	Coventry	Burton-on-Trent	17 Apr.	Windsor	scs l ear hnd
29	Barclay, R.	5095	3rd Highlnd LI	—	—	—	—	—	—	—	—	—	22 Apr.	Leith	
30	Bardon, Fred	6510	13th K. R. Rifs	23	5	5	—	—	mill band	27 July '15	Halifax	Shepley, Huddrsfld	15 Apr.	Aldershot	
31	Barnes, H.	1467	3rd R. Surr. R	21	—	—	—	—	—	labourer	20 Oct. '15	London	London	16 Apr.	Dover	
32	Barratt, Thomas	36502	3rd S. WalesBds	31	5	3½	—	—	haulier	3 Jan. '16	Pontypool	Aberaychan, Mon.	20 Apr.	H gbtown	scs lips nse insde rt knee
33	Barratt, W.	18	3rd 21st RaBtyRFA	30	5	5	—	—	labourer	4 May '15	Boyton	—	15 Apr.	Woolwich	3 poc mrks l arm
34	Baylis, Thos. Wm	43927	Art 4-AirDefnce	16	5	5	—	—	clerk	18 Dec. '14	Dover	Madras, India	17 Apr.	Dover	mdl l arms chst
35	Beach, Geo.	636	26thNorthdFus	30	5	3	—	—	farm labr	28 Dec. '15	Nwcsl-o-T	Islington	17 Apr.	Newcastle	
36	Bell, Alexander	133647	5 Depot RFA	30	5	5	—	—	carter	10 Apr. '16	Glasgow	Barony, Lanark	11 Apr.	Glasgow	sc l eybrw brokn nse
37	Belshew, John W.	16292	10th Border R	39	5	5	—	—	iron trnr	12 Nov. '14	Manchester	Manchester	16 Apr.	Seaford	
38	Berry, Wm	389	13th Re PlASC	31	5	3½ fair	lb brn	blue	—	—	—	—	18 Apr.	Fovant Cp	
39	Benson, George	493	18th Co. RGA	31	5	11	fresh	fair	blue	labourer	14 May '15	Manchester	Bramhall, Stockprt	19 Apr.	Bordon	
40	Blackmore, A.	9361	3rd R. Surr. R	37	—	—	—	—	—	hsweran	29 May '15	London	Greenwich	16 Apr.	Dover	
41	Bolt, —	70258	A Div A A TrnDp	—	5 8	fresh	fair	—	—	—	—	—	4 Apr.	Shoebryness	
42	Borland, Alexander	5135	3rd Scots Gds	29	5 11½	fresh	lb brn	bluegy	spirit sls m	8 Oct. '12	Glasgow	Greenock	7 Apr.	London	sc l shin
43	Bostock, A.	34580	30th Middlsx R	29	9½	—	—	—	tmkre cl'k	13 Feb. '16	Shoreditch	Birmingham	17 Apr.	Pirbright C	mole middl bck
44	Bouse, J.	16829	3rd Scots Rifs	23	5	2	allow	dark	brn	moulder	13 Nov. '14	Glasgow	Glasgow	17 Apr.	Ft. George	
45	Bowden, John	34439	2nd Can.Fld A.	39	5	5	dark	brn	brn	plumber	28 Sept. '14	Quebec	Oldham, Lancs	11 Apr.	Bradford	sallr rt arm ttd l frm
46	Bower, J.	8720	4th Gam'n Bls	19	5	6	allow	fair	blue	—	—	—	—	21 Apr.	Ripon	no teeth frnt
47	Bower, Walter	20641	11th Yorks L.I.	28	5	5½	—	—	labourer	7 Dec. '15	Sheffield	Sheffield	21 Apr.	RageleyCp	
48	Bowler, —	336	13th Bty RGA	27	5	6	—	—	labourer	24 Apr. '15	Manchester	Manchester	17 Apr.	Chstr-le-St	ttd rt wrst l frm scs rt shldr eybrw
49	Boyle, Thomas	13077	11th Yorks L.I.	32	5	7½ fresh	lb brn	hazel	labourer	24 Apr. '14	Sheffield	St. Pauls, Sheffield	23 Mar.	RageleyCp	scs knees abv rt knee bk hd
50	Bradwell, B.	31710	3rd GnK WlshFs	—	—	—	—	—	—	—	—	—	21 Apr.	Rock Ferry	
51	Brady, John	44305	I.A. Med. Corps	25	5	5	fresh	grey	grey	vanman	28 Oct. '14	Dublin	Glasnevin, Dublin	18 Apr.	Dundalk	
52	Brand, George	1847	8th North'd Fs	29	5	3½	—	—	fireman	4 Aug. '15	N. Shields	Tynemout	16 Apr.	Nwc tl-o-T	
53	Bratt, John	18120	3rd E. Yorks R	43	5	5	fresh	brn	blue	labourer	1 Sept. '14	Stoke	Hanley, Staffs	17 Apr.	Withrnsea	
54	Brenchly, Thos.	5846	3rd Highlnd LI	—	—	—	—	—	—	—	—	—	19 Apr.	Leith	
55	Bridge, W.	10191	10th WBurr. R	90	5	5	—	—	groom	9 Nov. '15	Nrthmptn	Hooley Hill, Lancs	19 Apr.	Aldershot	
56	Brooker, Richard	9123	3rd E. Yorks R	24	5	4	fresh	brn	—	labourer	13 Mar. '16	London	Rotherhithe	22 Apr.	Withrnsea	mke 1 LHB C l frm clspd hnds flg
57	Brooks, John	17406	4th ScottshRifs	31	5	5	—	—	enge drvr	16 Dec. '14	Manstield	Carlton, Notts	20 Apr.	M atilda	ttd arms Jack Brooks shp chst
58	Brophy, Michael	6756	3rd R.Irish Rs	25	5	5	—	—	gen labr	5 Nov. '15	Carlow	Bagalastown,Carlw	18 Apr.	Dublin	
59	Brown, Donald	28505	Army9er.Corps	28	5	5	allow	brn	grey	labourer	1 Nov. '15	Aberdeen	—	19 Apr.	B.E.F.	4 moles l thorax sc bk nck
60	Brown,'O. H.	19380	11th Yorks L.I.	35	5	4½ fair	lb brn	blue	labourer	28 Aug. '14	Pevensey	Christ Ch., Btn-o-T	28 Mar.	RageleyCp	sc rt hnd
61	Brown, George	26105	Dpt Middlsx R	22	5	5	allow	brn	brn	carman	17 Mar. '16	Finsbury	Hoxton	22 Apr.	Mil T Hill	sc l eye l thgh flwrs l arm 1 LMB rt
62	Brown, P.	16766	3rd R. Scots	—	—	—	—	—	—	labourer	6 May '15	London	—	17 Apr.	Glencorse	
63	Brown, Peter	11489	3rd Dpt Co. RE	24	5	7	—	—	carpenter	9 Nov. '15	Glasgow	Allos,Clackmanan	16 Apr.	Llandudno	
64	Brown, W. J.	40055	19th Bde RFA	26	5	8	—	—	carpenter	2 Nov. '15	London	—	16 Apr.	Aldershot	Unity bd figs l arm skull bones etc rt
65	Brownlie, James	2150	11th W.RidngeR	24	5	5	—	—	miner	15 Dec. '14	Hamilton	—	21 Apr.	Middlsbro'	
66	Bramwell, R. J.	13110	4th Dv'TyBty*	26	5	5	—	—	labourer	25 Mar. '16	Nwcsl-o-T	St. Dominics, Nwcsl	17 Apr.	Ripon	* R.F.A.
67	Bryans, John	29802	3rd E. Yorks R	35	5	5	—	—	labourer	10 July '09	Beverley	Hull	22 Apr.	Withrnsea	sc rt shin
68	Bryce, Robert	31372	304th Co. ASC	27	5	6	—	dark	blue	driller	8 Dec. '14	Perth	—	20 Apr.	Blackdwn	
69	Buckfield, —	10564	Dpt R. Surr. R	29	5	6	fresh	lb brn	blue	engineer	16 Aug. '14	Coatbridge	Old Monkland, Lark	20 Apr.	Ripon	scs l groin dorsum l ft *from BEF
70	Burke, T. J.	30031	I.A. ReVTrnCorp	25	5	5	—	—	electrician	16 Apr. '16	Lagerdhall	—	22 Apr.	Park Royal	
71	Burns, E. E.	100	6 ArmySer.Corps	30	5	7	—	—	labourer	6 May '15	London	Holloway	19 Dec.	Aldershot	sc l frm
72	Bursatti, J.	73382	1a Re Bds RFA	24	5	5	dark	brn	grey	carman	13 Jan. '16	S. Shields	Newk Shields	23 Apr.	Norwich	girls bd rt frm
73	Burt, F.	11121	327th ReBtyRFA	19	5	6	dark	brn	grey	cook	1 Jan. '16	S. Shields	Hebburn, Durham	17 Apr.	Norwich	
74	Burton, James	72315	327thReBtyRFA	21	5	5	—	—	steeplejack	8 Jan. '16	W. Hartlpl	—	17 Apr.	Norwich	
75	Burton, James	3854	1st North'd Fus	35	5	11	—	—	col ler	28 Jan. '16	Burtn-o-T	Langley Mill, Notts	11 Apr.	B.E.F.	horseshoe l frm c'spd hnds rt
76	Butler, John	46481	R.A. Med Corps	25	5	5	—	—	labourer	18 Aug. '14	Dublin	St. Catherine's,Dbln	15 Apr.	B.E.F.	sc l mk mole rt breast var. vns leg
77	Butterworth, J. T.	53	41st NrthmtnBds	33	5	8½ pale	lb brn	grey	brush mkr	1 May '14	Nrthmptn	Crewe	25 Feb.	Bury	sc l arm
78	Byrne, A.	9572	10th Beaf R	26	5	7	—	—	miner	22 Sept. '14	Coatbridge	Old Monkland, Lark	16 Apr.	Danfmline	sc rt eye TBLC l hnd *from France
79	Cuddle, James	1703	28thNorth'dFus	24	5	5	—	—	miner	29 Jan. '15	Cramlngtn	Wigton, Cumberlnd	22 Apr.	Nwestl-o-T	
80	Caine, James F.	65316	3rd Royal Fus	29	5	1½	—	—	miner	16 Apr. '16	Ashin-u-L	Bermondsey	16 Apr.	Hounslow	
81	Cairns, Thomas	63405	Mech Co Corps	22	5	5	—	—	miner	16 Apr. '16	Glasgow	—	16 Apr.	Ripon	
82	Cairns, W.	24446	17th Dpt Hghlnd LI	20	5	5	—	—	miner	16 Apr. '16	Hamilton	Old Monkland, Lark	17 Apr.	Dundalk	
83	Caldwell, J. H.	27072	Dpt Hghlnd LI	26	5	5	—	—	miner	2 Aug. '15	Glasgow	Barony, Glasgow	16 Apr.	Dumbarton	sc rt eye
84	Caldwell, J. M.	34112	1a Re Bds RFA	30	5	5	dark	fair	blue	cartr engsr	29 Sept. '15	Barony, Austrin	—	30 Apr.	Nwcstl-o-T	
85	Camplon, Thomas	1277	3rd Highlnd LI	24	5	3	—	—	labourer	31 Mar. '16	Edinburgh	Sth. Clcknts, Mdthn	18 Apr.	Leith	
86	Candy, Walter	494	3rd K. Kent R	20	5	7	—	—	timber	7 Dec. '14	Dover	Brighton	18 Apr.	Dover	ttd chst
87	Carey, J.	30631	14th Cheshire R	34	5	5	—	—	labourer	1 Nov. '15	Chester	—	18 Apr.	Oswestry	
88	Carmichael, Wm	20043	1st Gn. Yorks R	32	5	6	—	—	labourer	11 Dec. '15	Hull	Dairycoatr, Yorks	21 Apr.	Beverley	
89	Carnegie, Alex	2506	ArmySer.Corps	25	5	5	medm	brn	blue	labourer	16 Apr. '16	Glasgow	Barony, Glasgow	16 Apr.	B.E.F.	ttd bth frms sc rt bttck

Front page of the Police Gazette *supplement of 2 May 1916. The weekly list of deserters and absentees grew longer with the introduction of conscription.* (The British Newspaper Archive)

Gus Platts, the Sheffield boxer, took 'French leave' to fight in the ring rather than on the battlefield. Right: *Platts on his wedding day.* (Sheffield Independent, 9 October 1915, courtesy Sheffield Newspapers); Below left: *Platts as pictured in cigarette cards – this one from Cope's.* (Author's own collection); Below right: *And this from the Ogden series.* (Author's own collection)

Gus Platts, of the City Battalion and the well-known Sheffield boxer, was yesterday quietly married in Sheffield to Miss A. Bowden.

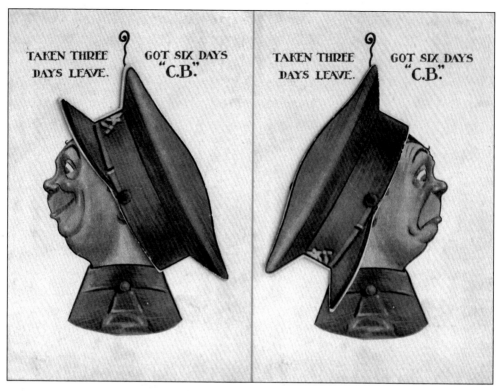

'Taken 3 day's leave/Got 6 day's C.B.' Two views of the same postcard, the soldier's cap being hinged to swap his facial expressions. (Author's own collection)

Deserter or 'absent tea'? These postcards are indicative of a more casual attitude towards absence held by the general public than that displayed by the British Army. (Author's own collection)

Above left: *'Conscription for me? Not likely!' Of course, children were not conscripted, but 250,000 enlisted voluntarily, some to desert when the reality of army life became apparent.* (Author's own collection)

Above right: *Leonard Ewart Nixon's gravestone at Lawnswood Cemetery in Leeds. Nixon was not a soldier, but a conscientious objector.* (Andrea Hetherington)

Right: *Medical examinations at recruiting offices were often perfunctory.* (Author's own collection)

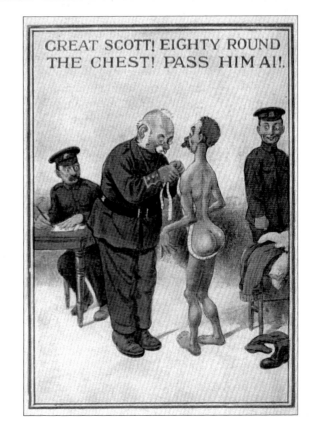

Above left: John Bull *mocked the ease with which 'Farmer's Boys' escaped conscription.* (British Newspaper Archive)

Above right: *Fred Spurgin produced many patriotic postcards during the war years. His brother, Maurice, would find himself at odds with the authorities in his bid to avoid khaki.* (Author's own collection)

Cowling, the 'Deserters' Village'. (Author's own collection)

Canadian camp on Salisbury Plain. A rare sunny day on 'a wind-swept waste where darkness lasted fourteen hours a day and all was wetness, mud, and misery'. (Author's own collection)

The Canadians meet for Sunday prayers. The soldier sending the cards back to Canada addressed this one to his mother . . . (Author's own collection)

And this one to his father . . . (Author's own collection)

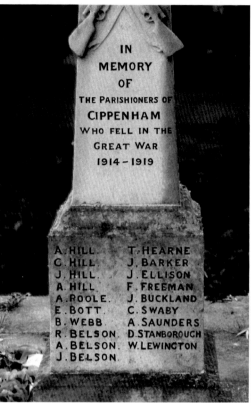

Above left: *The Beaver Hut was a magnet for Canadian soldiers and those interested in meeting them, sometimes with dubious motives.* (https://commons.wikimedia.org/wiki/File:Beaver_Hut_Canada_YMCA.jpg)

Above right: *The Cippenham War Memorial. Walter John Lewington's name appears, but he was a deserter, not a casualty.* (Courtesy of June and Peter Underwood)

Frank Lennard Walters, second row, smoking a pipe, at Bray in France with 52nd Battery Royal Field Artillery – 'The Bengal Rocket Troop'. A Regular army soldier, Walters would desert before his official discharge. (The Liddle Collection, University of Leeds)

Others committed offences which were simply incidental to their mission to return home, the theft of bicycles by deserters being common. There were several reasons for this – firstly, bicycles were easy to steal and numerous in these days before motorized personal transport was common. Secondly, they could be easily sold on once their use was at an end. Thomas Benzeval, serial deserter from Jersey, travelled around the towns of the South-West of England by bicycle, hiring a machine in each town and selling it in the next.[21] Ernest Dunn, in a state of desertion for two years, was arrested in Enfield where he seems to have made a living by stealing and reselling bicycles. The police claimed that twenty-seven bicycles had gone missing from outside the public library since Dunn had been in town.[22] Another reason for the popularity of bicycle thefts among deserters was that travelling by train was fraught with danger. The Military Police enjoyed a good level of co-operation from railway officials around the country in their hunt for deserters and it was difficult to board a train without a leave pass and ticket.

As the war continued and the realities of life in the trenches became known, the suspicion was that some men were committing crime on the home front to avoid overseas service. Albert Ellis deserted from the 3rd Sherwood Foresters in September 1915 and told the police that he had offended because he thought prison would be a warmer place to spend the winter than the trenches.[23] When the police arrived at his house to arrest him on behalf of the army, he immediately confessed to a burglary for which he was not a suspect. *John Bull* commented on the phenomenon in January 1916 with conscription imminent, questioning the practice of the army in discharging criminals back to civvy street once they had served their sentences. The paper claimed that the 'large numbers' of men deliberately committing crime to take advantage of this 'should be sent straight to the firing line'.[24]

This was, in fact, what was happening to soldiers in Britain who were receiving sentences of detention at courts martial. Alarmed at the prospect of losing the services of 39,000 men who had been given varying periods of detention in 1915 alone, the War Office instructed commanding officers to include the names of all trained men in detention barracks to be sent abroad immediately. It was acknowledged that there were men deliberately committing offences to avoid being sent to the Front and in 1916 763 men identified as being in this category were sent to India, their sentences remitted from the date of sailing. This was an example of the long-standing British Army practice of sending men abroad to 'regain their character'. Official records suggest that about 56,000 soldiers were removed from detention in

Britain to service overseas between 1916 and the Armistice.[25] The civilian courts were also less inclined to oblige deserters with protective prison sentences as the war went on. Harry Jacobs admitted breaking a jeweller's window and stealing £80 worth of rings in order to be sent to prison and not back to the army. The court did not go along with his grand plan, simply binding him over to be of good behaviour in the future and handing him to a military escort.[26]

For more serious offending the courts had to make an example regardless of the need for manpower on the Western Front. Frank Griffin Hodson was a serial fraudster and deserter from the Royal Fusiliers. He had already stolen £50 from the YMCA and committed a fraud in which he sold tickets for non-existent Red Cross fundraising shows when he hit on a new scheme in 1917. Wearing a Regimental Sergeant Major's uniform, Private Hodson went door to door nationwide pretending to be authorized by the army to sell surplus coal to the poor at reduced prices. Small amounts of money were sought as deposits for coal deliveries that never arrived. Even more audaciously, he turned up in Bognor Regis claiming that he was there to arrange billets for 2,000 officers. Hodson was on the run for a year before the authorities caught up with him. Eventually sentenced to three year's penal servitude, according to reports, he left the dock with a smile on his face knowing he was safely out of the firing line for the foreseeable future. The officer attending his civilian trial showed no desire to take Hodson back into the army and he served his full sentence and was discharged with ignominy in 1920. His military career was at an end but his criminal career continued and he received several prison sentences for burglaries of shop premises in the 1920s.[27]

Criminals could be heroes when the occasion arose. Richard Albert Langley of the East Surrey Regiment appeared before Old Street Police Court in January 1918 as a deserter and a thief. Langley had been missing from the ranks since March 1917 and was working instead as a porter for a soap manufacturer. Unable to resist temptation he had stolen £284 worth of goods from his employer, at which point his deserter status had been detected. Langley had won the Military Medal for leading an assault on a German pill box after his superior officers were incapacitated and showed the medal to the court, pleading for an opportunity to return to the Front. The magistrate did his best, declining to punish 'such a brave soldier' and simply ordered that he be handed back to the military. The army were less impressed with Langley. It wasn't his first desertion and his previous sentence of six months' detention was doubled at his court martial. Langley continued 'acquiring' goods that did not belong to him after the war: in 1920 he went to prison for stealing eighty turkeys just before Christmas.[28]

Anthony Babington comments that, 'It was usual for a deserter, like any absconding fugitive, to seek the anonymity of the commonplace rather than to indulge himself in a form of vainglorious display.'[29] It could be argued that in a country increasingly in khaki a wounded man in uniform was commonplace. Fake collecting tins and unnecessary bandages were fairly simple ruses, but some deserters constructed more elaborate and audacious frauds deliberately seeking the limelight rather than anonymity.

John O'Brien, also known as Edmond Joseph Walsh, was one example. He travelled the country pretending to be a 9th Lancer wounded at Mons, taking part in photo opportunities with eminent people, and even leading a recruitment parade in Streatham which resulted in 100 men joining up, all whilst being in a state of desertion from his real regiment.[30] Alfred Norman of Rotherham cheekily did an interview with a Chesterfield journalist under the name of Corporal Martin, claiming to have been wounded five times at the Front. When the police caught up with him and he appeared in court, these stories were exposed as 'fairy tales'. Norman had been to France but did not have a scratch on him, having been sent home sick twice and disposing of his uniform on the trip across the Channel.[31] Alfred Barker felt the need to show his war wounds to a local journalist to scotch rumours that he was a deserter. Barker claimed to have been sent home from the Front with wounds caused by a German bayonet and was enjoying the hospitality of Hebden Bridge, including a sum of £6 raised for him by a group of townswomen. The truth was that his impressive war wounds consisted of an appendectomy scar and an old injury sustained in a bicycle accident: Barker had never left the country let alone been impaled by a German bayonet. He was a deserter from the Lancashire Fusiliers and had forged his own leave pass to escape from camp at Lichfield.[32] Lancelot Dickinson Chapman was an army reservist who was called up in August 1914 but had deserted by November. He had never been to France but had for some time been cavorting around Camberwell claiming to be a holder of the Victoria Cross, the Order of Leopold and the Medal Militaire. He had bought these honours in curio shops, paying 30s. for the Victoria Cross and a lot less for the foreign medals. Chapman had even appeared in a music hall tableau celebrating his achievements and had his photograph printed in newspapers as a war hero. His war stories and his medals had been employed to obtain money and services by deception whilst he was on the run.[33] Laurie Bell aka Lorenzo Reginald Bell was employed by a recruiting officer in Bradford during his travels round the country as a deserter. Bell pretended to be an officer, and committed frauds in various locations, the cheekiest being that of forging an order from the War Office to be able to go and select a revolver from the Tower of London, no less.[34]

Corporal Fred Cropper pretended to be Scotland and Manchester United footballer Alec Menzies to prolong his period of freedom from the army. Cropper absconded from the Border Regiment at Grantham and made his way back to Manchester claiming to have war wounds. He had been conning a few pennies out of people, telling them that he knew their soldier relatives and showing them an Iron Cross he had allegedly taken from a German soldier to boost his veracity. The medal can't have been a very good copy, as the Stipendiary Magistrate who eventually dealt with Cropper in December 1914 laughed when the trinket was handed to him. Cropper kept up the pretence that he was Menzies, speaking in a Scottish accent and claiming that Heart of Midlothian, his former club, had bought him out of the army. George Wall, a Manchester United footballer, was brought to court to say that the defendant was not his former teammate.[35]

If people were more likely to trust a man in uniform in wartime, that trust would be doubly extended to a man in an officer's uniform. In a society that was in thrall to the class system, presenting oneself as an officer would buy a considerable amount of time before any fraud was detected, the word of a 'gentleman' trusted above and beyond that of an ordinary Tommy. A fraudster could happily write cheques to be drawn on an account at Cox's Bank knowing that by the time they were dishonoured he could be at the other end of the country doing the same thing to some other unsuspecting hotelier. Young women were particularly impressed by an officer's uniform. A number of writers have recorded that when troops were billeted on a town or village, there was a scramble to offer the household to officers, especially if there were women of marriageable age in the house.[36] Unlike the other ranks, officers ordered their own uniforms from a tailor, opening up more opportunity to deceive. Lionel Arthur Reeves Ball aka E.T. King had obtained his officer's uniform in this way and, suitably attired, the dapper Lieutenant hired expensive motor cars to take women on day trips to the seaside at Westcliffe and Herne Bay. He paid for all this with a cheque book belonging to someone else, as he himself was a lowly deserter from the London Rifle Brigade. Ball's deceptions continued throughout the war, most latterly touring the country claiming to be a US pilot.[37] Impersonating an officer of His Majesty's Army was an offence in itself but if a soldier was already a deserter the charge would add little to the overall sentence at a court martial. It is little wonder that some deserters chose to masquerade in plain sight as officers rather than hide away in civilian clothing. Offences of the impersonation of officers by ordinary soldiers were so prevalent that newspapers described them as 'one of the features of the present war'.[38]

Glaswegian Sam Rutherford deserted from the Royal Army Medical Corps when he was dumped by his girlfriend after buying her a ring with a fraudulent cheque. He went to London in the guise of an officer from the Black Watch. More bouncing cheques were used to buy military equipment and uniforms from Moss Bros to use in future frauds. At Matlock Hydro he rubbed metal polish on his skin to mimic the effects of poison gas and started a new relationship with a woman from Sunderland. His run ended when he was recognized by a police inspector at Paddington Station. Even then Rutherford would not come clean, trying to deter the inspector by claiming to be on his way to Buckingham Palace to receive the Victoria Cross. Rutherford found himself with twenty-one months' imprisonment for his deceptions. Discharged from the army as a result of this sentence, he fraudulently enlisted in the London Regiment in the name Alexander Menzies Murray. In February 1918 he appeared at the North London Police Court charged with wearing wound stripes, medal ribbons and an officer's uniform without authority. He was again involved in a relationship, this time about to be married to his landlady's daughter.[39]

Francis Turner, deserter from the Royal Engineers, obtained his officer's uniform from what looks suspiciously like a homosexual encounter in June 1915. The officer to whom the uniform legitimately belonged had allegedly missed his train one night, forcing him to stay with Good Samaritan Corporal Turner in his flat off Tottenham Court Road. Waking the next morning the officer found Turner gone, along with his uniform and all of his money. Turner then took an actress out to tea in his new finery. The wonderfully named Bunny Dix was resplendent in jewellery and a fancy watch, all of which Turner asked to try on. Having acceded to this request she never saw the items again.[40]

Though the stories above are just a few examples of the many ordinary soldiers claiming to be officers for nefarious purposes, real officers were not averse to desertion and deception. In January 1916, Second Lieutenant Turner-Smith of the Highland Light Infantry was disappointed when the latest list of names to go abroad on active service did not include his own. He saw a chance to be called after all because one of the officers on the list, Lieutenant Clayton, was absent without leave. Turner-Smith describes him as 'a heavy drinker and a thoroughly bad fellow' and Richard Stopford Clayton had certainly left a trail of destruction in his wake over the years. From a respectable banking family, who lived at Wylam Hall, Northumberland, Clayton was something of a disappointment, not doing well at Eton and being sent to Canada in 1899 for a fresh start. He did not make a success of the ranch his father had bought him and returned to England in 1913. Clayton soon found himself before the court for bouncing cheques but was discharged when his family promised to make restitution. A commission in the army did nothing to ease Clayton's financial situation. He saw action abroad and was sent home with a shrapnel wound from which he made a full recovery. Heavily in debt he now decided that the best way to solve his problem was to marry a rich woman. The slight flaw in his plan was that he already had a wife in Vancouver. Nevertheless, Clayton found a suitable candidate and set about impressing his target and her parents. He hired an expensive motor car to take his new beloved around and issued a series of bad cheques with which to pay for it. His marriage proposal was accepted, the banns were read in church and Clayton absconded from his battalion to seal the deal. His fiancée's parents now found out that his cheques had bounced and his flashy motor car had been repossessed, and they cancelled the wedding. Holed up in the Royal Hotel in Edinburgh, Clayton heard that he had been warned on a draft to go to the Mediterranean and was now seen as a deserter. Tracked down by the Military Police, as a courtesy to his rank he was placed on open arrest. With his world crashing down around him, Clayton shot himself in his hotel room. His account with Cox & Co. was overdrawn by nearly £24.[41]

The meanest deceptions were committed by deserters who deliberately targeted the families of men serving abroad. Claiming to be wounded soldiers, these deserters would turn up in a town and make the acquaintance of women who were waiting for news of their husbands. The new arrival would claim to have served with the husband and have greetings and instructions from him, hoping to obtain free food, accommodation and possibly money in return. James McGhee of Glasgow pretended to be just home from France and defrauded several army wives in this way in 1915. He had deserted the King's Own Scottish Borderers only a month after enlisting, failing to return from leave in September 1914.[42] This kind of fraud was particularly cruel when it involved the families of men who had been reported missing, families easily identifiable from a cursory glance at the local newspaper of whichever town the deserter happened to be passing through. Some fraudsters went further than merely claiming to have known the missing men.

Thomas Baker was a King's bad bargain, discharged from the army before the war due to his criminal convictions. He joined up again, enlisting in the Royal Field Artillery in August 1914 but was discharged by January 1915 as someone 'unlikely to make a good and efficient soldier'. Undeterred, Baker re-enlisted in the Royal Field Artillery two months later under the name Johnson. After being attached to the Seaforth Highlanders in Cromarty he deserted in the summer of 1915 and made his way to London. Claiming to have been gassed at the Front he took advantage of strangers who gave him accommodation and money. One such stranger was Mr Hazell, whose daughter-in-law, Sarah, had a brother called John James Smyrk, a Corporal in the 2nd Essex Regiment, currently a prisoner of war in Germany. When Sarah visited the house and met Baker, she said that he was the spitting image of 'our Jack'. Baker seemed initially content to simply claim that he knew 'Jack', but when shown a photograph of the man, he took the deception a stage further and now said that he was, in fact, John Smyrk. Sarah became convinced that Baker **was** Smyrk. Amazingly when the imposter was taken to Smyrk's mother she was similarly fooled, as was his fiancée, Nellie Reed, both believing that he was the real thing. Robert Smyrk, the real man's uncle, was similarly content with the identification and all were delighted to have 'Jack' home again.

Not satisfied with duping two families, Baker also defrauded the War Office, seeking backpay owed to Corporal Smyrk and the £5 remittance he was due as an exchanged prisoner of war. Robert Smyrk, the real man's uncle, began to have second thoughts about this soldier's true identity and reported him to the police in August 1915. By that stage Baker was lodging with his fiancée's family who were still insistent he was Smyrk. The real Smyrk had tattoos on his arm in tribute to his sweetheart Nellie – Baker did not and claimed that the Germans had removed them whilst he was a POW. Conveniently, the Germans had also tattooed him with new markings. Baker was eventually tripped up by the simple fact that he did not know Smyrk's middle name. He maintained the deception, supported by the Reed family, until the police brought his real mother to Clerkenwell Police Court to identify him. He finally admitted his identity and was given a rather lenient sentence of six months' imprisonment with hard labour for his deception. There was a happy ending to the story – the real John Smyrk came home safely and married Nellie Reed in December 1918.[43]

A more tragic outcome was seen in another impersonation case in Manchester. In the summer of 1915, Sarah Jane Dandy was eagerly awaiting news of her husband, Sergeant Herbert Dandy, who had embarked with the

Manchester Regiment to fight at Gallipoli. On 16 July 1915 a soldier came
into Mrs Dandy's grocery shop in West Gorton, Manchester, claiming to be
Herbert. He did bear a resemblance to her husband but also looked different,
most notably being shorter than the Herbert she remembered. Sarah Jane
challenged him on the changes but was given the answer 'You would have
altered if you had gone through what I have.' 'Herbert' claimed to have been
stranded in the Egyptian desert without food or water for 72 hours and had
also sustained a leg injury resulting in some bone being removed. He blamed
this ordeal not only for his changed looks, but for his loss of memory that
made him unable to answer personal questions about the couple's history.
Mrs Dandy noticed that identifying marks which would have proved he was
her husband were no longer there. 'Herbert' claimed to have had his tattoos
and a scar surgically removed. Initially Mrs Dandy does not appear to have
been completely convinced, but the encouragement of her neighbours and
Sergeant Dandy's own sister led her to accept the man as her husband.
'Herbert' stayed at her house for a week and told her he had run off from
Netley Hospital because they were threatening him with detention as a mental
patient and he could not stand the thought of being unable to see her and their
four children again. On 9 August her doubts got the better of her and she
asked him to prove his identity. The police now became involved. Mrs Dandy
had saved every postcard and letter written to her from Egypt by her husband
and the man claiming to be Herbert Dandy was told to complete a handwriting
test. The handwriting did not match. The man was arrested and six soldiers
who had served with Herbert Dandy were brought to see him: 'Herbert' could
not name any of them. Though the soldiers acknowledged that the man bore a
resemblance to Sergeant Dandy, they were clear that he was not their former
comrade. Indeed he was not – he was a deserter from the Lancashire Fusiliers
by the name of George Parkin Hall and he already had a wife and six children
in Patricroft, just 8 miles from the Dandy's shop. Hall was convicted of rape
for his fraudulent intimacy with Mrs Dandy and was sentenced to three years'
penal servitude in November 1915. By the time of the trial Mrs Dandy was
wearing mourning clothes: she had received the news that Sergeant Herbert
Dandy had been killed at Gallipoli in June.[44]

The end of hostilities did not put an end to deserter's frauds. In fact, it
provided new and lucrative opportunities to make money from the gullible.
Arthur Lomas, of Mytholmroyd, operated a scam by which he took out
advertisements in newspapers offering to sell large numbers of wooden
army surplus boards. Deposits were required before the boards would be

sent, after which time the advertiser disappeared. Lomas was a deserter who had escaped from hospital in Oswestry and had a poor disciplinary record. Exploiting the existence of a genuine market in army surplus goods, his fraudulent advertisements had earned him the huge sum of £2,000 before he was arrested.[45]

Beggars, confidence tricksters, fraudsters and burglars abounded in the ranks of home-front deserters. Less common were those much more dangerous men who committed the most serious offence in the criminal calendar during their time on the run. By the second week of the war, Private Donald Lesbini of the Worcestershire Regiment had his first kill. The victim was not a German soldier but a young woman working at 'Fairyland', an amusement arcade on Tottenham Court Road where Lesbini had gone to practise his marksmanship. He certainly had no intention of using his skill on the Germans, as he had deserted from his regiment days before war was declared.

Lesbini was a serial deserter who joined the army straight from borstal in 1911. A tailor in the regiment, Lesbini complained that he had been subjected to constant antisemitic bullying and that this had caused him to desert. He strongly objected to this treatment, not on the grounds that it was racist, but because he was not Jewish, claiming Greek descent. On 12 August 1914 Lesbini turned up at Fairyland and took exception to attendant Alice Storey referring to him as 'Ikey' – a derogatory term for someone of Jewish descent. Though she apologized when challenged, Lesbini chased her through the premises and shot her in the chest from close range, killing her almost instantly. He later said he had gone to the range that day to kill himself because he was miserable 'at being despised and looked down upon no matter where I went'. He claimed that the revolver had gone off accidentally. Lesbini must have presented a pathetic figure at the Old Bailey, as although he was quickly found guilty, the jury made a recommendation for mercy. He was sentenced to hang and later refused leave to appeal his conviction, though days before his scheduled execution date the death sentence was commuted to life imprisonment. Lesbini's behaviour in prison became increasingly paranoid and odd and in 1931 he was finally certified as insane and transferred to Broadmoor.[46]

In February 1917 in Liverpool, deserter James O'Neill of the Royal Welch Fusiliers murdered his own brother. The two had been involved in a drink-fuelled argument which ended with William O'Neill leaving the house and going to the police station to report his brother as a deserter. When arrested at the family home, James slashed William's throat with a razor on his way out of the door. James O'Neill pleaded not guilty to murder and the trial judge was sympathetic in his summing up to the jury, advising them that it may have been accidental that William was killed rather than sustaining a minor facial wound. Taking the hint, the jury did not even leave court to deliberate before returning a verdict of manslaughter. James O'Neill was sentenced to seven years' penal servitude.[47]

One morning in November 1917, Captain Edward Tighe was found at home at Winkfield Lodge, Wimbledon with severe head wounds, dying of his injuries a few days later. The newspapers speculated wildly about the reasons for the tragedy, coined 'The Wimbledon Mystery'. The *Pall Mall Gazette* headline asked 'Did A German Murder Captain Tighe?'. Irish revolutionaries were also suspected given that Tighe owned an estate in Ireland, or perhaps it was a soldier with a grievance against the recently retired Captain.[48] The truth turned out to be a little less sensational: Tighe was murdered by a deserter who was burgling the house. Arthur Harry Victor De Stamir/Stanier – real name Arthur Stamrowski – was the culprit, items from the burglary being found in his lodgings. He had told the landlady that he was attached to the Military Police at Whitehall, but in reality he was a deserter from the Imperial London Yeomanry who had spent more time in custody than in khaki during his army career. Stamrowski immediately confessed to the police that he had been present at the scene of the crime but denied being the one who inflicted the fatal blows. At his trial at the Old Bailey, he claimed that the real culprit was an Australian soldier called Reginald Fisher who usually made his living by doping soldiers with opium and robbing them. The jury decided that Fisher was fictitious and found Stamrowski guilty of the murder. An appeal was unsuccessful and he was executed on 12 February 1918.

On 16 August 1918 the market town of Pontefract was shocked by a murder in broad daylight. Widow Rhoda Walker, the owner of a jeweller's shop near the town centre, was found lying in the heavily bloodstained premises with serious injuries. She died in hospital without regaining full consciousness and the search for her murderers commenced. There were few clues for the police other than the fact that Mrs Walker kept sighing 'Oh, George!' as she lay dying in hospital. Pontefract had long been a garrison town and soldiers were a common sight. Mrs Walker was said to be generous to the wounded soldiers who frequented the Soldier's Home close to her shop. Witnesses had seen a soldier looking into the window of the jeweller's shop that afternoon, noting that he was sporting wound stripes on his uniform. Suspicion fell on George Walter Cardwell and Percy George Barrett, deserters from the Army Service Corps who had been working at Hemsworth Colliery. The two fugitives had returned to their lodgings with their army greatcoats on after the murder and were noted to have carefully washed themselves before leaving. Information was received that they were on their way to London. Cardwell was found at the address of a girlfriend on the Old Kent Road, and Barrett was picked up in a public house a short time later. Both men were in possession of bloodstained jewellery taken from Mrs Walker's shop and were charged with her murder. Their first appearance at Pontefract Magistrates' Court attracted crowds bolstered by local miners who happened to be on strike at the time. At their subsequent trial each defendant blamed the other for inflicting the injuries on Mrs Walker; the jury retired for just 7 minutes before convicting them both. The judge had no option but to impose the death penalty and an appeal against the conviction was unsuccessful. Both men were executed in January 1919.

George Cardwell was one of the individuals who had been released from custody at the outbreak of war under the Royal Prerogative of Mercy. He was serving a sentence of borstal detention and was released early on the condition he enlisted in the army. Joining the Royal Berkshire Regiment, Cardwell reportedly had a good record as a soldier, being recommended for medals for gallantry. He couldn't keep up his behaviour for the duration of the war, deserting in June 1918. Cardwell maintained his innocence to the last and expressed the hope that his actions in the front line would save his reputation, if not his life. In one of his last letters to his father, he wrote, 'If I have to face this disgraceful death you can always say that I fought for a few years in France, and that no man can call me a coward who has ever been led by me in action out there.'[49]

Chapter 8
Conscription – The Net Tightens

Every male British subject who –
(a) On the fifteenth day of August nineteen hundred and fifteen was
    ordinarily resident in Great Britain, and had attained the age of
    eighteen years and had not attained the age of forty-one years;
    and
(b) on the second day of November nineteen hundred and fifteen
    was unmarried or was a widower without any child dependent
    on him; shall, unless he is either within the exceptions set out
    in the First Schedule to this Act . . . be deemed as from the
    appointed date to have been duly enlisted in His Majesty's
    regular forces . . .

Military Service Act, 1916, c104

By the Summer of 1915 any idea that joining the army was going to mean a
few months in khaki before the Germans surrendered was now acknowledged
as pure fantasy. Recruitment numbers had dropped considerably and despite
the traditional reluctance in Britain to enforce military service, conscription
was inevitable. Less drastic measures were introduced under the guise of
improving 'national efficiency' before compulsion was enforced, the first
being the creation of the National Register in August 1915. The Register was
compiled from questionnaires issued to all citizens between the ages of 15 and
65 asking for their personal details, skills, employment status and if they were
willing to attest. Though the accuracy of the information was in question,
some observers claiming that the register contained 1 million errors, when the
results were analysed, a pool of 2,700,000 men were deemed to be eligible for
military service.[1] The machinery to get those men into uniform now cranked
into gear.

At first this was still on a voluntary footing. Lord Derby was appointed
Head of Recruiting and the scheme which took his name asked all men of
military age to indicate whether they were willing to join the army when
called for. Married men were assured that they would not be called until the

supply of single men had been exhausted, meaning that many of them happily attested in the belief that they would never actually be needed. If the aim of the Derby Scheme had been to avoid the need for conscription, then it was a failure. Only half of the 2 million single men identified through the National Register indicated their willingness to serve, and of those a mere 343,386 were actually in a position to do so, the rest being already engaged on work of national importance or physically unfit for war service.[2] With the daily casualty rate continuing to climb, this was nowhere near enough to satisfy the demands of the military machine. In January 1916 the government introduced a conscription bill to apply to single men and childless widowers only, the bill becoming an Act at the end of that month. For men who had rushed into marriage before November 1915 to protect their civilian status the honeymoon was brief and in May 1916 conscription was extended to all men between the ages of 18 and 41.

The provisions of the Military Service Act 1916 stipulated that men 'ordinarily resident' in Great Britain on (or since) 15 August 1915 and aged between 18 and 41 were deemed to have enlisted as of 2 March 1916 and been technically transferred to the Army Reserve to await further instructions. A call-up notice would be sent out in due course with instructions for when and where to report for military service. Tribunals allowed appeals against the call-up on four grounds:

1. That you were of more use to the nation in your current occupation
2. That serious hardship would occur to your family were you to be called up
3. That you were suffering from ill health
4. That you were a conscientious objector to war

Exemptions could be granted completely or temporarily, depending on the reasons for the application. Should a conscientious objector be considered to have a genuinely held belief, the Tribunal could grant him total exemption – in practice quite rare – or a conditional or partial exemption that would oblige him either to take part in military service in a non-combatant role, or to instead be employed in work of national importance. Applicants were entitled to appeal any failure to grant them the level of exemption sought, firstly to a Regional Tribunal and then to the Central Tribunal which also issued directives and sample cases to guide the lower bodies.

A man who did not answer his call-up was not yet considered a deserter, though the intention of many who did not respond to the letters sent to them was undoubtedly to avoid service in the army completely. These men were not court-martialled but simply fined up to 40s. by the civilian court before being handed over to the military. They do not, therefore, form part of the official statistics on discipline published in *Statistics of the Military Effort of the British Empire*. Some indication of the level of non-co-operation with conscription can be found in a memorandum from the Chief of the Imperial General Staff, Sir William Robertson, to the Cabinet on 21 March 1916 in which he stated that 'of 193,891 men called up under the Military Service Act no fewer than 57,416 have failed to appear'.[3] The Army Council also recorded similar disappointment, noting that 'only a very small percentage' of men called up had actually been secured.[4] The *Police Gazette* of 2 May 1916 listed the names and addresses of 920 men who had failed to answer their call-up papers.[5] Every week a list of new names of similar volume was printed as the call-up notices went unheeded. The lists were not necessarily accurate as they were compiled from information that was months out of date in certain cases. Some of the men summoned may not have been in a position to answer the country's call: as of 1 July 1916 3,000 enlistment notices had been sent out to men who were already dead.

The importance attached to the task of obtaining new recruits can be seen by the measures introduced alongside conscription itself. Firstly, instructions were issued that men who had already been discharged from the services for misconduct or due to a civilian prison sentence would now be called up once again. This included officers who had previously been cashiered out of the service.[6] The same document specified that British-born men of foreign parentage or those who were now naturalized British citizens would also be conscripted, though if they were of German or Austrian origin they must only be sent to labour battalions. Regular soldiers were no longer to be discharged on the expiry of their original term of service unless they had served more than twelve years and were over the age of 41. Workhouses would be scoured for recruits: Poor Law Guardians were told that all single men applying for relief must be reported to their local recruiting officer immediately.[7] This was a far cry from the attitude displayed in October 1914 when a court dismissed the charge brought against a pauper of failing to maintain himself by refusing to join the army. The North London Police Court declared that an invitation from a recruiting officer was not an offer of work per se and that 'an unwilling man was not the sort of man wanted in the British Army'.[8] By 1916 any man was wanted in the army, willing or unwilling.

A change was also made in May 1916 to Section 153 of the Army Act, the legislation which made harbouring or encouraging deserters a criminal offence. From now on, it was not necessary to prove that an individual before the court for assisting a deserter knew that the man was a fugitive from the military. The statute was now to operate until the end of the war with the following clause: 'a person shall be deemed to have knowledge [of a deserter's status] unless he proves he had not knowledge'.[9] This reversal of the burden of proof meant that the chances of putting forward a successful defence to the charge of harbouring a deserter were now slim.

Opposition to conscription was widespread, certainly in the early part of the war. Political parties and even the War Cabinet itself were split on the issue. Dissent sometimes came from unexpected sources. Two articles were published in *John Bull* in early 1916 supposedly by a father opposed to the conscription of his 'delicate' son. 'The Slander of the Slacker' claimed that unfit ordinary men were being forced into the army whilst those in high places were securing cushy non-combat roles for their own physically fit sons. The writer made the point that not everyone was suited to the military and could better serve their country in a different capacity.[10] Though it was claimed the articles did not necessarily represent *John Bull*'s editorial view, the pieces repeated themes that the paper focused on throughout the war – ineffective bureaucracy and the 'scrimshanking' of those in positions of power. Conscription was 'Prussian' – the very antithesis of all Britain was fighting for. Once the measure was in force, *John Bull* was often critical of tribunals that failed to grant exemptions to self-employed men with families to support. The organization most famously opposed to compulsory military service was the No Conscription Fellowship (NCF), established in November 1914 under the direction of two members of the Independent Labour Party, Fenner Brockway and Clifford Allen. In addition to lobbying against the introduction of conscription, the NCF frequently asserted that their members would be glad to hide deserters and absentees. Once conscription was in force the NCF were keener to have men who objected to military service on conscientious grounds attend tribunals rather than simply run away once their call-up notices were received. The reporting of proceedings in the press would give those opposed to the war a platform to air their views.[11]

The majority of conscientious objectors (COs) opposed the war on what could be described as political, not religious grounds: three out of every four men imprisoned for their CO stance were political objectors.[12] It was harder for these men to demonstrate to the satisfaction of the tribunals that they held a genuine conscientious objection to military service than it was for members of a particular religious faith. In fact, if a man's convictions were purely political, the Central Tribunal took the view that 'such a conscientious objection, no matter how strongly held, was not one which came within the provisions of the Military Service Acts'.[13]

On the first day it was open to the press, the Leeds Military Service Tribunal dealt with 228 cases. On 13 March 1916 it heard 350 cases during the day's sitting.[14] The level of scrutiny applied to each case must have been minimal. The fact that applicants were already engaged in war work yet claimed to have a conscientious objection to the war itself was frequently used by the tribunal to thwart their arguments. Tribunals took the view that it was a short ideological step between sewing a uniform and wearing one. This was especially relevant in a city like Leeds that was making a huge contribution to the war effort through its industries. Tribunals did grant exemptions and certain parts of the country were more open to the idea of the conscientious objector – York, for example, was reputed to grant exemptions to Quakers fairly easily.[15] Maurice Rowntree of the famous Quaker family had the misfortune to be working in Leeds when he applied to the Military Service Tribunal and his application was refused though friends doing the same work in York were considered exempt.[16] In Cabinet it was acknowledged that it was a matter of luck whether a man was granted any exemption by the Military Service Tribunals and what form it would take.[17] An exemption that compelled a man to take part in work of national importance was something of a poisoned chalice. The Pelham Committee was set up to find suitable work for these individuals with the stipulation that they should not be allowed to remain in their home towns and 'should be required to make some sacrifice', conditions designed to deter men from claiming CO status.[18]

The process of applying for exemptions provided intervals for the unwilling to make themselves scarce and a new category of deserter now came into existence – the deserter of conscience. Some refused even to take part in the registration process in the first place, declining to offer their details for the National Register. Others disappeared once conscription was announced whilst those keener to display their principles would appear before the Military Service Tribunals and plead for exemption, only to remove themselves from the vicinity if their applications were refused. Some COs, having been granted exemption by a Tribunal in exchange for Pelham Committee work would absent themselves from that employment and go on the run. Others who were released from sentences of imprisonment as COs on the grounds that they would carry out road repairs, forestry, quarrying or farm labour under the auspices of the Brace Committee made themselves scarce from work centres around the country.[19] *Statistics of the Military Effort of the British Empire during the Great War 1914–1920* (*SMEBEGW*) records that 444 men employed under the Brace Committee scheme were arrested or recalled to the army for absconding or other misbehaviour, about 11 per cent of the men working under these conditions.[20] Whilst roughly 20,000 men did appear before Military Service Tribunals and claim a conscientious objection to war, it is hard to estimate the number of those with similar beliefs who decided that the better tactic was to disappear. Cyril Pearce estimates that at any one time between 1916 and 1919 there were several hundred COs roaming free around the country who were deserters or absentees. The NCF claimed that 6,745 men failed to answer their call-up papers on the grounds of conscientious objection with 175 managing to escape detection completely for the duration of the war.[21]

Ingenious hiding places were secured, often with the assistance of politically motivated associates. A cave under the premises of a cycle shop in Bristol became a refuge for deserters and the Wheeldon family's help in Derby for those on the run would see them ultimately accused of a plot to kill Lloyd George.[22] A CO who escaped from the Princetown Work Centre, more usually known as Dartmoor Prison, was found sleeping on a snooker table at the Independent Labour Party Institute in Newport. The most colourful version of the story suggested that the man was using a Union Jack as a blanket[23] It is worth noting that this story appeared at a time when striking miners were being described in the press in similar terms to deserters and COs, 'shirkers' all. The Newport ILP had played a prominent role in a recent strike and the fact that no names are mentioned in this story in any of the publications in which it appears suggests that it may be apocryphal. Albert Bryan took hiding in plain sight to a new level by attending the court martial of one of his fellow COs. Bryan was promptly arrested as an absentee himself, much to his apparent surprise.[24] There was something of an underground railroad in existence amongst those opposed to the war, transporting absentees and deserters around the country to safer locations and sometimes to Ireland and America. Harry McShane wrote that after his desertion he was taken in by an anarchist barber in Glasgow Green whilst he awaited funds to escape further afield. McShane had been given a letter of recommendation to James Connolly, leader of the Irish Citizen Army, and was also offered assistance from another socialist friend to travel to America.[25] Some fugitive COs found hiding places much closer to home.

In the tranquil grounds of Lawnswood Cemetery in Leeds, not far from the war memorial, stands the grave of Leonard Ewart Nixon who died in April 1924 aged 25. His epitaph reads 'B.Com. He gave his life for peace'. Leonard Nixon was not from 'B Company' of any regiment in the British armed forces – 'B.Com' stands for Bachelor of Commerce, the subject Nixon studied at the University of Leeds. He did not die of wounds sustained on some foreign field whilst fighting for the Empire, but of influenza at his home address in Leeds, his health ruined by a sentence of imprisonment at Wormwood Scrubs in 1918 as a conscientious objector. The son of a sweet-factory owner, Leonard and his brother, Frank, were part of what has been described by one of the group as a 'collection of idealists, cranks and practical revolutionaries' who met at the Anarchist Club in Elmwood Street in the Little London area of Leeds.[26] Though records of Leonard Nixon's progress through the local tribunal system no longer exist, his friend Michael Lipman reports that Leonard had applied for exemption on the grounds of conscience but had been turned down. He ran away rather than answer his call-up notice, though he did not go far, camping in a tent pitched in Adel, a northern suburb of Leeds just a couple of miles from his home address. Nixon was arrested there in July 1918 and appeared before the magistrates where he again claimed to be a CO. It was not the court's concern to investigate his claims by this stage and he was fined 40s. and taken to Fulford Barracks in York.[27] As was often the case with COs, he refused to follow orders and was court-martialled, receiving six months' imprisonment with hard labour in August 1918, one of 5,797 COs committed to prison from 1916 up to the end of 1918.[28] Subsequently interviewed by the Central Tribunal to ascertain the strength of his beliefs, Leonard's conscientious objections to service were not considered valid and he served the rest of his prison sentence rather than being offered Brace Committee work.

The level of opprobrium directed towards COs was far greater than that to the ordinary deserter. In June 1916 the Prime Minister had addressed Parliament on the subject, outlining two propositions he wished the country to follow. Firstly, the idea that a man who held an 'honest conviction' against war service should be allowed to rely upon that to claim the statutory exemption. Secondly, he stated that those who claimed such convictions dishonestly were 'guilty of the double offence of cowardice and hypocrisy' and should be treated 'with the utmost rigour'.[29] The popular press seem to have taken only the second proposition to heart, treating all who claimed CO status as criminals. Despite the paper's ambivalence towards conscription, *John Bull* was scathing in its condemnation of those seeking to take advantage of the conscience clause to avoid military service. 'Conchies' were 'shirkers' and much more deserving of criticism than men who had served before deserting. Strikes and protests occurred in factories if COs were sent there to carry out their allotted work of national importance. In May 1918 workers at a clothing factory in Mytholmroyd downed tools for this reason, as did those at Bibby's Oil and Cake works in Liverpool who objected to 100 COs being assigned to the workplace.[30] COs had been working at Bibby's for around eighteen months by this time and, being men of principle, now found themselves in the position of having to go on strike themselves to avoid being blacklegs. There was also a serious disturbance at Knutsford in 1918 where a group of COs housed in a former police station were besieged by a mob. The court dealt with the rioters leniently, blaming the COs for the fact they were attacked.[31] Princetown Work Centre was regularly portrayed in the press as something akin to a holiday resort for COs and questions were regularly raised in Parliament about 'soft jobs for shirkers'.[32] Walter Long, President of the Local Government Board, felt confident enough to tell the Cabinet in 1917 that should a CO die in prison 'there would be no substantial outcry'.[33] Prison conditions for COs were certainly not lenient: an estimated 71 CO.s died either during their prison sentences or shortly after release and many more would be left with permanent health problems. Leonard Nixon, dying in 1924, is not included in those statistics though his epitaph clearly demonstrates where his family felt the blame lay for his early death. In certain areas of the country support for COs was stronger. Cyril Pearce writes about the town of Huddersfield in *Comrades in Conscience*, presenting evidence that the community was much more tolerant of opposition to the war than the national picture would suggest.[34] As already noted, the existence of a Quaker community in York meant more favourable treatment for those purporting to be COs before the Military Service Tribunal in that city than elsewhere.

The introduction of conscription gave new impetus to police raids on popular entertainment venues. For those evading military service it would become increasingly difficult to avoid detection and live a normal life. This did not deter those who hoped to ignore the obligations now placed upon them, and the poor response to conscription reported in March 1916 continued. By July 1916 just over 66,000 men in Britain had failed to answer their call-up papers and a further 33,000 were listed by the army as 'unaccounted for'.[35] This was 30 per cent of those who were required to report and represented a significant loss of manpower. It was against this background that a number of raids were made around the country in autumn 1916 to try and flush these men out of their hiding places and spread fear amongst the ranks of those who had not yet answered the country's call.

In Leeds in September 1916, the police interrogated crowds outside theatres and other places of amusement, looking for men of military age and asking to check their papers. Similar raids happened nationwide, concentrating on theatres and cinemas. The moral backlash then brewing against the cinema did not help the cause of those indignant at the interruption of their evening's entertainment. Several hundred men in Leeds were said to be unable to produce their 'bona fides' at the time of the first raid and were asked to report with the relevant documentation later. Fifty men were detained at the town hall whilst checks were made, and sixteen subsequently appeared before the court as deserters or absentees. Between 200 and 300 men did report as required over the coming days, most producing documents in the form of exemption cards or leave passes to get them off the hook.[36] The 1916 raids were not popular in some quarters: *John Bull* in particular criticized the action, calling it 'unjustified and unjustifiable' even if it did pick up a few 'shirkers'.[37] The number of absentees and deserters obtained from these exercises, as in Leeds, was negligible, usually consisting of only a handful of soldiers from hundreds of men questioned.

This did not necessarily mean that these hundreds of men were legitimately exempt. Exemption cards did not include photographs, leaving endless potential for deception. Giving an exempt man's name when arrested in a mass raid could be enough to secure release with instructions to attend the station with paperwork later. Failure to turn up may send the police looking for the exempt man, but he had little to fear from their visit. More ingenious ruses were employed by organizations opposed to conscription, protecting on-the-run members by making sure that when out in public they were accompanied by someone legitimately exempt from service. In the case of police raids on public places, exemption cards would be passed to the deserters and absentees, who would flash them at the constables and be released. The absconders would then go straight to the home addresses of those lending them the cards and leave the documents there. The truly exempt men could tell the police that their paperwork was at home, and should the police bother to check they would find it there.[38] Another trick when faced with a lone policeman was for the exempt man to make a run for it, inevitably to be pursued by the constable whilst the true absentee made himself scarce. If the policeman caught the runner he would find him to be in possession of a full set of paperwork. There was a market in selling army discharge certificates with the going rate being in the region of 10s.. Ernest Folkes of Luton was working in a munitions factory following his release from the army, and lent his discharge papers to a deserter called Gustavus Streeton. When the missing soldier was found hiding in a ceiling void in possession of the certificate Folkes was fined £6 for his part in the deception and Streeton was sent back to the army. The Assistant Provost Martial told the court, 'This practice of obtaining and trafficking in discharge papers is a thing that is growing and is a practice of a most dangerous and unpatriotic description and requires very severe penalties in order to put it down.'[39]

One of the arrestees in the Leeds raid, Horace Cliff, produced a medical exemption certificate but was still detained because the police believed the paperwork was forged. A few days later the certificate was confirmed as genuine and Cliff was released.[40] The willingness of the police to believe that the certificate was bogus is an indication of the widespread availability of forged documents. Every time the War Office or Ministry of National Service came up with a badge, certificate or pass which would allow a man to prove his exemption from military service, there was a forger waiting in the wings to provide fakes to those prepared to pay the necessary fee. The introduction of the wound stripe as a badge of honour in 1916 gave fraudsters another item to sew on their uniforms to bolster their claims of heroic service and defray questions over their current status. Silver war badges, issued to those who had been invalided out of the war, were bought or stolen from those legitimately entitled to wear the symbol. Gerald Keen of the South Staffordshire Regiment, for example, was arrested as a deserter whilst wearing a silver war badge in March 1917. Keen had deserted from a hospital and claimed to have found the badge in the street.[41] MI5 reported that they came across a lot of passports forged with the sole intention of evading military service.[42] In July 1917 *The Times* published an article outlining the ways in which criminals assisted in the avoidance of military obligations. It claimed that the introduction of conscription had increased crime, stating, 'The cheat and the charlatan found a new field of operations . . . and the forger found the fears of the few a splendid foundation for new rascality'.[43] Army rejection certificates were much sought after, being stolen or bought from those in legitimate possession, whilst blank certificates of all kinds were stolen from recruiting offices. Merchant seamen's papers were particularly prized, especially those of US nationals, as merchant seamen were exempt from conscription. In addition to the traffic in certificates, *The Times* noted the extent of bribery and corruption which had taken place, with army clerks and doctors being offered money to provide the right documentation to let a man avoid service. The paper declared that, 'Master minds have been, and are, at work. Every degree of rascality has been suspected and proved.'

Following the introduction of the Military Service (Review of Exceptions) Act 1917, which allowed the authorities to re-examine men who had previously been rejected on medical grounds, simulation of disabilities of all kinds was rife, with men harming themselves temporarily to fool medical boards. Major General Sir W.G. Macpherson wrote after the war that men had managed to pull the wool over the eyes of examiners by 'Fraud, bribery, impersonation, doping, or chemical and bacterial maiming'.[44] In the summer of 1917 Dr George Bishop of London was convicted of fraud, allegedly taking money to place men in a lower medical category than their level of fitness suggested. According to the evidence heard at the trial, a complete exemption certificate could be bought for £120. Bishop had allegedly given a man pills to make his heart race faster so he could fool a fellow doctor that he was unfit. Bishop went to prison for twelve months.[45] Controversially, the new Act also included potential re-examination of men who had been discharged after being wounded or contracting an illness or disease on active service. The widespread view was that these men had 'done their bit' and should not be forced back into the fray whilst others stood idly by. Several deserters who had been recalled under this provision would appear before the courts from 1917 onwards. Robert Butler of the Manchester Regiment certainly felt he had already done his duty. After serving in the Balkans he was discharged in 1916 with a gunshot wound to his knee. Still wishing to contribute he then joined up again for home service only. When he was reclassified as 'A1' and put down for overseas service, he deserted.[46]

Many men accepted into the military during the war were either physically or mentally unfit to serve. Recruiting offices were overwhelmed by the initial enthusiasm to enlistment and examinations could be perfunctory. Even after the problem was realized the response was somewhat inadequate: doctors were told they had to reduce the number of examinations to six or eight per hour, or thirty to forty a day! It is difficult to see how any effective medical examination could take place within these timescales.[47] A contributory factor no doubt was that doctors were paid 2s. 6d. per recruit passed fit for service. Truly unfit men were a liability to the army, so doctors were later warned that these amounts could be reclaimed if the man turned out to be unfit. In practice, the money was rarely recovered unless 'distinct carelessness' could be shown on the part of the doctor.[48] Accepting men into the armed forces whose health quickly broke down would tell heavily on the country's war pension budget in years to come despite the Treasury's attempts to evade liability in many cases.[49] Two men arrested in the Leeds raid of September 1916 should never have been passed fit for service: William Henry Wadsworth suffered from epileptic fits and was discharged in 1917 as a result, whilst Sidney Addleman was released within six months of his arrest due to a heart complaint.[50]

Some of these unfit men would inevitably desert. Gustavus Streeton, the Luton deserter, was one of them. Streeton had signed up under the Derby Scheme in December 1915 and was called for service the following year. He had deserted before the escapade with his friend's discharge certificate but was spared imprisonment on that occasion due to his medical condition. Streeton had a congenital skull defect which caused him considerable pain, and in addition he may have had some learning difficulties as he was unable to read and write. He told a court martial that he had suffered from debilitating headaches his whole life and that they caused him to be confused about his actions. Placed before a medical board after his arrest in 1916, he was declared unfit to undergo imprisonment or further service in the army and his immediate discharge was recommended. Streeton was not discharged but transferred to another regiment, from which he again absconded within 24 hours. He was eventually transferred to a Labour Company in 1917 and, following his arrest in the Luton incident, would twice escape from confinement before he could be punished. Streeton was eventually sentenced to two years' detention, half of that then being remitted. He would desert again in 1919.[51]

A recurrent theme in the pages of *John Bull* in 1917 was the War Office's conscription of men who were already dead. The paper printed the story of Leonard Williamson, whose widow received his call-up papers and went to Dewsbury Town Hall to tell them that unfortunately her man had died. Further demands were sent and eventually the police turned up on her doorstep to arrest Leonard as a deserter.[52] Another example from Tottenham described a call-up notice being sent to a dead man at his former address in a tuberculosis sanatorium. *John Bull* joked that Britain was so short of manpower than the police were now intending to dig up the dead and put them in uniform.[53]

The Leeds police did not confine themselves to raiding the city centre, also targeting the substantial travelling fairs visiting the city. Holbeck Feast was one of the largest in the country and its September 1916 staging saw several absentees arrested. Timothy Kayes was one – a lion tamer arrested as he was about to enter the cage for that evening's performance. Just 5ft tall, Kayes caused some hilarity when he appeared before the magistrates in Leeds.

He claimed to have been detained on two previous occasions and declared too short to serve but the army now told the court he would be accepted. The officer in charge at the barracks kindly gave Kayes a fortnight's grace to sort out his affairs.[54] Timothy Kayes did not return as agreed but carrying on his profession made it difficult to hide from the authorities and he was arrested again a couple of weeks later, this time at the feast on Woodhouse Moor in Leeds. His 70-year-old father, William, appealed to the court to release his son as he was going to have grave difficulties running the business without him. Before the war the circus consisted of 23 men, 100 horses and a number of wild animals. At the time son Timothy was before the court the show was reduced to three lions, a monkey and fifteen ponies. All of the circus employees had been called up, including Mr Kayes' elder sons and the proprietor had six children under the age of 14 to support. The magistrates had no choice but to detain Timothy Kayes.[55] He survived the war and judging by the array of different addresses held for him by the pension authorities, then appears to have taken up his previous employment as a travelling showman.

The pressure to increase the recruitment figures meant that a practice called 'combing out' periodically took place, the needs of businesses being reassessed to see if anyone could be released for military service. Every announcement that a round of this was to take place undoubtedly prompted some to make themselves scarce before the assessing tribunal made its way to their workplace. 'Combing out' appears to have been selectively used by some employers to rid themselves of men they considered to be troublesome. In October 1917 Neil Livingstone of Glasgow was convicted of being an absentee and fraudulently claiming to have an exemption from military service. Livingstone was a joiner, making aeroplane parts, and had previously been employed at a shell-filling factory. He was also an active trade unionist. His brother wrote to the Prime Minister to protest his detention, warning that there may be dire consequences as a result: 'At the present time the unrest on the Clyde has reached an acute stage: only a spark is needed to cause a conflagration.' The reply on file from the Recruiting Officer who ordered the arrest suggested a motive beyond the simple need for manpower: 'from what I gather from the police, there will be less unrest if there is any when Livingstone is enlisted'.[56]

The blizzard of paperwork now flying about between tribunals, medical boards, the army and employers meant that mistakes were made, allowing some to escape service altogether whilst others were forced into uniform. Fred Jameson was arrested in the Leeds city centre raid in September 1916 and fined 40s. for failing to answer his call-up notice after being combed out from his employers. It later transpired that he was not guilty of the offence at all and his employers applied to the court to have his fine remitted. Previously exempt from military service as his garden tool manufacturing workplace was now making entrenching tools instead, Jameson was one of three employees now deemed available for enlistment. His workplace was told to keep the men on until further instructions: no further instructions had yet been forthcoming. After a weekend in custody and without legal representation 19-year- old Jameson was convicted of being an absentee. By the time his employers realized what had happened, he had been taken away by the military escort. The court could not remit his fine, and a formal appeal against his conviction was impossible without his involvement but the magistrates ordered that the fine should not be collected, declaring that the teenager no longer had 'a stain on his character'.[57] Fred Jameson was killed in action in Belgium in October 1917. He was his parents' only child.

Conscription caused problems in rural areas where it was difficult to maintain a sufficiently large male work force to allow communities to function normally. The attitude towards the military in these areas was not always one of co-operation. The Revd Andrew Clark recorded that agricultural workers in Essex became frustrated with the constant badgering to enlist and that recruiting posters in the area were regularly destroyed.[58] *John Bull* meanwhile mocked the ease with which it was believed that farmers' sons could obtain exemptions from Military Service Tribunals, publishing a cartoon with the following verse:

> Although the nation is at War,
> I do not think it's right
> To ask a man of twenty four
> Like me to go and fight;
> My father he has taken me
> Into his own employ,
> And away from the fray I mean to stay
> And be a farmer's boy[59]

Some 'farmer's boys' did not wish to take their chance at the tribunals and took matters into their own hands.

The village of Cowling, near Skipton in North Yorkshire had long held a reputation for obstinance and independence. The village had a population of less than 2,000 in 1911 and had a strong Baptist and Methodist influence.

Philip Snowden MP, soon to become the champion of COs at Westminster, was born and raised in the village. Nestled between Lancashire and Yorkshire, the surrounding valley is said to have been a hiding place for those fleeing the Scottish invasions of the seventeenth and eighteenth centuries. Cowling would serve a similar role during the First World War, this time for those wishing to evade the British Army.

Conscription hit the village hard and by the summer of 1917, concerns were being expressed as to how the community was to cope with the coming winter. 'A prominent citizen' remarked at a local council meeting that with all of the carters now having been called up so it was going to be very difficult to have coal brought to the farms.[60] Some families took the view that their needs were greater than those of the British Army, and by July 1917 the *Yorkshire Evening Post* was calling Cowling 'The Deserter's Village'. The surrounding hills were said to offer admirable hiding places from the law and at that stage five men from Cowling were in a state of desertion with others threatening the same if they were called up. It was believed that the villagers were providing the men with food and that the absentees were all armed.[61] Captain William Whittington, Sub Area Commander of the local recruiting district, frequently expressed his frustration at the situation when appearing at military service tribunals and threatened to bring a company of soldiers onto the moors to round the men up.[62]

The police had been humiliated in their attempts to retrieve the absentees. Hannah Wilkinson had allegedly been boasting in the village that none of her sons would serve in the army and she went to extreme lengths to make good her promise. Son Martin was stopped by the police in July 1917 and challenged as to why he was not in uniform. Martin claimed to have an exemption from the Board of Agriculture that he was more than willing to show the officers if they would only come back to his house. As soon as he was close to home the absentee shouted to his mother to get the shotgun and ran inside. He bolted the door and left his mother outside fending off the police with a stick. Hannah kept them at bay for over an hour, attracting a large crowd and giving Martin enough time to make good his escape.[63] Thomas Emmott, a dry stone waller of Beckfoot Farm in Cowling, concealed his two sons, Jonathan and William, when they failed to answer their call-up papers. The police were hot on Jonathan's trail in October 1917, just missing him when they raided Fiddling Clough Farm in Thornton, where he was working. Footsteps were heard approaching the farmhouse whilst the police were questioning the housekeeper inside, but when the front door was opened, there was no one to be seen. The police had to settle for charging the farmer, Thomas Pinder, with failing to post a notice of his employees.[64] Jonathan Emmott's luck ran out a week later when he was found hiding in a kitchen cupboard at his father's farm, though brother William was nowhere to be seen. Superintendent Vaughan told the subsequent court hearing that there were now believed to be seven men from Cowling hiding in the district in various 'outlandish' places. Vaughan said there was 'more bother with the village of Cowling than all the other places in the Division'.[65]

The defiance continued into 1918, and a Cowling grocer who had asked for an exemption from military service to run his business seems to have fallen foul of the village's reputation. His brother was said to be one of five deserters in hiding in the area at that time and the Skipton Rural Tribunal questioned him closely as to the man's whereabouts and means of survival. The grocer couldn't or wouldn't give them any details, saying 'I think that everyone has to stand on his own bottom'. The Chair of the Tribunal declared that the deserters were bringing disgrace on the village and refused the request for an exemption, claiming that the grocer's wife and 16-year-old son were perfectly capable of running the business on his behalf.[66] The grocer appealed to the West Riding Tribunal in Leeds, where he was represented by solicitor Arthur Willey.[67] With a little bit of distance from the local area tempering any feelings of shame at Cowling's reputation, the Leeds Tribunal agreed with Willey's plea that the applicant should not suffer through the actions of his brother, granting the grocer a conditional exemption until the end of October 1918.[68]

There must have been a significant degree of assistance given by the villagers to the missing men of Cowling to allow them to survive undetected. One fugitive, James Emmott, was called up in August 1916 and deserted from the Duke of Wellington's Regiment that December. He was not arrested until December 1918 when the police detained him after he got into a fight with another Cowling resident. His status was quickly ascertained and he proudly told the police that he had enjoyed 'a good run', going undetected for two years.[69] The need for manpower on the farms and in the local mills often outweighed any sense of patriotic duty on the part of employers. The name Emmott was a common one in the area and a number of Emmotts from Cowling appear to have been deserters. It must also be pointed that that a number of men sharing the surname did serve and die during the conflict as local war memorials will attest.

Not everyone took the same view of conscription as the villagers of Cowling, especially if they already had family members serving their country. London taxi driver Joseph Buckingham was arrested after a local man with two sons serving at the Front wrote to the police, incensed with talk he had overheard at the taxi garage. The man alleged that a gang of drivers of military age had been boasting about not reporting for duty when their call-up papers arrived. Acting on the tip-off, the police arrested Buckingham. The magistrate at Marylebone Police Court said he 'did not wonder at the man's disgust that this sort of thing should go on while loyal, decent men were risking their lives in the trenches for us'.[70]

A friend in a Military Service Tribunal office was a friend indeed if you were seeking to avoid being called up. In July 1918 two young women who had been working in the Stepney office were found to have been fraudulently issuing exemption certificates. By way of contrast to the fees demanded by unscrupulous doctors like George Bishop, Ida Lillian Carter and her colleague Miss Terleshky performed this service for 2s. 6d. and some sweets and ice cream.

In July 1918 there was a perception that there were lots of fit-looking young men on the streets of Stepney who should have been in uniform. Reports claimed that 8,000 men in the East End were challenged that month as to why they were not in the army: 400 turned out to be deserters and 7,000 were men who hadn't answered their call-up papers. It was claimed that 5 per cent of those illegally at large were in possession of documents stolen from the Stepney Tribunal offices. The problem was traced to the two employees, who had been forging the signature of the clerk to the Tribunal on blank exemption certificates. Ida Carter was only 17 when she started working at the Tribunal two years earlier and was susceptible to the sweet talk and sweet treats provided by the hopeful absentees. Ida's solicitor said that both defendants were 'good looking young girls, and they have been flattered and cajoled by the young men who came to the office, and who wished to dodge the army'.[71] By the time the fraud was discovered, Ida Carter was no longer working at the Tribunal, ironically having been sacked for absenteeism. She had found herself a new job at the Ministry of Munitions. When questioned she immediately confessed, resulting in the arrest of her brother who was found to be in possession of a full set of exemption forms in an assumed name. Ida's parents were said to be respectable people, but this did not save their daughter – she was sent to prison for a month. The *Manchester Guardian* wrote that this was too harsh and blamed the Chief Clerk's carelessness for the offending.[72] Stung by the criticism both of his office and his district, the Chairman of the Stepney Tribunal defended his clerk and challenged the figures given by the prosecution in the case against Ida Carter, pointing out that 40,000 men from Stepney had enlisted in the armed forces, a huge number considering the industrial nature of the district.[73]

By 1918 the Chairman must have become accustomed to the accusation that the East End was not doing its bit. Stories of thousands of Russian Jews enjoying the privileges of British residency without any of its obligations frequently appeared in the press and in Parliament, Russian citizens being banned from serving in the British forces. It was claimed that there were 30,000 Russian Jews of military age in Britain, the majority living in the East End. The area was depicted as a haven for shirkers, with the Under Secretary for War telling Parliament in May 1917 that 500 absentees and deserters had been apprehended there in the previous 6 months.[74] A few weeks later, he was forced admit that in two raids in the East End in April and May 1917 a total of 856 men were arrested but only 13 of them were charged with offences under the Military Service Act and only 4 of those men were handed over to the army as deserters or absentees.[75] A few weeks later the Military Service (Conventions with Allied States) Act 1917 was passed requiring all men born in a country with whom Britain had a convention, and who were eligible for military service, to either enlist in the British forces or return to their country of birth. Only if a man elected to be eligible for the British Army would the usual exemptions from service apply and special 'Russian Tribunals' were convened to deal with appeals from the newly eligible. If no appeal was made by 21 September 1917, a man would be deemed available for immediate call-up by Britain. The Leeds Russian Tribunal had dealt with about 1,000 applications by May 1918, granting 60 per cent of the exemptions claimed.[76] One of those falling foul of the regulations was Maurice Spurgin, a London-based Russian and the brother of Fred Spurgin, renowned illustrator. Maurice was managing director of the Art and Humour Publishing Company Ltd, which marketed designs under the Fred Spurgin name, including many patriotic postcards. Maurice was arrested in Blackpool as an absentee from military service in August 1918. He belatedly made an application for exemption from service but had not done so before the deadline for Russian applications. Further appeals were not allowed, and Maurice Spurgin had to serve his time in the Labour Corps.[77]

Conscription did have an effect on the desertion figures recorded by the army, though not in the way one might expect. Rather than a ballooning of numbers of men walking away from uniform, the introduction of conscription saw the figures fall dramatically. In April 1915 the number of men lost to desertion was 3,444: in April 1916 this figure was 1,369. The net loss to the army from desertion on all fronts plummeted from 2,635 to 559 in the same period.[78] The reasons for the drop may be as much to do with under recording as with better behaviour on the part of soldiers. The increase in the numbers of military policemen on the home front also made it more likely that absentees would be arrested quickly before they could formally be struck from the strength as deserters. The use of suspended sentences and the early release of men from detention saw the military machine become much more efficient at getting men back into uniform, thereby reducing the net loss. Conscription did not, however, solve Britain's manpower problem. The availability of exemptions from service on various grounds combined with the numbers who did not answer their call-up papers meant that the expected targets were never reached. In the first year of their operation the Military Service Tribunals granted exemptions to 779,936 men, compelling less than half that figure to don a uniform of any kind.[79] Further measures were introduced to widen the pool of recruits. In April 1918 the upper age limit was raised to 50 and exemptions removed completely from all men under the age of 23 and a quarter years. The net had tightened but large numbers of men continued to slip through it.

Chapter 9

Irish Issues

When is an Irishman not an Irishman?
Linlithgowshire Gazette,
10 November 1916

On 6 November 1915 there were disorderly scenes at the docks in Liverpool when a Cunard line ship bound for New York was prevented from sailing by the ship's firemen and crew. The reason for their refusal to leave shore was not due to an industrial dispute but to the fact that the crew did not approve of the passenger list. Around 600 men of military age had arrived at the Cunard offices hoping to buy tickets to board the *Saxonia*, the vast majority of them being Irishmen. Passenger ships to America were not sailing from Ireland itself at the time, so anyone seeking to emigrate would have to travel to England or Scotland to board a boat. Rumours abounded that conscription was to be introduced to Ireland as well as the rest of the United Kingdom, and the assertion was made in the press that these men were seeking to escape before that happened. The men were described by the local newspapers as 'young, athletic fellows, every one of them from a cursory glance fit for a soldier's work'.[1] The *Liverpool Echo* reported that the men were all from the south and south-west of Ireland and went so far as to call them 'Sinn Féiners'. The *Dundee People's Journal* went even further, suggesting that their passages had been paid by Germany.[2] Women handed out white feathers to the queue of Irishmen whilst recruiting sergeants berated and cajoled them in an attempt to have them enlist instead of emigrate. The *Saxonia* crew were not prepared to allow Irishmen to escape their military duties by sailing to America. Ultimately the Cunard company refused to honour the men's tickets and announced that no further bookings would be accepted from men of military age. There were similar scenes in Glasgow where 200 Irishmen from northern counties were seeking to board the *California*.[3] Those passengers were allowed to sail but the boat's operators, the Anchor Line, said they would follow Cunard's new policy from now on.

The uproar which followed the *Saxonia* incident reverberated as far as Whitehall. Just two days before the sailing, Parliament had been assured that there had been no need to introduce measures preventing men of military age from leaving the country.[4] The Cabinet was now provided with figures showing that the number of men of military age travelling to America had risen significantly in the previous month. Though emigration figures were still below pre-war averages, in October 1915, 3,735 British subjects of military age had travelled to destinations outside of Europe, the number getting proportionally larger as the month went on. Of this number, 990 were said to be from Ireland – a whole battalion's worth of manpower.[5] New regulations were now introduced to make it mandatory to have a passport before embarking on a voyage across the Atlantic. (Passports were already required for trips to Europe, having been introduced in February 1915.) The Passport Office would refuse to issue documents to men of military age unless they had a good reason for their trip.

The reality was that whilst the numbers were undoubtedly inflated by the spectre of conscription, the autumn season always saw an exodus of young men from the farming communities of Ireland, as the harvest was now in and there was little work available.[6] A significant proportion of the *Saxonia* crew members seeking to prevent the emigration were themselves Irish, and it was reported that a good number of the crowd harassing the passengers came from the Liverpool Irish community. The *Liverpool Daily Post* emphasized that it was not suggesting that the *Saxonia* passengers were representative of the Irish people in general – 'They are not, as both the recruiting statistics of Ireland and the gallantry of Irish soldiers in the field amply demonstrate.'[7]

The *Saxonia* incident highlighted the problem the British Army would have throughout the war with the status of Ireland and Irishmen. Though ostensibly part of the United Kingdom, progress towards home rule for Ireland had only been stopped due to the outbreak of war. Compulsory military service was too incendiary a measure to introduce in those circumstances. The failure to apply conscription to Ireland in 1916 made the country a potential haven for fugitives from the British and Dominion forces and made the status of Irishmen a hot topic in the rest of the United Kingdom.

Ireland had traditionally supplied the British Army with large numbers of recruits. In 1878 Irishmen had constituted 22 per cent of the British Army. This figure had dropped significantly in the early years of the twentieth century and in 1909 only 9 per cent of British soldiers were Irish.[8] The relationship between Irish citizens and the British Army was complex and sometimes ambivalent. Whilst to many the British Army were oppressors, to others they were benefactors, providing employment opportunities, housing and other facilities which transformed towns and villages where soldiers were stationed. When war was declared on Germany there were riots in Ireland as well as England with damage caused to German-owned shops and businesses. Even in the heat of the Easter Rising, significant numbers of Dublin residents were openly hostile to the rebels. Heavy Irish losses at Gallipoli in 1915 had sullied the reputation of those of military age who had stayed at home, whilst the very practical difficulties of obtaining separation allowance when the General Post Office was being occupied by the rebels had a bearing on levels of support for the Rising.[9] Those arrested after the Easter Rising recalled a mixture of responses from the crowds in the street, from the singing of rebel songs in support of the prisoners to the throwing of rotten fruit at them for the trouble they had caused. Edward Casey's account of his service with the Royal Dublin Fusiliers as a Cockney of Irish descent records that his reception as a British soldier in Ireland varied over time and location from enthusiastic greeting to being confined to barracks for his own safety.[10]

When war was declared Irish men of all religious persuasions and geographic locations did enlist in the British Army. Motivations for doing so were diverse, from the Protestant Ulsterman keen to defend the Empire and the Union to the Irish Republican wanting to help the fellow 'small nation' of Belgium and make a case for Irish independence. Political leaders of both Unionist and Nationalist parties urged their followers to enlist. Both parties already had an armed wing of their own – the Ulster Volunteer Force on one side and the Irish Volunteers on the other. Both parties offered their militia for the defence of Ireland itself, allowing the British Army to remove the current contingent and send them to the battlefields. This was never going to be an attractive proposition for the British government and the offer was rejected. There was a split in the Nationalist movement as a result when John Redmond then offered the party's Irish Volunteers for full service in the British Army. Those who saw this as a capitulation to British rule split from the party, taking the name 'Irish Volunteers' and 11,000 men with them. Those remaining under Redmond's banner were renamed the National Volunteers, numbering around 170,000, and large numbers of them did go on to enlist in the British Army. Figures vary as to how many Irishmen served in British colours during the war. Thomas Dooley states that 140,460 men from the north and south of

Ireland **enlisted** in the British Army in Ireland in the period 1914–18.[11] Peter Karsten, however, claims that as many as 300,000 Irishmen served in total.[12] Recruitment figures were lower for the south of Ireland but this was largely due to the overwhelmingly rural nature of the area rather than opposition to service.

Some Irishmen joined the British Army specifically to get access to weapons, especially following the ban on importation of arms to Ireland in December 1915. The presence of large numbers of soldiers in Ireland provided a ready made source of weaponry for the armed factions on both sides of the political divide. British Army soldiers going on leave in Ireland were instructed to leave their weapons at the barracks, or, failing that, to hand them in to the nearest police station to their home address, to be collected on their way back to duty. This instruction was not always followed, sometimes through forgetfulness and sometimes deliberately as buyers for a British Army rifle were not hard to find. This was a particular concern when a man deserted in Ireland. Civilian James Byrne was sentenced to six months' imprisonment with hard labour by the Southern Police Court in Dublin in May 1916 when it was discovered that he had bought a gun from a deserter called Matthew Kelly. Kelly had escaped from the ranks of the Royal Munster Fusiliers with his Lee–Enfield rifle which he sold to Byrne. A prison sentence was inevitable when the police told the court that Byrne had a full Irish Volunteers uniform in his closet.[13] He was arrested just two days before the Easter Rising. Matthew Kelly was sentenced to a year's imprisonment at his court martial, appearing on the same page of the record as several Sinn Féiners initially sentenced to death for their part in the rebellion.[14] The acquisition of British weapons from Irish soldiers was not a solely southern Irish phenomenon – when two youths appeared before the court in Belfast in January 1916 for buying a rifle from Gerard Brady, deserter from the Royal Irish Rifles, the prosecuting police officer claimed that these offences were becoming very prevalent in the area.[15]

The pressure on Irish recruits to desert the British Army must have been considerable in certain parts of the country. Opposition to Irish men serving in the British ranks would be demonstrated by sharp words and the pointed singing of rebel songs to physical attacks on British soldiers and intimidation of the families of the Irish born who wore khaki. Soldier's wife Alice Russell of Rathkeane in Limerick was shunned in her local community thanks to her husband's service in the British Army. She responded by making wild allegations about her neighbours in a confidential letter to the King himself, claiming that there were deserters on the loose in the town and that the police were not doing their job properly. When an investigation took place she retracted her original story and the police came to the conclusion that she was simply lashing out because of the harassment she had suffered.[16] Once Ireland was under martial law after the Easter Rising, civilians were not infrequently prosecuted for displaying opposition to Irish involvement in the war through posters, leaflets, flags or by attempts to disrupt recruiting. Gentle persuasion of soldiers to desert was also a common tactic. Private George Joseph Cullen of the Royal Marine Light Infantry admitted desertion at a court martial in Plymouth in September 1919 saying that when he had gone on leave to Dublin in March 1918 some Sinn Féin friends had persuaded him to desert on the promise of good employment.[17] Some needed less persuasion than others: Privates Conroy and O'Brien had already left the ranks of the Royal Irish Regiment when met by James Fraher, later to become an IRA commander in Waterford. Fraher persuaded the two to enlist again under new names so that they could procure arms for the Republican movement. Fraher was prosecuted in 1918 for aiding and abetting the deserters but the case collapsed when the soldiers refused to give evidence against him.[18]

Rural areas of Ireland were a good place for men on the run to evade the authorities, and agricultural work was often available without too many awkward questions. Private Harkin of the Inniskilling Fusiliers enlisted in October 1914 and spent most of the next four years as a deserter. After being released from one sentence of detention for desertion he was on his way to France when he managed to escape again in Londonderry. He spent 1917 moving between Plumbridge and Strabane, posing as a labourer, and once evaded capture by hiding in a field of oats which was being harvested, somehow managing to stay out of the range of the scythe. On another occasion he knocked on the door of a house in Glenroan to seek refreshment before realising to his horror it was the police barrack house. He didn't wait for an answer to his knock.[19] Alf Monahan of the Irish Republican Brotherhood recalled hiding from the authorities after the Easter Rising on a farm in Ballysheedy where the owners welcomed Republican fugitives. Monahan claims that one of his colleagues was a British Army deserter called Denis O'Beirne, an officer who claimed to have absented himself from duty before the Easter Rising to avoid fighting his own countrymen.[20] An examination of O'Beirne's army records reveals that the truth was a little less heroic. He was a deserter, having been a Second Lieutenant in the Royal Irish Regiment, but he did not receive his commission until November 1916. He deserted from the Anti-Gas School in Dublin in

December 1916, having been warned to report for the Front. O'Beirne was raised in England where his family still lived, but extensive enquiries with them failed to reveal his whereabouts. Ironically, his family had a lifetime of service with the British state – his father was a customs inspector, one brother worked for the Inland Revenue and a sister worked for the Post Office. By February 1917 O'Beirne was officially released from service despite the fact that he was still missing.[21] Denis O'Beirne moved to Amsterdam in November 1920 and seems to have remained there until the outbreak of the Second World War when his trail goes cold.

Desertion was an issue for the police all over Ireland. District Inspector Ryan told the court in Derry in November 1915 that they had brought in 125 missing soldiers that year to date and that many were found with great difficulty.[22] On Bridge Street in Derry in May 1917 Edward Thompson and Adam Smith from the Inniskilling Fusiliers were arrested after quite a struggle. The pair were hidden in a special compartment between the ceiling of a house and the roof tiles, requiring the police to enlarge the entrance hole before they could be dragged out. The officers were then assaulted by the women of the house, one constable needing stitches after being hit on the head with a bowl.[23]

Watching the apprehension of difficult deserters could be a good day's sport. Deserter Private Fraher of the South Irish Horse was found in a village near Tipperary and ran away from the police. He was pursued by a police officer with a reputation as a sprinter but evaded him by jumping across the River Arra. When the speedy policeman caught him up again Fraher climbed a tree and threw missiles onto his pursuers below. The ferocity of the attacks meant it was difficult to use a ladder to retrieve him. Cutting the tree down was the next option but Fraher made it clear they would have to cut down every tree in the row, swinging from bough to bough. Dinnertime intervened so the policemen left, leaving a few soldiers to keep a less than watchful eye on Fraher, who managed to steal the ladder himself, hauling it up into the branches. He finally gave himself up 6 hours later when some troops arrived with a fire engine and threatened to blast him out of his perch with water.[24]

Sometimes crowds did more than simply watch, taking an active role in assisting the deserter. In July 1915 there was a riot on Grafton Street in Dublin when a deserter called Michael Colburn was apprehended. A crowd estimated to be 200-strong attacked the police, allowing Colburn to escape, though he was later rearrested. After sentencing four of the offenders to terms up of up to six months' imprisonment with hard labour, the magistrate at the Southern Police Court said of the defendants, 'They are afraid. They are much better off throwing stones at the police than fighting the Germans. The brave men are at the front, the cowards are staying at home.'[25]

In January 1918 an escort party took advantage of the country's reputation for assisting deserters by blaming a crowd of locals for the loss of their prisoners at a train station. 'The Burtonport Affair' involved the rescue of deserters Private Ward and Private Duffy by a mob at Kincasslagh Road Station. The two prisoners had been arrested at a dance and were being escorted back to Ebrington Barracks. The escort party, Lance Sergeant Robert Shaw and his subordinates Privates Henderson and Holland, returned to the barracks empty handed and claimed that they had been overwhelmed by a hostile crowd who had rescued the prisoners. The story coming from Burtonport itself was somewhat different and Lance Sergeant Shaw was court-martialled. The District Court Martial heard from witnesses that all three soldiers had been drinking, Holland staggering in the street and Henderson being so inebriated that he had to be walked to the station by two civilians. There was a crowd of up to 150 people at the station, though it was not unusual to see large crowds there to see off passengers and the numbers were swollen by the fact that there was a fair in the town that day. When a train door opened to allow a passenger to alight, the two deserters jumped from the carriage and ran down the tracks in handcuffs. The escort party found themselves completely incapable of preventing their escape or chasing them at all.

Lance Sergeant Shaw told the court that as soon as he and his colleagues arrived in the town to collect the prisoners they were booed and jeered on the streets. He claimed that the mob at the station were armed with sticks and dragged the escapees from the carriage, preventing his men from chasing them thereafter. In short, it was the crowd that had made it impossible for them to catch the escapees, not the drink. The *Northern Whig* claimed that Sinn Féin had organized the rescue and stormed the train: the court martial preferred the evidence of the civilian witnesses appearing before them, finding Shaw guilty of misconduct. He was sentenced to fifty-six days' detention, half of it being remitted, and lost his sergeant's stripes. Evidence available from the Bureau of Military History in Eire suggests that Shaw and his colleagues were badly treated, as witness statements taken from participants in the struggle for Irish independence confirm that the episode was indeed an organized rescue by armed Irish Volunteers.[26]

The Irish police and military not only had to contend with soldiers deserting from their barracks in Ireland, but with the influx of British men seeking to avoid conscription. The failure to extend conscription to Ireland in 1916 meant that if a man could get across the Irish Sea before he was forced into uniform he had a good chance of avoiding service altogether. Men were not only taking the usual ferry or passenger ships from ports on the western coast of Britain but were also allegedly being taken across in smaller numbers in fishing boats, paying the crews the appropriate bribe for their passage. The escapees were a mixture of those who objected to war on religious grounds, those who were politically opposed to a capitalist war and those who simply did not fancy joining the British Army. Arthur Horner, later to become General Secretary of the National Union of Mineworkers, was one of the political refuseniks who escaped to Dublin to evade conscription. Horner was a trade unionist and anti-war activist who lost his protected status as a miner when he was dismissed for his union activities. He managed to get a job in the coalfield under a false name, but realising it was only a matter of time before he was discovered, escaped to Ireland in 1917. There he joined the Irish Citizen Army and worked under another false name before tiring of the charade in the summer of 1918 and returning to Wales. Horner was arrested as soon as he landed at Holyhead.[27]

As with the incendiary coverage of the East End of London, Jewish men were disproportionately reported as being on the run in Ireland. In April 1916 the *Belfast News-Letter* reported the arrest of eighteen young Jewish men, recent arrivals in the city, as absentees. They were all from the same part of Leeds and there were several sets of brothers amongst their number. Solicitors for the accused argued that as the Military Service Act did not apply to Ireland, their clients had been wrongfully arrested. The defendants all claimed to have return tickets to Leeds and very much resented the label of deserter. Some claimed they had not received a call-up notice and others said they were awaiting an appeal to the Military Service Tribunal. Only one of the men, Louis Harris, voiced any opposition to the principle of serving in the army, stating 'I don't believe in war'. All were remanded to await a military escort back to England. At least four of the defendants were killed in action in the next three years. The Harris brothers all served in the army with reluctant soldier Louis being one of the casualties of the last week of the war whilst serving with the 10th West Yorkshire Regiment.[28]

The *Pall Mall Gazette* published a story in 1918 that would have been clearly recognized as a joke by its wartime readership. A young Jewish man escaped the clutches of the military by the good fortune of having his barber come to court. The man said he had been a resident of Ireland since March 1915 and was therefore not subject to conscription. The barber testified that this was true, as he had shaved the man on St Patrick's Day that year. He remembered it clearly because his customer had given him a racing tip – a horse called Lie Low. The horse won. When the Dublin magistrates had this information checked they discovered that the horse had indeed won that day and discharged the defendant.[29] This antisemitism was not just the province of the popular press. The idea that Jewish men were escaping to Ireland en masse was also broadcast in the corridors of Whitehall. In autumn 1917 an extraordinary memo was written from the Ministry of National Service on the topic of British Army reservists escaping to Ireland. Entitled 'English Conscription Slackers in Ireland', the writer claimed that English Jewish men were in Dublin in great numbers and were congregating at racecourses. These 'young well to do Jews' were said to be 'undesirable visitors' and it was claimed that a crackdown from Britain which resulted in their removal would not be resisted by the Irish.[30]

The issue of whether the Military Service Act applied to Ireland exercised the minds of many in the legal community and in government. The official legal advice to the government was that although the Military Service Act did not apply to Ireland as a country, it did apply to certain **people** living in Ireland, i.e. those who had been 'ordinarily resident' in Great Britain on or since 14 August 1915.[31] Courts in all jurisdictions were now called upon to answer the question 'When is an Irishman not an Irishman?' The results were inconsistent. The *Freeman's Journal* claimed that magistrates in Wicklow, Derry and Kiltimagh were determining this question themselves, releasing the majority of men as they were satisfied they were not 'ordinarily resident' in Great Britain, whilst the single justice in Longford was simply remanding all men for collection by the army, taking the view that their eligibility for conscription was a matter out of his jurisdiction.[32]

Irishmen were now being arrested on both sides of the Irish Sea because they had been working in England, Scotland or Wales at or since the relevant date for registration. Irishmen had always travelled to Britain to work, especially in agriculture at key times of the year, and manpower shortages meant that this flow of labour needed to continue without restriction. Irishmen travelling to England to assist with the harvest for a short period of time were not to be subject to the Military Service Act. They were examples instead of men in Britain temporarily for a 'special purpose', which would preclude their enlistment. Large numbers of workers came from Ireland to work in English munitions factories and they could also be argued to be in Britain for a 'special purpose.' With no precise definition of the terms 'ordinarily resident' and 'special purpose' in the Military Service Act itself, their meaning was tested at every court hearing.

Some courts were using the fact that a man had completed National Registration forms in Britain as proof that he was resident there, though it was stated in Parliament that this was not of any evidential use in deciding the question.[33] Patrick Boyle appeared before the Londonderry Police Court charged with being an absentee. He claimed to be ordinarily resident in Londonderry but had been temporarily in Glasgow for the state of his health in August 1915 when registration forms were issued and he was told it was obligatory for everyone to sign them. He had then come home as planned but was now being treated as an absentee. Boyle, one of three similar cases before the Derry bench on that day alone, was eventually discharged by the magistrates who decided that his ordinary place of residence was not Great Britain.[34] The very same court decided a case the other way in similar circumstances just a few weeks later. John Clarke from Londonderry had also been in Glasgow temporarily for work in two short stints between June and November 1915. He had returned to Ireland, got married and was now working in a distillery in his hometown. On this occasion the magistrates decided that he was ordinarily resident in Glasgow at the relevant time and remanded him for a military escort. Clarke had the last laugh when he was rejected as medically unfit for service.[35]

Touring actors seemed particularly vulnerable to arrest for evading conscription with several cases of Irishmen in theatrical productions being detained. The hearings did not produce uniform results. David Corken, a member of an opera company, was arrested at rehearsals at the Northampton Opera House in September 1916 and though he claimed residence in Ireland the magistrates found that he was liable for service in the British Army.[36] A month later, Walter Roy convinced Marylebone Police Court that he was a resident of Cork, simply spending time in England and Scotland in the course of producing and starring in theatrical productions.[37]

English courts often made scathing remarks about the Irish and their special exemption from service even on occasions when they found in favour of the Irishman in front of them. In the case of James Burns, another employee of a theatrical touring company, the magistrate announced his decision as follows:

The defendant . . . claims to be defended by the British Army and the British Navy while he fools about the country with a party of players who in sterner Puritan days would be regarded as rogues and vagabonds and would be placed in the stocks on their appearance in any town. Curiously, he is only claiming his right. So he will be discharged to continue his foolery, while Englishmen, Scotsmen and Welshmen do the fighting.[38]

The status of Irishmen working in Britain after conscription was precarious. The idea that there were many thousands of Irishmen working in lucrative munitions jobs rather than fighting for the Empire was frequently mentioned in English newspapers. Publishing one such complaint, *John Bull* described England as 'a fine country for Irishmen to make a living in. For an Irishman who will not wear khaki it is now a finer country than ever.'[39] The prospect of high wages and immunity from conscription were undoubtedly attractions for Irish workers coming to Britain. However, it also seems likely that there were large numbers of Irishmen being exploited by their British employers with the threat of being handed over to the authorities. In the same way employers put forward troublesome men for 'combing out', Irish workers were at risk of being reported to the military should they complain about their pay and conditions. An example is the case of David Sweenie from Donegal who was working on a farm near Linlithgow in Scotland in 1916. Sweenie had worked at Haugh Farm for three months when he told his employer, George Padkin, that he was leaving because he had a more lucrative employment offer elsewhere. Padkin's response was to lock Sweenie in a barn and call the police. Sweenie was subsequently arrested and placed before the court where he quickly proved he was not subject to the Military Service Act and was released. He sued Padkin for the distress and inconvenience of his arrest and overnight detention. Padkin's solicitor was not shy of trying to prejudice the Sherriff against Sweenie because of his nationality, declaring, 'Here is an Irishman exempted from fighting, while the men of my own country have to fight . . . There has been a great feeling about this differentiation.' The lawyer claimed that Padkin had done no more than his patriotic duty in detaining Sweenie. The 'great feeling' about the easier life allowed to Irishmen had, of course, not deterred Padkin from employing Sweenie to get the harvest in. Given the penalties for employing fugitives from military service the farmer must have been satisfied that Sweenie was not in that category else he would have been placing himself in danger of prosecution. The Sherriff advised the parties to meet privately and come to a settlement.[40]

Despite assurances that only Irishmen who were ordinarily resident in Great Britain and not there for a special purpose would be caught in the conscription net, in practice this was not the case. Fifty Irishmen were arrested in Mossend near Motherwell in August 1916 and handed over to the military. Parliament was told that the men had been rounded up from farms, munition factories and boarding houses, the local Sherriff refusing to inquire into their status and telling them they would have to tell their stories once they were at Hamilton Barracks.[41] John Murphy and James Manning were arrested in Ireland as absentees on the basis that they had worked in Cheshire for a short time as harvesters. The fact that one of the pair had a letter in his pocket from MP John Dillon confirming his immunity from conscription did not save them from being detained for the army. Just as in Motherwell, the presiding magistrate wrongly took the view that the issue of their eligibility was not his concern.[42]

In autumn 1916 another group of Irishmen was taken to court in England to be charged as absentees under the Military Service Act. These men would also claim that they were not subject to conscription as they were not ordinarily resident in Britain. However, these men were not only allegedly dodging their military responsibilities to the British Empire but were actively fighting against it: they were rebels involved in the Easter Rising who had been interned in England.

After the Rebellion 1,846 men and women were arrested and taken to detention facilities in Britain, being interned under the Defence of the Realm Act without trial as there was not enough evidence against them to justify courts martial. In June 1916 an Advisory Committee was set up under the control of Sir John Sankey to weed out the true rebels, releasing nearly three-quarters of the detainees. The 549 men remaining were sent to Frongoch Detention Centre near Bala in North Wales. The Frongoch detainees included Michael Collins and other leading lights of the Republican movement but also men who had nothing to do with the Easter Rising and were simply in the wrong place at the wrong time. The British government believed that around sixty of the internees were evaders of military service and the authorities tried to compile a definitive list. Those eligible for conscription were referred to as 'refugees' by the prisoners and were protected by their fellow internees. Fifteen men from Frongoch were court-martialled simply for failing to identify themselves and their hut mates. A list of twenty-seven names was eventually produced by the authorities, though there were undoubtedly many more 'refugees' than this in the camp. Police in London, Liverpool and Glasgow were tasked with tracking the histories of these men to find evidence that they were subject to the Military Service Act. Once positive information came back from the police they were sent to court to be prosecuted. Of course, the penalty for failing to report for conscription was a fine of up to 40s., the offender to then be handed over to the military. It seems ludicrous to suggest that these men, recently involved in an armed insurrection against British soldiers, should be integrated into the ranks of the British Army, but Home Secretary Herbert Samuel directed that this be done.[43]

The personal histories of some of the men placed before the courts shows the utter futility of this move. Neill Kerr was from a staunch Republican family in Liverpool and had been one of the Irish Volunteers who had seized the Jacob's Biscuit Factory premises during the Rebellion. His stepmother, Elizabeth Kerr, was a member of Cumann na mBan, the women's wing of the Republican movement. She had treated Republican wounded during the Rising and was one of the first people to visit the internees in Knutsford and then at Frongoch. Neill Kerr's father, also called Neill, was later responsible for importing arms for the Irish Republican Army. The Kerr home sheltered deserters and Irish fugitives during and after the war, including Michael Collins and Eamon de Valera. Kerr senior was sentenced to ten years' imprisonment in November 1920 for conspiracy to commit murder and arson after the IRA burnt down timber yards in Liverpool.[44] By this time Neill junior was dead – not gunned down by a British soldier or policeman but accidentally shooting himself whilst waiting for an arms shipment to arrive at a house in Liverpool. He was buried at Glasnevin Cemetery in Dublin with full Irish Volunteer honours, his funeral attracting a large crowd.[45]

Patrick King was one of three Liverpool-born Irish brothers also sent to the police court from the internment camp. The three had fought at the very heart of the Easter Rising, in the General Post Office building. After lengthy legal argument all three were fined 40s. as absentees from military service and handed over to the British Army. One brother, John, was found to be unfit for military service due to wounds he had received during the fight for the GPO. Patrick and George passed their medicals and were sent to the King's Liverpool Regiment. Unsurprisingly these IRA men spent their army careers in continuous detention for failing to obey orders before being discharged in January 1917, their 'services being no longer required'.[46] By March 1917 the War Office realized that these recruits were far more trouble than they were worth and released them from military service. They were free to re-join the other internees, who had been suddenly freed on 23 December 1916 to allow them to be home in time for Christmas. Patrick King would spend his career in the army, but it would not be a British one – King retired with the rank of Acting Major in the Irish Army in 1929.

Despite the widespread belief that any conscription in Ireland would result in bloodshed and civil war, in April 1918 a bill to extend conscription to Ireland was passed. There was widespread protest and concerted opposition from people of all political persuasion, from those in Ireland who wanted no part in Britain's war to those in England who felt that Irishmen who were forced into the army could not be trusted.[47] It was now felt necessary to solve the problem of Englishmen escaping to Ireland once and for all. Failing to make any attempt to retrieve Englishmen who had already shirked their duties by coming to Ireland would have provided a propaganda boost to those seeking to oppose compulsory military service for Irishmen.

British newspapers continually referred to the supposed large numbers of men living in Ireland to evade conscription. In May 1918 the *Yorkshire Evening Post* claimed that the many Leeds men in Dublin 'have caused Sackville Street to be likened to Briggate' (Leeds' main shopping street).[48] A proclamation was issued in July 1918 requiring all men who had come to Ireland from Britain and had been deemed to have enlisted under the Military Service Act to report to local recruitment offices or face arrest as absentees. Military police at the ports of Liverpool, Glasgow and Holyhead were told to be alert for 'fly boys' now reversing their flight and trying to escape from Ireland to areas of Britain that were under less scrutiny. Police at Holyhead had arrested twenty such men from one boat on a particular day. A letter printed in *John Bull* from a man called Noah Rigby described the purge, saying that 'the Irish people and authorities practically searched every nook and corner with the one object of getting in all Englishmen so as to save their own skins from conscription'. Rigby himself had fled to Ireland to avoid military service and was working as a maths professor in a Dublin college. He did not want the publicity of an arrest, so handed himself in. *John Bull* was interested in the case because Rigby's sister-in-law was the Lady Mayoress of St Helens. She and her husband had performed the usual tub thumping and fundraising during the war years and the paper wanted to expose their hypocrisy in assisting their own family member to avoid his military obligations. The Mayor, Dr H.B. Bates, told the paper that he had played no part in Rigby's escape and that it had caused a family rift, but *John Bull* got hold of further letters which showed that the family were now trying to pull strings to have Private Rigby released from the army. The paper called Rigby 'worse than a conchy' – a real insult in *John Bull's* world.[49]

As with most measures designed to force men into the army who did not want to be there, the numbers ultimately raised from the exercise of combing out Ireland looking for Englishmen fell far short of those anticipated.[50] By the time of the July proclamation the plan to extend conscription to Ireland was dead, the country instead being divided into ten recruiting districts with quotas of volunteers expected from each area. Unsurprisingly the number of Irish recruits produced by this process was negligible.

Chapter 10

Wild Colonial Boys

It was amazing the number of women relatives some of the Overseas
men had in London!

Mary S. Allen, *The Pioneer Policewoman*

Britain's Dominions not only boosted Allied manpower on the battlefield but
also increased the number of deserters on the home front. The three main
Dominion forces provided over 800,000 men: Canada sent 415,017 troops to
Britain whilst 331,814 Australians and 98,950 New Zealand soldiers and sailors
served abroad. At the highpoint of November 1916, nearly 216,000 Dominion
troops were stationed on British soil.[1] Though other forces made a significant
contribution to the war, for example the Indian Army, they were never present
in the United Kingdom in such numbers and therefore do not feature in this
study.

The Canadian Expeditionary Force (CEF) was the first overseas contingent
to arrive in great numbers, setting foot on British shores in autumn 1914. The
first Canadians were all volunteers and almost 70 per cent of their number
were British born. In some units the percentage of Britons was even higher;
Princess Patricia's Canadian Light Infantry comprised 31 officers and 1,100
other ranks and it was said that only 100 of the men were Canadian by birth.[2]
Patriotism for the defence of the mother country was no doubt fuelled for
some by the fact that Canada was in the middle of a depression. Some of the
British-born recruits may also have been taking advantage of free passage back
to their country of origin either for a visit or a permanent return. Charitable
agencies had a long tradition of sending working class British children to
Canada and 6,000 of these 'Home Children' joined the Canadian armed forces
during the war, some to escape colonial circumstances which had failed to live
up to the sunny promises of childhood.[3] Local newspapers around Britain
proudly reported the names of men from their towns who had joined the
Canadian forces and were on their way home to fight the Germans. The CEF
arrived in Plymouth in mid-October 1914 and was enthusiastically received.
Crowds assembled at train stations to watch the Canadians pass through,

showering them with gifts, and the Prime Minister and the King and Queen visited their camps to welcome them.

The CEF tried to weed out the unreliable before the First Contingent left Canada. At Valcartier, training base for the departing troops, 227 were discharged before the Contingent sailed.[4] This did not stop misbehaviour in Britain and, concerned about their image, by the beginning of December 1914 the CEF had identified a number of other recruits as undesirables and sent them home. When British-born deserter Private James McKenna appeared before the civilian court for stealing rings from shops in Bristol the CEF representative in court was at great pains to point out that McKenna was **not** a Canadian, lest the reputation of the country be sullied by his actions.[5] McKenna spent most of his service in detention of one sort or another before being discharged in 1915 for misconduct.[6] He remained in the United Kingdom, but 153 men would be returned to Canada from the First Contingent for disciplinary reasons.[7]

By mid-December 1914 there were 33,000 Canadian troops on Salisbury Plain, where they experienced the same miserable autumn and winter under canvas as their British counterparts. The Canadians, at least, were uniformed and armed. Salisbury Plain had regularly been used by the military, but for the summer training of Territorial Army units, not as a winter base. An inch of rain fell in one day during the Canadians' first month in England, turning the camps – one aptly called Pond Farm Camp – into swamps. The water was 6in deep in some areas and the men's uniforms were constantly wet.[8] The delay in the hut-building programme meant that there were 11,000 Canadians still under canvas in December 1914, and they were billeted on the local populace until the permanent accommodation was ready. Even when built, conditions in the huts were unsatisfactory, and twenty-eight Canadians died on Salisbury Plain in February 1915 after an outbreak of meningitis.[9]

Within a month of the CEF's arrival, the first cases of desertion began to appear before the local magistrates' courts. Private Arthur Edwin Lawrence, a British-born Canadian from Cheltenham, was brought before the magistrates in November 1914 for 'enjoying a somewhat prolonged stay amongst old friends' incompatible with his military duties.[10] British-born 'Canadoos' presented a disciplinary problem as it was difficult to keep men in camp when they had friends and relatives to visit. The British Canadians would have no problems in finding welcoming hiding places if required. The overstaying of leave by men unused to having their movements curtailed was said to be a particular issue.[11]

The Canadian troops wasted no time in spending their money freely in the towns and villages around their training camps. In the first few weeks on Salisbury Plain there was a lot of drunkenness and rule breaking, chiefly carried out by the British-born recruits who found the temptation of cheap beer too much to resist. Patrols went to pubs in Salisbury every night to find absent and drunken Canadians, both officers and men, and were not short of arrestees.[12] Drink played a part in a significant proportion of the cases of desertion and absenteeism that resulted in court-martial proceedings. Prostitution became rife in the towns circling Salisbury Plain. During the time the Canadians were accommodated in the area, there were 14,000 admissions to hospital from their ranks – 1,249 of them for venereal disease.[13] Venereal disease was sometimes a factor in a man's desertion as he did not want to face punishment or exposure for contracting the condition. Conversely, it encouraged some deserters to surrender themselves to obtain treatment. In early November 1914 in a bid to keep the Canadians on site alcohol was made available in the previously 'dry' camp canteens. The innovation was reported to be a success, with trouble in the neighbouring villages ending now soldiers could drink in camp.[14] Attempts were made to tackle prostitution with regulations under the Defence of the Realm Act, including a ban on women with convictions for soliciting being resident in an area where large numbers of troops were stationed.[15] In a measure designed to boost morale and curtail unofficial wandering, all ranks were granted six days' leave and a free rail ticket to anywhere in the British Isles. Many went to London where their behaviour was so poor that it resulted in the numbers of recruits granted leave being cut. Colonel Nicholson's history records that some of the First Contingent on leave 'found their way into English homes to form permanent friendships and to enjoy the warm hospitality extended to the visitors from overseas'.[16] For some soldiers the hospitality was so warm that then never found their way out of English homes again unless it was under arrest.

The official history of the Canadian forces states that ninety-four men were struck off the strength for desertion during the Salisbury Plain period, 18 October 1914–15 February 1915.[17] These are the men who were gone long enough to be declared deserters and this figure minimizes the problem the CEF had with men who went missing for shorter periods. Half of all military offences committed at Salisbury Plain were for absence without leave, which the CEF dealt with as a minor offence at this time. Private Lawrence's case is a good example, as his only punishment was to forfeit eleven days' pay for his period of absence.[18] The official history of the CEF explained that this lenient attitude was because it was understood that 'determination was needed to forsake the bright lights of London or the kindly warmth of home and friends, when the alternative was a tent on a wind-swept waste where darkness lasted fourteen hours a day and all was wetness, mud, and misery'.[19]

The First Contingent began to leave for France in December 1914. Given the issues with the accommodation on Salisbury Plain, the Second Contingent would be based at Shorncliffe in Kent, a long-established and well-equipped training location for the British Army which was now moved out in favour of the Canadians. Other towns in the South of England acquired resident Canadians too and letters home now came from Witley, Bramshott, Seaford and other new locations. The change to better accommodation did not stop absentees and deserters from leaving the Canadian ranks. David Campbell's study of the 2nd Canadian Division reveals that 484 cases of absence were recorded in the 19th Battalion of the CEF in just three months in summer 1915.[20] The 19th Battalion had arrived from Canada in May 1915 and had gone straight to the comparative luxury of Shorncliffe so did not have the poor conditions at Salisbury Plain as an excuse for their absenteeism.

British-born Canadians continued to wander. Private John Somerville Bisgrove of the 27th Winnipeg Battalion was a typical example. Granted leave from Shorncliffe in 1915, he went to visit an aunt in Kent. Missing his train back to camp he went to London instead, spending time with a cousin who was on leave from the navy. He told the subsequent court martial that he did not return to camp because he was afraid of the punishment he would receive, having been told that miscreants were being sent back to Canada. A law clerk in civilian life, Bisgrove may have been particularly sensitive to the reaction his return may provoke. By way of the huge coincidence which often seemed to happen to deserters and absentees, Bisgrove said he was on his way to hand himself in when he was apprehended by Canadian Military Police. His account on this point was undermined by the arresting officers who were clear that, far from admitting his sin, Bisgrove tried to fool them by claiming he was undergoing treatment at St Thomas' Hospital. For his month on the run Bisgrove received twenty-eight days' detention but his fears of being returned to Canada in disgrace were not realized.[21]

The difficulties experienced by the CEF on Salisbury Plain meant that plans for soldiers coming from Australia and New Zealand to train there were abandoned, the troops instead going to Egypt. The towns and villages around Salisbury Plain may well have had a lucky escape in 1915, as the discipline of the ANZACs in Egypt was poor. Their ranks contained large numbers of troublemakers who caused problems before the force even reached its destination by jumping ship and even rioting at sea. There were instances of serious disorder and looting in Cairo involving both Australians and New Zealanders, and widespread drunkenness and absenteeism. The situation regarding missing soldiers was so bad that all leave was stopped for ANZAC troops in January 1915 to allow the 'stragglers' to be rounded up.[22] Like the CEF, the Australian Imperial Force (AIF) used the punishment of being sent home to deal with bad behaviour at the start of the war. This threat was a deterrent to some as the idea of being sent home in disgrace rather than triumph was something which the average volunteer soldier wished to avoid. By the end of April 1915, over 150 Australian soldiers had been sent home for misconduct.[23]

ANZAC troops started to come to England in late 1915 once their main field of operations had been changed from Gallipoli to the Western Front. By November 1915 there were 10,000 such men in Britain, many in convalescent hospitals. Camps in Hampshire, Dorset and Wiltshire housed ANZAC soldiers for the rest of the war. Salisbury Plain was eventually utilized as the horrendous conditions experienced by the Canadians had now been resolved. The ANZACs arrived as heroes, their exploits at Gallipoli becoming legendary despite the catastrophic campaign. A valedictory parade for the newly established 'ANZAC Day' was held in London on 25 April 1916 and the troops taking part were greeted by huge crowds. Michael McKernan says that this was the high point of the ANZACs' popularity in Britain and things swiftly went downhill thereafter.[24] The Australian soldier in Britain got a reputation as a troublemaker and there were reports of hoteliers refusing to take his business. In 1917 *John Bull* claimed to have a mailbag full of complaints from ANZACs about their treatment in England. Citing a specific example where soldiers were refused service at a billiard hall, the column declared, 'A nation's soldiers must not, and shall not, be insulted because a few larrikins disgrace their uniform.' The writer somewhat undermined his own argument by suggesting that if such treatment continued the ANZACs may well riot.[25]

The military authorities shared the concerns of the civilian population. When the Australian forces were first moved to France, they were encouraged to take their leave in Britain in order to strengthen the bond to the old country; by the end of the war they were banned from staying overnight in London due to fears of bad behaviour. As with the Canadians, venereal disease was a big problem and a special hospital for Australian troops suffering from the condition was established at Bulford Camp. Half of the offences reported to the Military Police up until July 1916 involving Australians were cases of men overstaying their leave in England.[26] The Australian military police in England dealt with approximately 45,000 cases and more than 6,000 courts martial in the two years to December 1918.[27] This issue of discipline whilst in England was not confined to the Australians: when the New Zealand forces headquarters was moved to England in early 1916, there were serious concerns over the ability to maintain order amongst the troops. The New Zealanders didn't match the Aussies in terms of their bad reputation, though as Christopher Pugsley suggests, this may partly be down to the fact that the British public couldn't tell the difference between the two nationalities, meaning that Aussies were blamed for New Zealanders' misdemeanours.[28]

The prospect of being sent home in disgrace lost its sting once battle conditions were experienced. A month in the heat of Gallipoli or the mud of Flanders would certainly change the mind of many who would now see being sent home as a goal rather than a punishment. Recognizing this, by November 1916 the AIF decided that criminals would not be sent home but would instead serve their sentences in detention camps or prisons in Britain or on the fronts. As with all of the Dominion armies, officers were not infrequently sent home as an alternative to being court-martialled. Second Lieutenant Thomas Ray Crooks of the AIF, for example, was sent home to Australia for disciplinary reasons in March 1918 after going absent for four days. Crooks had won the Military Cross a year earlier.[29] Unlike soldiers from the other Dominions, Australians were not at risk of the death penalty. Though technically available at court martial, such sentences had to be ratified by the Governor General of Australia before they could be carried out. The strength of public opinion in Australia meant that this would not happen so all sentences of death were commuted to imprisonment instead. In November 1917 the AIF stopped imposing the death penalty, recognizing its futility. The lengthy prison sentences to be served in its place were served in Britain; Lewes Gaol now handed over for the exclusive use of the AIF. Conditions in Lewes and the other nine detention centres around the south coast of England were meant to be harsh to deter others from going down the same path. Prisoners were put to monotonous work sewing mail bags and potato sacks in addition to undergoing military training. In the two years of its operation, 5,600 military prisoners would pass through the gates at Lewes.[30]

Douglas Haig recorded that twice as many Aussies proportionally were in prison in March 1918 than British soldiers in their worst disciplinary period.[31]

Haig believed that this was entirely down to poor discipline which could be blamed on the absence of the death penalty as a deterrent. Less contentiously, no death penalty meant that Australian courts martial tended to impose longer sentences in serious cases and they also did not use suspended sentences as liberally, meaning it is inevitable that the numbers of Australian soldiers actually serving prison sentences would be greater.[32] By way of contrast only 41 per cent of New Zealand soldiers sentenced to a term of imprisonment would actually pass through the prison doors, the vast majority having sentences suspended or commuted to Field Punishment.[33] By the end of the war there were seven times as many Australians, proportionally, in prison than the other Dominion forces.

The fact that the Australians were true volunteers may have led to a less submissive approach to military discipline. With their ranks containing large numbers of trade unionists, Australian soldiers were not slow to complain if conditions did not suit and were prepared to withdraw their labour in appropriate circumstances. They reportedly clung to the concept of the 8-hour day as being the golden rule, even on active service.[34] Glen Wahlert characterizes the Australian soldier's outlook as one of 'stalwart civilianism'.[35] Christopher Pugsley attributes high levels of desertion amongst the AIF in 1918 to the fact that soldiers had not been given enough rest, their ranks unable to be refilled by conscription.[36] Not every AIF deserter in Britain in 1918 was a battle-scarred veteran: some had only arrived from Australia as the war was coming to an end and had never set foot on a battlefield. Though the practice of sending offenders back to Australia had ended two years earlier, shaming at home was still threatened to errant soldiers. The AIF declared in 1918 that the names of all those convicted of desertion would be sent to Australian newspapers so that friends and neighbours could see exactly how a man had spent his war service.

Though the AIF did not have the same concentration of British-born volunteers as the Canadian contingent, with around 25 per cent of the recruits being born in the United Kingdom, the vast majority of the intake were first-generation Australians with British roots.[37] If British Canadians were keen to visit family they had left behind, the Australians were determined to find family they had never met. Michael McKernan writes that the search for relatives became a hobby with the Australians, some hoping in vain that they would find some money at the end of this particular UK–Australian rainbow.[38] Taking the view that this may be the only chance they got to visit Britain for free, the ANZACs were determined to make the most of it, becoming enthusiastic tourists, not just of London but the whole of the United Kingdom.[39] When Harry H. Plant was arrested as a deserter in Derby in January 1918 he had been missing for nearly six months and, armed with a number of fraudulent leave passes, had travelled to Scotland, London, Gloucester and Leeds.[40] Ireland was particularly popular and difficult to police, so in 1918 all ANZAC leave to Ireland was banned. Christopher Pugsley writes that there was a rumour that half the bus drivers in Dublin were ANZACs, and one NZ deserter arrested in 1919 was said to have attained a high rank in the Irish Republican Army.[41] More than 26,000 Australian soldiers were dealt with by the ANZAC Provost Corps in England for either absence or desertion between January 1917 and December 1918.[42]

Dominion deserters displayed the same criminality seen amongst other forces. Thousands of miles away from home with army pay cut off it was probably even more difficult for a colonial deserter to stay on the run without resorting to crime. Australians in particular became notorious for criminal activities and, as we saw in the case of the 'Wimbledon Mystery', were sometimes handy scapegoats for others' misdemeanours. Looking at the records of some AIF miscreants it is hardly surprising that they acquired such a bad reputation. Alfred Ambrose, described as a mechanic, appeared before the civilian courts in London in February 1918 for receiving stolen motor cars. He was actually an Australian deserter called Oscar Fitzroy Kendall, a serial offender who the AIF struggled to contain. Kendall had served in Gallipoli and France, being evacuated to England in September 1916 and diagnosed with shell shock. He was first in disciplinary trouble in November 1916, going absent and travelling to London without a ticket. Mixed with various military offences from then onwards until his eventual return to Australia in late 1919 were several offences committed against civilians whilst he was absent without leave, for which he received prison sentences of varying lengths. He spent time at Bulford VD hospital and at Lewes in addition to the civilian prisons he frequented, so had all the ANZAC larrikin badges of dishonour. His service was not rewarded with medals from the AIF. Sentenced to eighteen months' imprisonment with hard labour in June 1919 for desertion and resisting an escort, Kendall was sent back to Australia in custody and in disgrace. In one last adventure he escaped from the cells on his ship when it docked at Durban, South Africa and was missing for a further month.[43]

ANZAC deserters resorting to criminality were not always Antipodean outdoorsmen with a healthy disdain for British institutions – some of them were British born and bred. In the grand tradition of transporting troublesome young men to the colonies, Ralph Clement Davies had sailed to Australia in 1912 after a failed apprenticeship in the Merchant Marine and an equally unsuccessful stint in the British Army. His father had been a vicar in the Church of England. A second-class ticket to Melbourne would hopefully give him a fresh start. Davies made a start on a criminal career in Melbourne in 1913 and served several prison sentences before joining the AIF in October 1916. He was back on British shores in Australian uniform in January 1917 and by the end of March had gone absent without leave for the first time. In early 1918 whilst in a state of desertion he appeared before Marylebone Police Court for stealing two violins and falsely charging his mother's account at Harrods. Davies received twelve months' imprisonment with hard labour, though half of the sentence was remitted to allow him to re-join the ranks. As was standard practice with AIF miscreants, he was sent to France before he could get himself into further trouble.[44]

An officer's uniform from any Allied army was always a bonus to those trying to fool the British public into taking their word as a gentleman. Australian 'officer' Henry South visited a number of jewellers' shops in Yorkshire in late spring 1917 and bought several rings. Henry Louis Hart was his real name and he was no officer but a carpenter from Manly – an ordinary private and deserter who was paying for the jewellery with worthless cheques. Eventually, the firm of Fattorini & Sons in Bradford called the police when 'Captain South' bought a ring from them and immediately pawned it elsewhere in the city for less than half its cost.[45] Arrested in Stockport, 'South' told the court that he had served in Egypt, France and Gallipoli and that his criminality was solely because he was prevented from earning an honest living without an army discharge certificate. The court showed some sympathy for the defendant and bound him over for the criminal offences so he could be handed to the AIF straightaway.[46] It was not that simple, as 'South' was wanted all over the country for thefts and deceptions. The *Police Gazette* struggled to keep up with his aliases: Captain Cecil Muir, Captain A.N. Hingley and John Niven were just a few of his names. It was in the name of John Niven that he was eventually sent to gaol by a civilian court in October 1917 when he was sentenced to eighteen months' imprisonment with hard labour.[47]

Canadian deserter Charles J. Soden was one of those rejected as undesirable before his regiment left Canada, but he sneaked into the CEF under a new name and was then sent to England. He deserted in June 1915 and travelled the country committing frauds and thefts. Buying a captain's uniform in

London allowed him to go in and out of barracks nationwide, seemingly without challenge. Whilst there he would help himself to pairs of binoculars which he then sold, claiming to the buyers that he had recovered them from the battlefield. Soden was eventually detained near Birmingham and was sentenced to eighteen months in prison by the civilian court.[48]

Real officers were not saints. The court-martial records for Canadian officers show that the most prevalent offence was that of drunkenness, though absenteeism was also common and was not infrequently preceded by a bout of cheque fraud, the officer issuing worthless cheques from overdrawn accounts that the Bank of Montreal refused to honour. This was such a problem that circulars were issued by the Canadian top brass in March 1916 warning officers that they must stop bouncing cheques else they would face proceedings under Section 11 of the Army Act for failing to obey a general order. The phenomenon continued. Lieutenant William Bailey passed bad cheques at a jeweller's in Regent Street, London in October 1917 and then disappeared for a week. He was dismissed as a result.[49] Captain Hugh Price Davies issued a series of cheques around Shoreham and London, one to a trusting woman he had just met who agreed to advance him some cash on the strength of the useless paper from the Bank of Montreal. Davies promptly went on a drinking spree then enlisted in a new regiment, joining the King Edward's Horse as a lowly private. Ironically, he listed his profession on his new attestation form as 'accountant.' Charged with desertion, Davies was ultimately convicted of absence instead and this, in addition to the conduct unbecoming an officer that was shown by his cavalier attitude to the cheques, was enough to see him dismissed from the service.[50]

British deserters would sometimes claim colonial status to take advantage of hospitality that may not otherwise have been offered. Walter Woodward of Sheffield pretended to be a Canadian soldier when he obtained lodgings with Mary Wood in Leeds. He was nothing of the sort, being a deserter from the Gordon Highlanders, and repaid his landlady's trust by failing to pay his rent and stealing a gold watch from the premises.[51] Canadian deserters sometimes claimed to be from the USA to allay suspicions that they were missing from the Dominion ranks. Henry O'Connor arrived in Bowness in style in a touring motor car in January 1917. Seeking to join friends working in a munitions factory where he had heard high wages were on offer, he took a room in the town, claiming to be a US citizen and producing a US passport. The game was up when the police found a khaki uniform amongst his belongings with the buttons and insignia cut off. O'Connor was forced to admit that he was a Canadian deserter with a wife and children in New Brunswick.[52]

For men thousands of miles from friends and family, the lure of British home comforts and female companionship was sometimes stronger than the call of duty. Deserters of all nationalities would use women as a source of financial support at a time when their own pay was being withheld. For British women, Dominion soldiers were an attractive and exotic prospect. They had more money than British soldiers and held the potential for a more exciting future abroad after the war. Should the worst happen, an Australian or Canadian private's widow was entitled to twice as much in pension payments as a British Tommy's spouse.

Facilities established to cater to the Dominion soldier in London were popular with British women. The Maple Leaf Club and the ANZAC Buffet refreshment rooms were just two of the places offering respite to soldiers, and the Australian YMCA rented the Aldwych Theatre in 1917 to cater specifically to the AIF. The Canadian YMCA established the Beaver Hut on the Strand in London for the CEF soldier on leave. The Beaver Hut, where it was said 'the soldier can satisfy his every want', had dormitories, a dining room, a theatre and a billiard room solely for the use of Canadian soldiers.[53] The site was soon besieged by women. The policewomen stationed in the area had the duty of moving the female visitors on, regardless of whether they were 'respectable or the reverse' to discourage them from congregating there. Many claimed to be relatives of the Canadians inside and policewoman Mary S. Allen wrote, 'It was amazing the number of women relatives some of the Overseas men had in London!'[54]

There appeared to be no shortage of English homes wanting to extend hospitality to Dominion deserters. In July 1915 the cramped streets of Finnis Hill were described by the magistrates of Dover as 'a nest of deserters'. Elizabeth Barnes was appearing before the court at the time on a charge of providing clothing to a Canadian fugitive. When the police raided her house they found four Canadian soldiers and several crates of beer. After her conviction the police representative in court asked that the local military commanders place Finnis Hill out of bounds to soldiers and sailors.[55] Louie Stride was a child living in the Dolemeads area of Bath, one of the poorest in the city, with a reputation as a hiding place for deserters. Known at one time as 'Mud Island', flooding was a constant problem in Dolemeads, conditions being all too familiar to any Canadians who had wintered on Salisbury Plain in 1914. Louie's mother eventually married a 'Canadoo' from a Royal Highlanders regiment who was born in Birmingham. ANZACs too found sanctuary in Dolemeads – Louie Stride babysat for a young woman who had given birth to an Australian soldier's child before an anonymous tip-off to the police led to his arrest.[56] Mabel Latcham, a war widow, was sent to prison in August 1919 for harbouring Australian deserter Rex Thomas. When the police turned up her protestations of innocence were undermined by the presence of a pair of khaki trousers and several pairs of army socks in the kitchen. Thomas, wearing civilian clothing, was arrested in a nearby public house.[57]

The stories of British women forming new relationships with Dominion soldiers did not always end in the romantic idyll of a new life across the seas. When Emily Crowe of Egham in Surrey appeared at court charged with concealing a deserter she had a baby in her arms. The child was the offspring of a Canadian deserter called Private Lawson, and the romance had cost Emily Crowe dearly. She was already married to a British soldier but had been reported to the authorities for her misbehaviour with Lawson, resulting in the removal of both her separation allowance and her elder child. Emily Crowe's story attracted no sympathy from the magistrates who sent her to prison for twenty-one days.[58] Aileen Passmore's relationship with CEF Gunner William Lindsay Hutton would have similar consequences. A war widow, she met Hutton, who was based at Witley in Surrey, in November 1916. The two were to be married and the banns had been read, the impending wedding causing Hutton to absent himself from duty at the end of March 1917. Aileen had already been fined and warned by a court for helping him evade the police when she was again found in his company, camping in Milton Woods near Eashing. She was now sentenced to three months' imprisonment with hard labour. Aileen loyally gave evidence at Hutton's court martial, supporting his claim that he was not a deserter and constantly went back to camp to check when his unit was being sent overseas. Hutton was convicted of desertion and sentenced to six months' imprisonment with hard labour. The couple never did marry and Aileen Passmore's misconduct saw her lose her widow's pension on her confinement to HMP Holloway, resulting in her being destitute and homeless.[59]

British women planning long-term relationships with Dominion soldiers sometimes found that their fiancés or husbands were already married. Bigamists were understandably determined to keep their two wives an ocean apart. In May 1919 William Marshall, a deserter from the Canadian Forestry Corps at Kemnay, appeared before court in Aberdeen charged with bigamy. Marshall was in a relationship with a war widow called Alice Gammie and, when she became pregnant with his child, agreed to marry her. A week after the ceremony – paid for by Alice – in October 1918, he disappeared and moved in with another woman. Alice went to see Marshall's commanding officer to find her man, unaware that her new husband was a deserter. She also now discovered that Marshall had a wife waiting for him in Canada. When the police arrested him they saw from letters in his possession that he was in the process of becoming engaged to yet another woman. Poor Alice Gammie lost her war widow's pension thanks to her bigamous marriage. The shocks kept on coming when she went to court to testify against Marshall and realized that he had also been lying about his age – he was not 29 years old as he had claimed but was nearly 40.[60]

By 1918 the problem of Dominion troops and bigamous marriages was so great that questions were being asked in Parliament. British women were giving up jobs, pensions and sometimes homes after marrying overseas men who already had families. One deceived woman wrote that the officer in command of the Canadian Discharge Depot at Buxton told her he had 'piles of letters' from women who had been tricked. The Scottish Registrar was well aware of the problem, writing that Dominion troops saw a trip to Scotland as 'a necessity to their "home" tour and they seem to find feminine friends everywhere'.[61] By 1919 prosecution figures for the offence of bigamy were nearly six times higher than in the last year before the war.[62]

As with soldiers on all sides, the content of a man's letters home did not necessarily reflect reality. If a man absconded and his wife's separation allowance was stopped, she would have a clue that he was up to no good, but with the ocean separating the different branches of the Dominion armies, it was not always this straightforward. Anastasia Thomas wrote to the AIF from Sydney in February 1920 seeking news of husband, Rex, because her allowance had suddenly been stopped. By this time Thomas had been missing from the ranks for six months. Thomas must have given the AIF the slip after his arrest near Mabel Latcham's house in Dolemeads in July 1919 as he was still at large.[63] Many a man would return home designated a local hero for his service when the reality was not quite so glorious. Fred Pitt served with the CEF and during 1917 persistently absconded from barracks in Britain and found his way back to the Portsmouth area where he and his wife had previously lived. At his eventual court martial Pitt said he was not a deserter but had gone 'to square up some business' with a woman who was threatening to write to his wife in Canada with details of their affair. Fred Pitt's good run ended and he served six months in prison for his desertion. In the meantime, Olive Pitt was keeping the local newspaper in Ontario up to date with her husband's exploits, the *Chatham Daily Planet* regularly publishing reports.

The letters were obviously somewhat economical with the truth. After the war the Imperial Order of the Daughters of the Empire, Chatham-Kent Branch published a book of remembrance for local veterans, taking their information from the newspaper and from family members. In the sanitized version of Fred Pitt's service that resulted, the whole difficult year of 1917 was brushed aside with the story that he had returned to Bramshott 'for further training'.[64]

London presented a disciplinary problem for the military in general and for Dominion Armies in particular. The attractions of the capital meant that overseas servicemen congregated there in large numbers whilst on leave and did not always return at the appointed time. It was easy to go missing in a city the size of London and sections of the local populace were by no means sympathetic to those seeking to arrest deserters. Certain establishments in the capital acquired a reputation as boltholes for overseas deserters. The Phoenix Hotel in Bishopgate Street was a safe haven for Australian deserters in particular. Australian Military Police raided in September 1917 and found AIF soldiers drinking at the bar. Passes were demanded and whilst they were examined, some of the uniformed drinkers managed to slink away. A thorough search of the premises found three more soldiers in a locked bedroom upstairs, all of them absent without leave from their units. In total, eight Australian deserters were found at the hotel. The proprietor, Louis Henry Golding, denied knowing they were deserters but was convicted of assisting them and sentenced to six weeks' imprisonment.[65]

London was also a dangerous place, full of those seeking to make money out of soldiers but particularly keen on overseas recruits who may have been more monied but also more naïve than the British Tommy. Sentencing a woman for soliciting soldiers for immoral purposes on Buckingham Palace Road in 1918, the presiding magistrate remarked, 'It is though these soldiers are set on by a pack of wolves.'[66] Parts of the city were renowned as hot spots for crime against soldiers: the Strand, for example, was known to the policewomen who patrolled the area as 'The Devil's Promenade'.[67] The AIF headquarters on Horseferry Road was also a notorious hotbed of criminality.[68] Incidents in these areas were not infrequently reported in the newspapers and sometimes put forward to courts martial as excuses for absence. In February 1918 CEF Lieutenant Wetmore was given a day's pass from Stafford Military Hospital in St Alban's to travel to London and buy a billiard table for the officers' recreation room. He was missing for three weeks. Wetmore had made the mistake of going to the Café Royal in Piccadilly, which was gaining a reputation as a haunt of unsavoury characters. In 1919 the venue would become known by the authorities as a hive of Australian confidence tricksters.[69] Wetmore had a drink with a stranger at the Café and claimed to have been drugged and robbed. He was too embarrassed to report to his superiors, especially as he had a responsible job as a banker at home. The court martial accepted his account and dealt with him simply by a severe reprimand and the forfeiture of some pay.[70] Though clearly at the other end of the punishment scale from imprisonment, a reprimand could be a serious matter for a young officer who was looking forward to any kind of career progression in the service. There was hardly time for this offence to be a hindrance to the young Canadian as Lieutenant Hastings de Blois Wetmore would be killed in action in September 1918 leading his platoon on the Canal du Nord.

London was so full of Dominion deserters that military police from the overseas contingents took part in raids alongside the police to assist with the identification and speedy return of their missing men.[71] A unit of New Zealand Military Police was stationed in London and spent most of its time tracing deserters and absentees. Given the numbers going missing, the New Zealand command made it clear that anyone going absent without leave in Britain would be posted straight to a front-line unit on arrest. Whilst this may have discouraged those who were thinking of wandering off, it did nothing to hasten the return of those who had already deserted, giving them instead an additional motivation for remaining undetected.

Identifying ANZAC deserters sometimes proved difficult. A man giving his name as William James made six appearances before the Marylebone Police Court in 1918 on a charge of failing to register as an enemy alien before his true identity was discovered. James was originally arrested because an off-duty police officer thought he looked like a German, and the man admitted he was an alien, pleading guilty to failing to register as required. The complication was the AIF were insistent that he was a deserter from the Australian forces. James denied this, claiming that he was not an Australian citizen and had never been in the army. He insisted he was German by birth and had a witness appear in court to corroborate this, and to swear that James had a music hall act before the war with a troupe of performing dogs! The police threatened to publish his photograph in order to invite people to identify him. Five weeks after his initial arrest James admitted that he was in fact Private 6946 William Heffernan, an orchard worker from Rochester, Victoria and a deserter from the AIF.[72]

The end of hostilities left hundreds of thousands of Dominion troops in Europe awaiting shipment back to their respective home countries. In November 1918 there were 220,073 Dominion troops in the United Kingdom.[73] Not all of those who survived the war were particularly keen to return home, whilst others were so impatient to do so that serious disorder took place. The original plan for the demobilization of the CEF was that it was to take place directly from France, but this was made too difficult by the numbers of British-born Canadians who wanted to come back to England before sailing across the Atlantic. Instead, the Canadians would return to Britain where they would be placed in camps to be sent back to Canada once ships became available. In the camps they would be medically examined and then granted demobilization leave of up to two weeks before being expected to return and await shipment home. It is some indication of the numbers of British-born Canadians that ultimately around 22,000 members of the CEF would be discharged in the United Kingdom despite the discouragement of the practice by the Canadian government.[74] John Somerville Bisgrove, the British-born deserter who overstayed his leave in London in 1915, continued to go missing from the ranks four years later whilst awaiting demobilization. He was eventually returned to Canada on a troop ship in November 1919. Some of his comrades didn't return at all and others caused so much unrest that the Canadian authorities may have regretted their decision to use Britain as a staging post. At Kinmel Park in March 1919 there was a riot which resulted in a great deal of damage to the camp and to civilian businesses and the deaths of five soldiers. At Epsom 800 Canadian patients from Woodcote Park Convalescent Hospital attacked the civilian police station to free two of their number, injuring several police officers and resulting in the death of one, Sergeant Green.

Britain's War Cabinet was in no doubt that the Australian contingent present in the United Kingdom needed to be repatriated as soon as possible. Trouble in London on Armistice Day was blamed on Dominion troops, with Sir Nevil Macready, the Metropolitan Police Commissioner, reporting to the Cabinet that, 'The main difficulty was with the Australians, who apparently intended their behaviour in Cairo in 1915 to be a standard for future action.' The same meeting was told that the Aussies had also misbehaved in Wiltshire, forcibly removing the gates at Lord Pembroke's estate at Wilton House, part of which had been turned into a war hospital.[75] Peter Stanley writes of the existence of a dangerous group of so-called 'sandbaggers' in Wiltshire in 1918 comprising Australian absentees who spent their time robbing and assaulting the local populace and even their own comrades.[76]

Rounding up ANZAC deserters after the war was particularly troublesome. Britain was a long way from Australia and New Zealand and many wanted to make the most of their stay. Like the Canadians, ANZACs were granted demobilization leave but hundreds did not return as required. In January 1919 there were 556 soldiers absent from the ranks of the New Zealand Expeditionary Force. Six months later there were still 357 men missing. Some were taking extended tourist trips but some had settled in the United Kingdom and had no intention of going home. The NZEF tried to encourage them to surrender by putting adverts in the newspapers making it clear that if they did not report by 31 July 1919, they would be struck off the strength and would not be entitled to free passage home, nor any war gratuity or other privilege.[77] In October 1918 Acting Australian Prime Minister William Watt made an offer to the state governments of Australia to pay half the separation allowances for families whose soldiers were in a state of desertion. He may have regretted that offer, as the *Sydney Morning Herald* claimed that as of 2 August 1919 there were 1,000 deserters from the AIF still unaccounted for. According to the newspaper, the majority were believed to be in France but between 200 and 300 were somewhere in Britain. The *Herald* reported the AIF's view that most of this number 'were never any good but they do not wish to leave undesirables behind'.[78] Rex Thomas was one deserter who did not return. Enlisting in June 1918, he hadn't arrived in Europe until getting off the boat in London three days after the Armistice. When he was still officially absent without leave at the end of March 1920, the AIF decreed that he should be discharged in absentia. Wife Anastasia's separation allowance never did recommence.

There were deserters from the Dominion forces who would be left behind as they were serving prison sentences in British gaols. Ernest Buck was sentenced at the Old Bailey to nine months' imprisonment with hard labour in December 1918 after financing his desertion by signing stolen cheques in the name of Australian Prime Minister W.M. Hughes. He did not return to Australia, dying in Wormwood Scrubs of peritonitis in May 1919. Despite his chequered military career, Buck was buried with full honours at Highgate Cemetery.[79] Some Australian soldiers were serving lengthy prison sentences, for example, Ernest Sharp and Thomas Maguire, serving seven years' and ten years' penal servitude respectively for the robbery of a Canadian soldier. Both Australians were in a state of desertion at the time of the offence in December 1917. Sharp had enlisted in a false name whilst McGuire, a professional boxer, had only been in Britain a few months and had never seen active service.[80] The CEF left thirty-four soldiers from their ranks serving sentences in British prisons whilst their comrades headed back across the Atlantic, including one murderer, Hackney born George Harman, who had killed his girlfriend,

Phyllis Earl. Originally sentenced to death, when the locals of Hackney submitted a petition for mercy to the Home Secretary, Harman's death sentence was commuted to penal servitude for life.[81]

Australian Albert James Fraser would not be so lucky. Fraser arrived in England direct from Australia in October 1918 and deserted shortly after the Armistice. He was arrested in June 1919 but absconded again less than two weeks later. This time when he resurfaced it was as a suspect in a murder case. 'The Queen's Park Murder' in February 1920 saw the death of an ex-soldier called Henry Senior, lured into the darkness of a Glasgow park by a woman on the promise of a sexual encounter. Once there he was set upon by two men, robbed and left to die. Albert Fraser and James Rollins, his co-accused, had both been soldiers, Rollins serving in the Irish Guards. They worked in conjunction with two young women, robbing the unwary who were foolish enough to follow them to secluded locations.[82] The quartet had fled to Belfast before they could be arrested. The AIF was present at the trial and reported that proceedings had been conducted entirely fairly and that it was never disclosed that Fraser was an Australian. The implication must be that the reputation of Australians was so poor at the time that the revelation of his nationality would have proved prejudicial. Fraser and Rollins were convicted of murder and hanged together at Duke Street Prison on 26 May 1920, a petition for mercy having been refused. A representative from the AIF was reportedly present at the execution to see the grisly end of this larrikin's wartime adventures.[83]

Chapter 11

After the War – Amnesties and Bad Army Characters

A terrible crime committed by terrible criminals.
Letter to the *Daily Herald*,
29 November 1919

After the Armistice, the British government faced the huge problem of demobilising the armed forces whilst keeping enough manpower to cover any resumption of the war and for the continuing operations in other arenas. An orderly and gradual demobilization was the ideal, but the actions of large numbers of soldiers at home and abroad forced a reconsideration of the government's original scheme. Excited by the end of the war and unimpressed with the army's plans to send troops to Russia, British and Dominion troops made their protests loudly, whilst some just quietly slipped away following their own timetable. Michael Knowles of the DLI was one man who made a very swift departure from the army, deserting on Armistice Day itself.[1]

Technically, Britain was still at war until a peace agreement was signed so troops could not be released wholesale and without conditions. An elaborate plan had been drawn up in 1917 to demobilize men in order of the importance of their profession in returning British society to business as usual. The Ministry of Labour divided soldiers into five categories, the first two being eligible for immediate release. In all categories, married men and those who had seen front-line service were meant to be given priority. Once physically released from the army a man was given a railway warrant, a ration book, a civilian clothing grant and twenty-eight days' home leave with pay and ration allowance. He was also given a Z11 'Protection Certificate and Certificate of Identity' to show that he was not a deserter – yet another valuable piece of paper for forgers to copy. After his leave he was automatically transferred to the Army Reserve and therefore technically demobilized and forbidden from wearing uniform.

The army needed a proportion of the war time volunteers to remain in the forces, not only to continue to occupy Germany until a peace agreement was signed, but also to bolster intervention in the Russian Civil War where the British government was determined that the Bolsheviks should be ousted. Conscription was suspended on Armistice Day for anyone who had not already received call-up papers so a fresh supply of recruits would not be forthcoming. Significant incentives were offered in terms of much higher pay and a lump sum as a bounty for re-enlisting. The level of the bounty varied with the length of service agreed – £20 for 2 years, £30 for 3 years and £50 for 4 years.[2] The lump sums were paid in instalments to dissuade men from deserting but, in time-honoured fashion, some would sign on the dotted line and immediately take off once the pay was in their pocket. Despite the extra money the request to re-enlist was not well received. The conflict in Russia was not the war any of the 1914–18 volunteers had signed up for, and an attack on the Bolsheviks was distasteful in the extreme to many on the Left. Arthur Horner claimed that he was told before the imposition of his sentence of imprisonment for refusing orders in 1919 that if he agreed to serve in Russia the matter would be forgotten. Horner preferred to serve his sentence in Carmarthen Prison where he wrote that most of his fellow inmates were soldiers, sailors and COs.[3] Andrew Rothstein recalls that a deputation seeking volunteers for Russia at his army camp on Salisbury Plain was greeted by only one hand going up from the hundreds assembled before them.[4] About 75,000 men did sign up for further service, but this still left a recruiting deficit when trying to fulfil Britain's remaining military commitments.[5]

The first man was not demobilized until 9 December 1918 and by the end of the year only 7 per cent of the army – just over 44,000 men – had been released. The number of men declared deserters showed its customary January spike in 1919, rising to 2,313 individuals by the end of that month.[6] Men began to revert to civilian behaviour now the war was over regardless of the fact they were still in uniform. Officers noticed a sudden failure to offer the necessary salutes to superiors, categorized by those in the Northern Command in York as 'the reassertion of civilian instincts'.[7] Servicemen began to show their displeasure in a wave of mutinies and strikes both at home and abroad. The strikes had begun in the civilian realm. A particularly tumultuous year for industrial unrest, 1918 saw 1,185 disputes nationwide compared with half that number in 1916, with even the police going on strike.[8] In early January 1919 at Folkestone, 3,000 soldiers refused to leave for France and a mob of 10,000 marched to the town hall to see the Mayor. Other Channel ports and military bases all over the country saw similar protests against the rate of demobilization and the rules as they were being applied. In February, when bad weather forced the postponement of a draft out to France and an administrative error meant that no accommodation was ready for them in London, over a thousand troops were involved in violent protest at Victoria Station and in Whitehall.

Assertion of rank no longer had the same effect on the average Tommy. Aaron Smith wrote to his family in 1919 from Bellmont Camp in Surrey: 'Since I've been here we've all been on strike. We are all for demobilisation and are all still sticking out for it . . . We have had different Generals up here to win us over but it's no good we just simply shout them down and tell them we don't want no more of it.'[9]

Sailors were particularly vociferous in their opposition to any further operations. In October 1919 the entire 1st Destroyer Flotilla refused to sail from Port Gordon to Russia and ninety-six of the men who left their ships were charged with offences against military discipline ranging from mutiny to desertion.[10] In the same month eighty-seven men from the Royal Marines were court-martialled for desertion in Russia when they refused to fight and walked back to base, and there were disturbances aboard HMS *Cicala*, HMS *Vindictive* and HMS *Delhi*.[11]

The unrest eventually saw the original demobilization plan scrapped in January 1919 with the promise of an accelerated process, though by February 1920 125,000 men were still waiting for their ticket out of the army.[12] Servicemen taking part in disobedience of this kind saw the incidents as industrial disputes, not as offences against military discipline. HM Prisons Inspector J.J. Knox reported that those serving sentences of penal servitude in Britain in 1919 for their involvement in mutinies at Rouen and Calais regarded the incidents as strikes.[13]

For those already serving sentences of imprisonment for desertion the end of hostilities must have brought hope that their detention would soon be over. Calls for an amnesty or a pardon for military offenders had been growing during 1918 and would continue to do so into 1919 and beyond. There was a precedent in that certain military offenders had been released from custody at the end of the Second Boer War in 1902. Amnesties had also been announced on special royal occasions, for example, Queen Victoria's Jubilee in 1887 and King George's accession to the throne in 1910. The appeals for an amnesty after the First World War largely fell on deaf ears. The pardoning of military offenders was unthinkable to the army, partly due to their actions in executing hundreds of British soldiers during the war for offences they were now being asked to overlook. A defence of the position they took in those cases was untenable if they now relented in the cases of men who suffered less than the ultimate punishment.

There were, of course, practical difficulties with releasing military offenders after the Armistice. The effect on public opinion and public order of releasing military criminals from prison before soldiers with unblemished service records were allowed to leave the army could be incendiary. Should those waiting for demobilization believe that no punishments would now be inflicted, wholesale desertions may well have taken place, fatally undermining the government's timetable. A general amnesty for imprisoned soldiers also raised the prospect of the military prisons in France and Belgium throwing open their doors and releasing thousands of desperate criminals on the local populace. Lieutenant General Asser, Commanding Officer of the Armies in France and Belgium, had no doubt that such a measure meant that these men 'would probably wreck the place and resume their gentle pastimes of robbery and violence'.[14]

The Director of Personal Services at the War Office gave an interview two weeks after the Armistice making the position crystal clear. Major General Sir Wyndham Childs reminded readers that the War Office did offer an amnesty at the beginning of the war to outstanding deserters, but that it was a very different and more serious matter to desert during a war. He claimed that virtually all of the soldiers imprisoned in the United Kingdom were actually serving time for civil, not military, offences and that the vast majority of men who were court-martialled were released from any sentence immediately under the Suspension of Sentences Act. He declared to the interviewer that, 'The deserter and the absentee are not popular with their comrades.'[15] If the War Office hoped that this article would put an end to the matter they were to be disappointed. The question of an amnesty was regularly raised in the press in the two years following the Armistice and was a constant demand of veterans' organizations. Members of Parliament made pleas for absolution shortly after the Armistice and prior to every significant development in the peace process thereafter, for example, during the planning of Peace Day, scheduled for 19 July 1919, and just before the anniversary of the Armistice in November 1919. In May 1920 Charles H. Palmer, MP and then editor of *John Bull*, demanded that the authorities 'Open wide the prison gates and set these poor captives free!'[16] Palmer declared that the end of hostilities meant that the hundreds of military criminals 'have been washed white in the glorious river of victory' and that the rank and file of the army agreed with him. Palmer's claim to speak for the Tommy met with some scorn from fellow MPs who pointed out that he had no army service himself. Austin Hopkinson, MP and Boer War veteran, said of Palmer, 'when he says he knows the feelings of the army he bases that statement entirely on letters received by him from soldiers convicted of crime and writing to him as editor of *John Bull*'.[17]

Publicly, the military authorities appeared dead set against an amnesty, but privately there had been a decision made to review the sentences of all men serving penal servitude or imprisonment for purely military offences. Wyndham Childs had embarked on this course in November 1918 at the same time as he was giving his interview decrying the call for an amnesty. He had already been instrumental in recycling soldiers who had been held in military detention, returning them to service at a rapid rate. At the date of the Armistice there were 3,500 men in military detention who were imminently to be sent to Aldershot and thereafter to France. Despite his public pronouncements, Wyndham Childs had a great deal of sympathy for these men. He wrote in a memo to the War Office that they were 'absentees off drafts, absentees off leave, and are in no way of a bad type'. Wyndham Childs took the traditional view that these men would 'make good soldiers when freed from the temptations which beset them in this country'.[18]

In May 1919 the scope of the Suspension of Sentences Act 1915 was widened. As demonstrated, this Act only applied to men on active service overseas who had been given imprisonment or penal servitude at their court martial. The Naval, Military and Air Forces Service Act 1919 extended this power to the home front and to all forms of detention, whether that was penal servitude, imprisonment or detention in barracks. This fell far short of a general amnesty, allowing the military to retain a man's services under the threat of a return to prison if there was further misbehaviour. A wholesale review of sentences of all kinds of military detention would now take place to reduce the numbers of soldiers in prison. James Emmott, one of the Cowling deserters, was a beneficiary of this review. Originally sentenced to two years' imprisonment with hard labour, when his sentence was promulgated it was reduced to eighteen months' imprisonment. Emmott served seven months at Aldershot detention barracks before his sentence was suspended in July 1919. He was discharged from the army completely in September 1919.[19]

There were reports of significant unrest amongst the ranks of military prisoners. It seems that there was a general belief amongst the men that there would be an amnesty and when this was not forthcoming after the Treaty of Versailles was signed, discipline within the prison walls became precarious.

The governors of both Dartmoor and Portland prisons wrote to the War Office in the summer of 1919 expressing their concerns. These prisons now contained soldiers who had been sentenced to periods of penal servitude. At the end of July 1919, 200 men at Portland Prison had refused to follow orders, resulting in the attendance of Prison Inspector J.J. Knox. He reported that the men felt abandoned and believed that Australian prisoners were receiving preferential treatment as a number of them had left Portland, presumably to be released. Knox recommended that prison sentences be reviewed across the board, that men who had deserted other than from the front line have their sentences remitted and that those serving time for their part in disturbances at Rouen and Calais be immediately released – this last suggestion earned three exclamation marks at the hands of the War Office reviewer wielding the blue pencil! Enquiries were made with the AIF and word came back that their men had not been released, simply returned to Australia to serve sentences there.[20]

The report into the prison disturbances also discloses the true numbers of men undergoing penal servitude, the figures being slightly different to those given to the press by government representatives. As of 1 August 1919 a total of 406 soldiers were in penal servitude, but contrary to the impression given by Wyndham Childs 8 months earlier, the majority were not serving sentences for 'civil' offences. Of this total, 99 men had committed civil offences and were punished either by court martial or a civilian court whilst 307 were serving for military offences. There were 216 men who had been sentenced for desertion and 2 particularly unlucky men for absence. Half of these prisoners were serving lengthy sentences from life imprisonment to ten years' penal servitude. Most of these men were likely to have been prisoners recently returned to Britain from military prisons in France and Belgium. One of the prisoners was the deserter given a warm welcome by his father-in-law, Gunner Herbert Caulder. Wyndham Childs had no sympathy whatsoever with these prisoners. He believed it would be fatal to army discipline if sentences for desertion were reduced or remitted and described the men as 'the scum of the Army and deserving of little if any consideration'.[21]

Concentration on those comparatively few men undergoing penal servitude obscured the real picture as far as military prisoners in Britain was concerned. District Courts Martial, the tribunal dealing with the vast majority of cases of desertion on the home front, were unable to award sentences of penal servitude, being restricted to a maximum of two years' imprisonment with or without hard labour. In the year between October 1918 and September 1919,

1,099 men had been sentenced to varying periods of imprisonment by a DCM in the United Kingdom.[22] Statistics from the Prison Commissioners show that nearly 700 men were received in civil prisons in the United Kingdom in the year between 1 April 1918 and 31 March 1919 after being sentenced at a court martial to a term of imprisonment. The Commissioners also recorded that, in addition to this number, local prisons had 'largely been utilized for the detention of military and naval offenders convicted of purely military offences, 2,394 such offenders having been committed during the year'.[23] There were clearly many more soldiers in custody in the United Kingdom than the government portrayed.

The review of sentences continued. In Cabinet discussions in early February 1920 to prepare War Secretary Winston Churchill for a meeting with the veterans' organizations that were calling for an amnesty, it was stated that there were still 260 soldiers undergoing sentences of penal servitude handed down during the war, 174 of them for desertion. Since the end of the war, just over 100 sentences of penal servitude had been remitted completely and the rest had been reduced in length. Almost 1,500 soldiers had also been released in that time from detention barracks where they were serving lesser sentences.[24] A month later Churchill told the Commons that there were now 171 soldiers left in penal servitude for offences committed during the war. He decried a general amnesty 'such as might be given by an oriental despot who had succeeded by violence to the throne and who took pleasure in releasing the political male factors with whom his predecessors had filled the gaol'.[25] Churchill was conveniently ignoring the earlier amnesties granted in Britain.[26] In the same month he made this assertion the Canadian government announced an amnesty for military offenders.

Conscientious objectors presented a headache for the government. Releasing these men immediately after the Armistice, either from prison or from their designated work of national importance would cause an uproar, being seen to give them a head start in the labour market above the British soldier who had fought for his country. The reality was that many COs would struggle to get employment of any kind due to their wartime stance, but the mere idea that they would be in a preferential position was unacceptable to many. The preponderance of political rather than religious COs in prison gave some pause for thought: Andrew Bonar Law said in Cabinet that these men would be only too eager to spill the blood of their fellow countrymen in a revolutionary struggle at home despite having refused to take arms against Germany.[27] At the end of the war there were 1,500 COs in prison. A further

606 COs were at Dartmoor and 761 in other camps around the country, both of these groups doing Brace Committee work. There were also 2,221 COs doing approved work of national importance around the country outside of work centres. Within five days of the Armistice thirty of the Brace Committee work camp men had run off and it was believed that there was a plot afoot amongst the Dartmoor men to make a mass escape. These men were all technically in the Army Reserve rather than being prisoners, so if they absconded little could be other than to recall them to the colours and then prosecute them as deserters if they did not show up.[28] Whilst the Cabinet deliberated, COs who had served their time in prison were released back to the army to be court-martialled again when they refused orders. Maurice Rowntree, for example, was released from one sentence to be given a further two years' imprisonment in March 1919 when he once more refused to put on uniform.[29] A decision was eventually taken to release COs who had served twenty months or more in prison and by August 1919 the last imprisoned CO was set free. Maurice Rowntree was in Germany by the end of September, working for the Society of Friends Emergency and War Victims Relief Committee.[30]

For those men who were still in a state of desertion when the Armistice was declared, the situation was unclear. *John Bull* had periodically suggested that deserters should be received back into the army without sanction whilst the war was ongoing and repeated the call now that the country was at peace. In May 1919 the paper called on the King to issue a pardon to deserters who were still outstanding as 'one great pledge of Peace'.[31] May 1919 was a date of particular significance, as the obligations of those who had signed on for the duration of the war only ran to six months after its end. If 11 November 1918 was seen as the date hostilities ceased, 11 May 1919 was the date on which such men should be released. Newspapers carried sensationalist headlines about the police discovering a plot to induce soldiers and sailors to mutiny or desert on 11 May, an organized faction of revolutionaries allegedly encouraging men to 'demobilise themselves' by walking out of barracks.[32] The mass walkout did not happen and the desertion figures for May and June 1919 do not show any particular spike. No arrests of dangerous revolutionary plotters were made. The numbers of men being struck off as deserters continued at an average rate of 1,657 men a month during 1919.[33]

Some men undoubtedly did take demobilization into their own hands and one wrote to the *Daily Herald* in November 1919 asking for an amnesty for outstanding deserters and military prisoners.

FROM A DESERTER

To the Editor of the *DAILY HERALD*.

Sir – Kicking their heels along the roads of the country they helped to save, harassed and driven from pillar to post, are thousands of soldiers who conscientiously refused to accept the extension of the Conscription Bill, and at the first opportunity after May 11, 1919, unofficially demobilized themselves.

Although these men have faithfully fulfilled their contract, i.e. 'three years or duration, and for a period not exceeding six months after the cessation of hostilities', efforts are still being made to trace them in order to arrest them on a charge of 'desertion'.

These men, let it be understood, did *not* desert in 'face of the enemy'. In the spirit and the letter they observed their agreement. Their crime, in the eyes of the military, is that they refused to allow themselves to be used for fresh and entirely unwarranted wars.

A terrible crime committed by terrible criminals – hence the relentless efforts of the police and military to trace them.

The methods adopted by the sleuths are characteristic of the Churchillian militarists. If the man is married his wife is subjected to periodical visits by the police, each visit being the occasion for veiled threats and unwarranted bullying, because the wife refuses to disclose her husband's whereabouts.

There should be a demand at once for the release of all military prisoners and the immediate cessation of efforts to trace post-war deserters.

Yours, etc.[34]

Officially there would be no amnesty for deserters at large post-war. Men could only be prosecuted by the army for offences committed less than three months before they ceased to be under military law, so for those who enlisted 'for the duration' there was a potential cut-off point ahead. Technically this limitation did not apply to the offences of mutiny, desertion or fraudulent enlistment, and did not apply to offences committed 'on active service' but as we have seen, pragmatism sometimes prevailed: absence without leave was often the charge of choice instead of desertion meaning the loophole was potentially available to write off large numbers of cases.[35]

In September 1919 a confidential letter was issued by the Admiralty stating that as they were keen to reduce the numbers of sailors in the service they would no longer be actively seeking deserters. When the news got out the government was forced to deny that the navy had issued an amnesty and the Admiralty officially cancelled the order a month later.[36] Despite the public declaration that naval deserters were still to be pursued, privately they were increasingly less likely to be reclaimed. The army was often now slow providing the necessary information to civilian courts when deserters appeared before them for criminal offences. These King's bad bargains were of no further use and the army was not going to waste time and manpower collecting them. Sometimes the court would adjourn cases repeatedly to request the attendance of a military representative. On other occasions courts simply ignored the desertion and sentenced the prisoner for the criminal offence alone or declined to detain men as deserters without an appearance by an army representative. This meant that those the army wanted to retain were as likely to escape as the King's bad bargains.

When the army failed to turn up for the case against George Hearne in February 1920, his solicitor was able to put forward his client's story without contradiction. The magistrates were told that Hearne had come from Argentina to join Kitchener's Army and was wounded and unfit for active service thereafter. He had offered to serve as an interpreter, only deserting when his offer was rejected, and even then continuing to do work of national importance. Hearne's story was not entirely true – he was born in Argentina but had been living in Brixton since 1910. He was evacuated to England on a hospital ship, but it was to deal with a bout of cystitis, not a serious war wound. He then applied for a discharge from the army claiming he was an Argentine citizen and could not be compelled to serve, disappearing before his request could be considered. Hearne had been arrested as a deserter once already but had fooled the police into thinking they had no right to detain him. Now, a breakdown in communication between the police and the army meant that no military representative attended any of the court hearings. Hearne was released from court. Where the fault lay was never ascertained, but the steam still rises from the pages written by the army in his service records – 'The man is of course free now and is extremely unlikely to let himself be caught again.' This was true and George Hearne quietly disappeared from view.[37]

The general public had more sympathy for deserters who had served in the armed forces than for those who had made themselves scarce fearing conscription or had seen out the war as COs. In Leeds, for example, the return of the 'fly boys' who had spent most of the war in Ireland caused some consternation. The *Yorkshire Evening Post* repeated the claim that large numbers of Leeds residents had been living in Dublin during the war and said that those who had managed to escape capture were now back home. These 'shirkers' were walking around freely, a notice having been issued to the police on Armistice Day that absentees under the Military Service Act were no longer to be arrested. Those who had done their bit were said to be aggrieved by the situation.[38] The suggestion that a man who had been a conscientious objector should be given back his job as a lecturer at Leeds School of Art led to a public outcry. Charles H. Broughton, a Congregational Methodist, who had accepted and completed work of national importance rather than serve in the army was in direct competition with a veteran who had won the Military Cross and Bar. There was said to be 'a very strong feeling in the city' against Broughton's appointment and though the Education Committee was brave enough to offer him the job, the City Council would not approve their selection.[39] This attitude was replicated around the country. Newport Education Committee was just one of many who refused to reinstate any teachers who had been COs, their stance being supported by the local newspapers. In contrast to the conciliatory tone taken towards deserters, *John Bull* was vociferous in its opposition to the employment of COs, carrying articles into 1920 criticizing local authorities for giving jobs to men who had failed to fight. George Coppuck had the temerity to apply for his old job back in Reading as a school attendance officer and was vilified in *John Bull* as 'a conchy in search of a war bonus'.[40]

The discrimination against COs was to some extent sanctioned by the government. The Representation of the People Act 1918 disenfranchised COs at the same time it gave votes to some women, suggesting that COs were now even less regarded as citizens. Anyone who had avoided military service by claiming to have a conscientious objection to war, or who had been court-martialled for disobeying orders and gave the same justification, was disqualified from voting for five years. An exception was made if a CO had engaged in work of national importance and had a certificate from a Military Service Tribunal to prove it.[41] This was an incredibly draconian punishment for men who had, after all, complied with the law in seeking the appropriate exemption. Ordinary deserters were not deprived of the vote regardless of how little service they may have provided to their country in wartime. It was bad law, a piece of retrospective legislation punishing men for actions taken at a time when this penalty did not apply. In practice, the rule appears to have been disregarded, either intentionally in some areas, or accidentally in others as Electoral Registration Officers were ignorant of the procedure. Leonard Nixon certainly appeared on the electoral register for 1919. His status also does not seem to have impacted upon the careers of his family members. At the same time as Leonard was eating prison food, his brother Frank was dining in Whitehall. Frank Nixon worked at the heart of government throughout the First World War and beyond, becoming an enthusiastic advocate and tireless worker for the League of Nations and was eventually knighted. Sister Hilda was later to become headmistress of Roundhay Girl's High School in Leeds.[42]

The public continued to be quick to come to the aid of deserters being arrested by the police. In May 1919 William Howard, a deserter from the 3rd East Yorkshire Regiment, was arrested at the Viaduct Bar in Leeds city centre. Once out on the street, Howard began to shout to a rapidly assembling crowd, 'This is what the . . . do after you have been fighting for them'. The mob attacked the officers to secure his release but were unsuccessful. Howard was not the most deserving candidate for their sympathy, having only been serving in the army as an alternative to a six-year sentence of preventative detention. He had deserted almost immediately.[43]

By the time a crowd came to the aid of deserter Private Robert Thomas Savage in Lambeth in April 1919, Savage was dying. Private Savage was one of a group of six prisoners being taken from detention in France to Portland Gaol to serve lengthy terms of penal servitude. Four escorts marched the men, handcuffed in pairs, to Waterloo Station to board the train to the West Country. Savage was a Londoner, a dock labourer by occupation and a staunch union man. He had a wife and three children in Islington. One of the children was only 5 months old and Savage had not yet seen the baby. Fellow prisoner Private Kitching told the subsequent inquest that Savage wanted to see his family before he went to Portland and told him that he would make a break for it if he saw an opportunity. Savage made his move and ran off, shoving his escort out of the way and Kitching had little choice but to go with him as they were handcuffed together. After a warning was shouted by the escort and ignored, 19-year-old Rifleman George Clarke was ordered to fire at the runners but to aim low. Clarke gave evidence at the inquest that he had fired at the man's boots: Savage bled to death from a chest wound. Understandably, the locals who witnessed the incident were not impressed. A crowd soon appeared, stones were thrown and the offending escort was attacked by one woman with a rolling pin. A taxi had to be quickly hailed to take Rifleman Clarke from the scene to safety.

Fear of the crowd of onlookers undoubtedly contributed to Savage's death. Lance Corporal De Bues, in charge of the escort, testified at the inquest that as soon as the men started to run, he 'felt sure the public would help them and not me'. There was unrest at the inquest itself, with the escorts being heckled and items thrown at them whenever they left the building: 'One woman, who had a jug of beer in one hand, threw mud with the other.'[44] The escorts were completely inexperienced and had only been asked to accompany the prisoners because they happened to be going back to England on leave at the time. It was against King's Regulations to march the men through the streets in handcuffs and the escorts appeared to have no instructions on the circumstances in which their rifles could be discharged. The lack of organization was a shock to the Coroner, who made much of the fact that De Bues was a jeweller by trade whilst Clarke was a shop assistant with a heart complaint. This was somewhat unfair on De Bues at least, who had seen action in France, Salonika and Egypt. The lengthy sentences being served by the prisoners also came as a surprise to the Coroner: Private Boyce of the Black Watch, was serving fifteen years' penal servitude for desertion.[45] Ironically, Savage was serving one of the lower sentences in the group – a mere five years' penal servitude – and may well have been a beneficiary of the general review now taking place. The inquest jury clearly had some sympathy for the escorts, returning a verdict of 'justifiable homicide'. The public gallery was incensed, one woman shouting to De Bues and Clarke, 'I hope he will haunt you tonight!'[46] No one ever faced criminal charges or court-martial proceedings over Private Savage's death.

The *Daily Herald* collected money for Private Savage's widow, Elizabeth. She had been offered a funeral with full military honours by the War Office but had refused to accept this arrangement. After the intervention of the *Daily Herald* the War Office agreed to pay the costs of a civilian funeral instead. Savage was buried in the chapel grounds at Islington Cemetery. Somewhat surprisingly, Elizabeth Savage did receive a war widow's pension. It is hard to discount the effect of the intervention of the newspapers and the huge amount of publicity given to what was described as 'The Lambeth Tragedy' in this decision. A British soldier, in handcuffs, had been shot in broad daylight on a London street by a man of the same uniform. The *Herald* claimed it was 'natural justice' that his widow should be catered for, though this concept was generally alien to the Ministry of Pensions.[47]

Deserters found life difficult in the post-war employment market. Demobilized men received an out-of-work donation of 24s. a week for each week they were unemployed to a maximum of twenty weeks, with additional sums for any children. The out-of-work donation was not available to men in a state of desertion because they had not been formally discharged from the army. Anyone discharged for misconduct was also ineligible. Deserters sometimes gave themselves away in attempts to claim the benefit. Private Corcoran of the Royal Irish Rifles made enquiries at his local labour exchange in Bray about getting the out-of-work donation before most men had even started the demobilization process. Staff called the police and Corcoran found himself serving a term of imprisonment as a deserter.[48] Fraudulent claiming of out-of-work benefit was a serious concern to the Ministry of Labour, largely because of 'the chorus of criticism' being levelled at the administration of the benefit generally and the cost to the nation. The amount of out-of-work donation paid between the Armistice and 18 June 1920, was £53,209,000, of which £30,813,000 was paid to ex-service men and women.[49] Those who claimed the benefit fraudulently were often harshly dealt with. Arthur William Cleary, a deserter from the London Irish Rifles, was sent to prison in May 1919 for claiming out-of-work benefit in the name of a discharged sailor called Joseph O'Donnell.[50] He got six months' imprisonment with hard labour with the court commenting on the number of these cases which were now appearing. In December 1918 the announcement of a war gratuity starting at £5 per man also saw deserters suddenly making contact with the War Office to get their dues.

The discharge or protection certificate – the Z11 – was a piece of paper prized by those who had no legitimate means of obtaining one. Employers needed to see an army discharge certificate before they could safely offer an ex-soldier work. William Butler deserted from the Machine Gun Corps in July 1918 and bought another man's discharge certificate for £10 to enable him to take up employment as a groom for Lady Frederick of Lamport Grange.[51] The trafficking of bogus army forms continued. Harold Trevena, Edward Smith, Francis Turner and John Smith appeared before the Tower Bridge Police Court in October 1919 charged with operating a scam selling forged documents to soldiers who wished to desert. The gang operated in the Waterloo district of London selling passes and stealing soldiers' greatcoats from YMCA huts and other establishments. The coats could be exchanged for 20s. each so were valuable items. Turner was previously employed as a clerk at Purfleet Camp where he had stolen a rubber stamp to authenticate the various forms – medical discharge certificates, protection certificates and railway passes – which were then sold to disaffected soldiers for a couple of shillings a time.[52]

A discharge certificate which specified that a man's expulsion from the army was on disciplinary grounds was a significant disadvantage in civilian life. Now that the war was over, soldiers sentenced to imprisonment who would previously have been forced to continue serving in the army were being dishonourably discharged. Churchill explained to the Commons in April 1919 that no soldier sent to prison was being taken back into the army 'because of the taint of the atmosphere of the gaol'.[53] It was an offence punishable with up to two years' imprisonment for these men to attempt to re-join the armed forces without disclosing the circumstances of their departure from the ranks. Deserters were reportedly hanging around demobilization camps into 1920 'in the hope of "scrounging" a "pucca discharge"'.[54] A man called W.C. Dawes wrote to *John Bull* in January 1920 bemoaning the fact that ex-servicemen found themselves 'seriously handicapped' when applying for work if they had bad 'army characters'.[55] Summonsed to court for deserting not the army but his wife and four children, a letter from Harold Sheppard explained he was not entitled to the out-of-work donation but that, 'No one will give me work with that discharge of mine.' Sheppard had been court-martialled on several occasions, sentenced to two years' imprisonment for desertion and was eventually dishonourably discharged.[56] The War Office was aware of the problems soldiers with poor conduct records faced in civilian life. In 1921 the Army Council wrote to Commanding Officers asking that in most cases men should no longer be discharged for misconduct after serving sentences of detention, the effects of a discharge under these circumstances being 'much more serious than they ever were before the war'.[57]

Those who had never been discharged at all faced similar problems as employers still risked prosecution if they took on a worker without seeing the relevant certificate. Frank Lennard Walters deserted from the Royal Field Artillery in October 1919 after eight years' service. He had written to the War Office asking to be transferred to the reserve, or alternatively, to be allowed to buy himself out of the army but had received a reply in the negative. In 1921 he needed a discharge certificate to satisfy an employer and wrote to Jack Mills MP, who had a reputation as a soldiers' advocate, to ask for assistance. Mills asked for advice from the then Secretary of State for War, Laming Worthington-Evans, and sought royal intervention from the Duke of York. The replies were not encouraging. Mills wrote to Walters in May 1921:

I have done my best, but apparently the only thing to do (according to Worthington-Evans) is to give yourself up and allow the court martial to decide as they think fit. He <u>thinks</u> they will deal with it very leniently, but I <u>also</u> gather from him that there are thousands of similar cases to your own known as 'honourable' as distinct from the dregs of the army. It would be equally well to 'let sleeping dogs lie' . . .

Mills advised Walters to take his employer into his confidence and admit he was a deserter, telling him that if the man was 'an ordinary Britisher with an ordinary sense of justice' he would understand the position and see that Walters honestly believed he had done his bit. Gunner Walters took the view that he needed a firm resolution to the problem and surrendered himself in July 1921. Laming Worthington-Evans' prediction came true and Walters was sentenced to fifty-six days' detention, later reduced to five.[58]

Deserters continued to come out of the woodwork in the years following the Armistice. Some had been missing for quite some time and were arrested by chance, whilst some had been waiting in vain for the declaration of an amnesty and decided to face the music when one was not forthcoming. Walter Buchanan of the Royal Fusiliers was lucky to be at large at the time he was arrested in February 1920, as he had been sentenced to life imprisonment for desertion two years earlier. On promulgation this was commuted to fifteen years' penal servitude and this sentence was suspended in July 1918. Somehow Buchanan managed to successfully desert again soon afterwards and stay away for eighteen months. He was now sentenced to two years' imprisonment with hard labour.[59] David Sommerfield, a Russian by birth, walked into the Central Recruiting Station in London in his British Army uniform in August 1920 to give himself up. Sommerfield had not returned to his unit from leave in July 1918 and though he had remained undetected, it was claimed that he found the suspense of life on the run so stressful that he preferred to surrender and take the consequences.[60] Sommerfield was one of a number of London deserters represented by none other than J. Scott Duckers, conscientious objector, who was only free to ply his trade because the War Office had been refused permission to strike him off the solicitors' roll.[61] Duckers would write to newspapers nationwide in November 1921 to plead for an amnesty for men like Sommerfield and to demand that military law now apply only to 'the professional soldiers who have voluntarily accepted military obligations'.[62]

The Duckers letter was partly inspired by the story of Walter John Lewington. In 1921 Lewington walked into his mother's house in the small village of Cippenham, near Slough, six years after the family had last heard from him. Leading Stoker Lewington's story appeared in purple prose in newspapers nationwide. His mother told the press that the family had believed he was missing in action and had caused lengthy enquiries to be made as to his whereabouts over the years, to no avail. Lewington, a career sailor, was unclear about his movements during his six years away, apparently having lost his memory. Vague references were made to being gassed and blinded and to taking part in the Battle of Jutland. Lewington's name had been transcribed on two local war memorials, in Cippenham, and also in the village of Burnham, as the family had given up hope that he could still be alive. One newspaper claimed the story was, 'What must for the present stand as the most extraordinary case of a war "missing" man turning up'.[63] Within days the news broke that Lewington was actually a deserter who had walked away from his ship in October 1915, the year before the Battle of Jutland. Lewington claimed to have deserted the navy to join the army instead, though the details of this service are unclear. As for his inscriptions on the war memorials, it was reported in some quarters that black paint now covered his name. The Cippenham war memorial still carries the name of W. Lewington as a First World War casualty.[64]

By this time of Duckers' letter men were not needed in the military in the same numbers and deserters were, on application to the War Office, being issued with what were confusingly called Protecting Certificates – Army Form B129 – 'not to be confused with Protection Certificates', said a government document, rather unhelpfully![65] The certificates gave a person's description and name and confirmed that though he was a deserter he was not required back by the army so should not be arrested.[66] When a request for a Protecting Certificate was made by a deserter, a stern letter was sent by the War Office, pointing out that the applicant was an absentee and therefore liable to court-martial proceedings. He was invited to fill in a confession and questionnaire about the circumstances of his desertion in the hope that he would not be prosecuted. Thereafter, a Protecting Certificate could be issued if the War Office agreed: if not, the man remained at risk of arrest and return to the army. Applications were sent out on enquiries made by deserters about their general entitlements as well as after specific requests for Protecting Certificates.

Under successive Royal Warrants only those who had been discharged from the armed forces were eligible for pensions. Those in a state of desertion were not discharged, so were not eligible. The issue was considered at some length in the early 1920s as cases began to appear of men who had fraudulently enlisted having already deserted another regiment or branch of the military. The problem was that the condition for which they were now seeking disability pensions was acquired during this first period of service, from which they had never officially been discharged. Driver Robert Glynn, for example, was a Regular soldier in the Manchester Regiment, stationed in India, when war broke out. By the end of August 1914, he and his battalion were on the Western Front where Glynn received gunshot wounds to the head before deserting in May 1915. Five months later he decided to return to the fray but fraudulently enlisted in the Royal Engineers as Frederick Carter, a name under which he served until February 1917 when he was discharged as no longer fit for war service. He was now seeking a pension for the injury suffered with the Manchester Regiment. It was harsh on a man like Glynn who may have given sterling service in his second regiment to lose his pension due to actions in his first unit. As was common practice at the Ministry of Pensions, a blanket grant for these men would not be entertained, with the decision being made that each case must be decided on its own merits. Permission was granted from the Treasury for pensions to be paid should a man be deemed worthy. The seven-year time limit for making a claim for a pension would, for these men, run from the date they had deserted from their original corps. Claims were not to be entertained by men who had run off from the navy and had not been punished or issued with Protecting Certificates – these men were to be told to hand themselves in to the police or contact the Admiralty for a certificate if they wished to make a pension claim.[67]

Men in a state of desertion were not entitled to medals. Numerous pages of every regiment's medal rolls contain the names of men who were not going to receive their service medals, mostly men who had never faced a court martial for their desertion as they had never been arrested: 'deserted – still at large' was a frequent annotation to the register. One volume of the DLI medal rolls contains thirty-one pages of nothing but deserters: 'No medals' is handwritten next to every name.[68] Applying for medals would potentially expose a man to arrest if he were a deserter and most of the missing men from the DLI at least do not appear to have ever made such applications. By the time medals started to be distributed in 1920 many men had moved on from their wartime experiences and did not necessarily want reminders. Medals became available in pawn shops as the 1920s and 1930s rolled on, many ex-servicemen having fallen on hard times and seeing more value in a few pounds for their medals than the supposed glory of wearing them. Eventually in 1921 the Army Council decided that deserters could have medals if they made application and it was considered they were worthy.[69] It took some men years to have their medals returned and some were ultimately unsuccessful in their applications. Despite the 'honourable' nature of his desertion, Gunner Frank Walters did not get his medals until 1939.

Some deserters established new lives after the war in names they had taken to avoid detection, often moving to new areas of the country where their new identity would not be questioned. Others did not go to such lengths: Robert Binns returned to his family in Hull without ever suffering any penalty for his desertion. After the war was officially over even the army acknowledged that their systems were imperfect and that not all men appearing in the *Police Gazette* as deserters deserved the label. In July 1920 army record offices were instructed that no action was to be taken against men apparently in a state of desertion making enquiries about their pensions, medals and back pay without prior War Office approval.[70] John Robert Vokes, deserter from the DLI, cheekily wrote to the War Office in 1936 asking for his discharge paper and any back pay due to him. Vokes had been at large for seventeen years.[71]

Conclusion

Desertion and absenteeism on the home front is a much neglected topic. The only deserters who have been given any significant attention are either those felt to have a strong moral base in the form of a conscientious objection to war or those shot at dawn who are portrayed as potentially suffering from shell shock and not being fully in control of their own actions. Much less is heard about those who slipped away from the army, temporarily or permanently, because it just did not suit them at a particular time.

There is still a stigma attached to wartime desertion. Even a century later few families want to have their ancestor labelled as such. Where memoirs do mention desertion it is usually significantly downplayed. Edward Casey did write candidly about his misdemeanours whilst serving with the Royal Dublin Fusiliers, but it is worth noting that he did so from the other side of the world under a false name, more than fifty years after the event. Casey was living in New Zealand in 1980 when he sent his memoirs to the Imperial War Museum under the pseudonym J.W. Roworth.[1]

Where desertion is discussed by veterans it is often framed as something other than a rejection of one's military duties. The former miners speaking to Peter Liddle and his team of researchers in Sunderland in the 1980s were more forthcoming about walking away from the army but saw themselves as strikers not shirkers.[2] Denis Winter, in explaining why there was no mass protest against serving in the army, claims that the inbred deference of early twentieth-century British society was key. Winter states that lots of soldiers had been servants in civilian life and were therefore accustomed to following orders.[3] This deference is overstated. There were huge numbers of trade-union men in the armed forces and they did protest when conditions were deemed unacceptable. Demonstrations of disobedience took place on a large scale at various stages of the war from the early stages of training to the demobilization process. Sometimes this was a group action and sometimes it was an individual act. Deference was conditional: where an implied contract was breached, men withdrew their labour. David Silbey says that the working classes were more invested in the British state pre-war than they had been historically due to welfare reforms which had targeted their lives, making them more eager to defend it.[4] An examination of deserter's motives shows that when these welfare safety nets were not accessible, for example, where separation allowances were not being paid to a man's family, individuals were more likely to withdraw their consent to fighting for the state.

Men brought standard operating procedures from their civilian industrial experience to the military sphere. Striking, casual employment and rest days after over-indulgence in alcohol were all an established part of working life but were alien to the military machine and carried potentially serious consequences. Absenteeism was a phenomenon in home-front industries that was reflected in home-front soldiering. The speed with which civilian instincts reasserted themselves after the Armistice is an indication of their persistence within the ranks of citizen soldiers.

Desertion and absenteeism were part of a range of responses which could be termed as oppositional to the war itself. The number of men who failed to respond to their call-up under the Military Service Act is an indication of the lack of willingness amongst a significant portion of the general population to take part in this war. Like desertion, this opposition has been largely under reported. For some men desertion or disobedience was the defining act of their military service and they would suffer serious consequences as a result in the form of imprisonment or even execution. For many more desertion was simply one part of their experience, a momentary lapse or a pragmatic response to a sudden difficulty, the rest of their military career being unblemished. Cowardice was not necessarily a factor: deserters could become heroes and some heroes later became deserters.

Desertion was sometimes merely an expression of individuality in the face of the army's insistence on the importance of the collective. George Coppard said of his own minor indiscretion in overstaying his leave that he felt, 'I owed it to myself to do something in defiance of authority'.[5]

Desertion was a small strike against the monotony of the military machine, a brief holiday from routine. It was a tactic for a man to negotiate or manoeuvre his way through a war which was mostly beyond his immediate control and it was a tactic utilized by many thousands of men.

John Keegan wrote, 'It is a function of the impersonality of modern war that the soldier is coerced more continuously and more harshly by vast unlocalized forces against which he may rail, but at which he cannot strike back and to which he must ultimately submit . . .'.[6] This study has shown that there were many thousands who, perhaps just for a brief period, did strike back.

Notes

Introduction

1. *Statistics of the Military Effort of the British Empire during the Great War 1914–1920* (London: HMSO, 1922) (hereafter *SMEBEGW*), p. 643.
2. *General Annual Report on the British Army for the year ending 30th September 1913* (1914), 1914, pp. 72 and 76.
3. Analysis of statistics from *SMEBEGW*, pp. 642–72.
4. See Dr Kate Grady, 'Disciplinary Offences at the Court Martial' [2016], *Crim L.R.*, Issue 10.
5. *SMEBEGW*, p. 741.
6. Joanna Bourke, *Dismembering the Male – Men's Bodies, Britain and the Great War* (London: Reaktion Books, 1996), p. 148.
7. W.R. Scott and J. Cunnison, *The Industries of the Clyde Valley During the War* (Oxford: The Clarendon Press, 1924).
8. E.P. Thompson, *The Making of the English Working Class* (London: Pelican Books 1986 edn), pp. 397–8.
9. John Brophy and Eric Partridge, *The Long Trail – Soldiers' Songs & Slang 1914–18* (London: Sphere Books, 1969).
10. J. Scott Duckers, *Handed Over – the Prison Experiences of Mr J. Scott Duckers, Solicitor, of Chancery Lane, under the Military Service Act* (London: C.W. Daniel Ltd, 1917).
11. Brophy and Partridge, *The Long Trail*, p. 117.
12. *Manual of Military Law* (6th edn, War Office, 1914) (hereafter *MML*), p. 188.
13. Robert Roberts, *The Classic Slum – Salford Life in the First Quarter of the Century* (London: Penguin Books edition, 1973), p. 93.

Chapter 1: Desertion and the Transition to War – Amnesties and King's Bad Bargains

1. See Alan Ramsay Skelley, *The Victorian Army at Home* (London: Croom Helm, 1977).
2. Branding was abolished in 1871 and flogging followed in 1881.

3. See several editions of *General Annual Reports on the British Army*, presented to Parliament every year.
4. Army Act, Section 83.
5. *MML*, p. 189.
6. Figures from *General Annual Report on the British Army for the year ending 30th September 1898* (1899), p. 27 and *General Annual Report on the British Army for the year ending 30th September 1913* (1914), p. 68.
7. *MML*, pp. 18–20.
8. Army Act, Section 152.
9. *MML*, p. 32. These powers were not available to punish officers and NCOs.
10. King's Regulations, 548 (ii) and Army Act Part 1, Section 12, n. 13.
11. Army Act, Section 73 – Army Form A46 can be found in a man's service record when this step was taken.
12. *MML*, p. 38.
13. *SMEBEGW*, p. 643.
14. A.F. Duguid, *Official History of the Canadian Forces in the Great War 1914–1919 – From the Outbreak of War to the Formation of the Canadian Corps, August 1914 to September 1915*, Vol. 1, Part 1, p. 58 (Ottawa: King's Printer, 1938)
15. The German Army issued a similar proclamation but gave their deserters three months to return.
16. The National Archives (hereafter TNA), HO 45/10765/271874. Navy procedure was different and unless a man's name had been published in the *Police Gazette* as a deserter he was to be sent home to await further instructions.
17. *Hull Daily Mail*, 6 August 1914.
18. *Dover Express*, 7 August 1914, TNA ADM 159/156/14939.
19. *SMEBEGW*, p. 83.
20. *Western Mail*, 5 September 1914.
21. *Aberdeen Press & Journal*, 24 August 1914.
22. TNA, WO 363, Army Service Records of Archibald Fletcher. He re-enlisted after his discharge in June 1919 and became part of the Graves Registration Unit taking part in exhumations on the Western Front. He had a clean service record with both corps.
23. *Chelmsford Chronicle*, 14 August 1914, *Globe*, 8 August 1914.
24. Robert Blatchford, *My Life in the Army* (London: Clarion Press, 1910), p. 101.

25. *Evening World*, 17 March 1915, *New York Times*, 28 March 1915.
26. *Yorkshire Evening Post*, 11 August 1914.
27. See Andrea Hetherington, *British Widows of the First World War – The Forgotten Legion* (Barnsley: Pen & Sword, 2018) for more details on pensions and allowances.
28. *Sheffield Daily Telegraph*, 12 September 1914.
29. *Nottingham Evening Post*, 31 August 1914.

Chapter 2: Training Camp Troubles

1. *SMEBEGW*, p. 364.
2. See Rachel Duffett, *The Stomach for Fighting: Food and the Soldiers of the Great War* (Manchester: Manchester University Press, 2012).
3. Corelli Barnett, *Britain and Her Army 1509–1970: A Military, Political and Social Survey* (London: Allen Lane, 1970), pp. 378–9.
4. *SMEBEGW*, p. 654.
5. Michael Martin, Liddle Collection, LIDDLE/WW1/TR/05/21.
6. At the outbreak of war the existing barracks in the United Kingdom could house 174,800 men. *SMEBEGW*, p. 833.
7. *Bucks Herald*, 10 October 1914.
8. Michael Martin, Liddle Collection, LIDDLE/WW1/TR/05/21.
9. *Bucks Herald*, 17 October 1914.
10. Stuart Cloete, *A Victorian Son: An Autobiography* (London: Collins, 1972), pp. 200–1.
11. *Bucks Herald*, 31 October 1914.
12. Michael Martin, Liddle Collection, LIDDLE/WW1/TR/05/21
13. Nelson had already accrued two earlier convictions for desertion of a few days' duration, the second attracting a sentence of penal servitude for life which was subsequently remitted. TNA, WO 72/488.
14. Albert Williamson, Diary, 13 January 1915, Liddle Collection, LIDDLE/WW1/RNMN/316.
15. Robert Graves, *Goodbye to All That* (1929; London: Penguin Books, 1960 edn), pp. 73–4.
16. See Duffett, *The Stomach for Fighting*, p. 74.
17. Ian Beckett, 'The Nation in Arms, 1914 to 18', in Ian Beckett and Keith Simpson (eds), *A Nation in Arms: A Social Study of the British Army in the First World War* (Manchester: Manchester University Press, 1985).
18. *Liverpool Echo*, 4 December 1914.

19. *SMEBEGW*, p. 837.
20. Major T.J. Mitchell and Miss G.M. Smith, *Medical Services – Casualties and Medical Statistics of the Great War* (London: HMSO, 1931), pp. 99–101.
21. W.N. Nicholson, *Behind the Lines: An Account of Administrative Staffwork in the British Army, 1914–18* (London: Jonathan Cape, 1939), p. 51.
22. Hansard, HC, 22 March 1920, Vol. 127, c161-162.
23. George Coppard, *With a Machine Gun to Cambrai* (London: HMSO, 1969), p. 15.
24. TNA, HO 45/10765/271874, Letter from the War Office to Metropolitan Police Commissioner, 11 December 1914.
25. Army Council Instruction 1665 of 1917.
26. TNA, HO 45/10765/271874, Letter of 12 November 1917 to the Clerks to the Justices from Edward Troup,
27. Figures and quotes are from Home Office, Scotch Office and Irish Office circular addressed to Clerks to the Justices, dated 15 June 1898,
28. *John Bull*, 28 August 1915.
29. Douglas Massey, 'The Police Strike 1919', quoted in A.V. Sellwood, *Police Strike – 1919* (London: W.H. Allen, 1978), p. 17.
30. *Yorkshire Evening Post*, 18 July 1918.
31. Andrew Clark, *Echoes of the Great War: The Diary of the Reverend Andrew Clark 1914–1919*, diary entry of 4 February 1918 (Oxford: Oxford University Press, 1985), p. 227.
32. Ernest Thurtle, *Military Discipline and Democracy* (London: C.W. Daniel, 1920), p. 24.
33. Lord Moran, *The Anatomy of Courage* (London: Constable, 1945), p. 24.
34. *Ibid.*, p. 20.
35. TNA, HO 45/10765/271874, Letter from Edward Troup to Metropolitan Police Commissioner, 14 May 1915.
36. Army Order 108/1760 of 14 May 1915.
37. TNA, HO 45/10765/271874, Letter to the War Office from R. Peacock, 22 July 1915.
38. *SMEBEGW*, p. 642.

Chapter 3: The Restless, the Feckless and the Brave

1. E.N. Woodbury, 'Causes for Military Desertion – A Study in Criminal Motives', *Journal of Criminal Law and Criminology*, Vol. 12, Issue 2, Article 7, 1921.
2. Alan Thomas, *A Life Apart* (London: Victor Gollancz, 1968), p. 71.

3. *Report of the War Office Committee of Enquiry into 'Shell Shock'* (1922) (hereafter noted as the Southborough Committee).

4. J.C. Penton, 'Lessons from the Army for Penal Reformers', *Howard Journal of Criminal Justice*, Vol. 7, Issue 2, July 1947, pp. 81–5.

5. *Gloucestershire Echo, Globe*, 7 August 1915.

6. *Manchester Guardian*, 9 August 1915.

7. TNA, WO 339/6287.

8. IWM Sound Archive, Arthur John Bonney, 8226.

9. IWM Sound Archive, Horace Calvert, 9955.

10. *Daily Mirror, Leeds Mercury*, 20 September 1916. It should be noted that it was reported in some papers that Brooks had deserted because he felt badly treated in the Royal Welch, not solely to get to the Front more quickly.

11. TNA, WO 363, Army Service Records and *Rochdale Observer*, 10 July 1915.

12. Library & Archives Canada, (hereafter LAC) Canadian Expeditionary Force records, RG 150 [Online] [Accessed 10 October 2019], available at https://www.bac-lac.gc.ca/eng/discover/military-heritage/first-world-war/personnel-records/Pages/personnel-records.aspx.

13. *Western Mail*, 3 November 1914.

14. *SMEBEGW*, p. 83. This figure did not include any officers who may have deserted.

15. *Yorkshire Post*, for example, 15 October 1914.

16. Coppard, *With a Machine Gun to Cambrai*, p. 2.

17. *Sunday Mirror*, 14 March 1915.

18. *Northern Whig*, 25 March 1915.

19. *Birmingham Daily Post*, 20 October 1914.

20. *The Times*, 11 September 1918.

21. *John Bull*, 21 September 1918.

22. *Hull Daily Mail*, 29 June 1917, TNA, WO 363, Army Service Records of Charles John Thurston aka Charles John George, Naval Service Records of Charles John George, TNA, ADM 188/731/42053.

23. *Manchester Evening News*, 6 December 1915.

24. *Middlesex Chronicle*, 13 March 1915, *Pall Mall Gazette*, 22 February 1916.

25. *Rochdale Observer*, 24 July 1915, TNA, WO 363, Army Service Records of James Veevers.

26. *Daily Gazette for Middlesbrough*, 1 December 1914.

27. *Drogheda Independent*, 28 November 1914.

28. *Coal Mining Organisation Committee. Report of the Departmental Committee Appointed to Inquire into the Conditions Prevailing in the Coal Mining Industry Due to the War. Part 1 – Report* (1916), Vol. 28, p. 14.

29. *Shipbuilding, munitions and transport areas. Copy of 'report and statistics of bad time kept in shipbuilding, munitions and transport areas'* (1916), Vol. 55, paper 220, pp. 3 and 17.

30. Woodbury, 'Causes for Military Desertion'.

31. *Globe*, 4 March 1915.

32. *Thanet Advertiser* 4 October 1919.

33. *Sussex Agricultural Express*, 24 September 1915 and TNA, WO 86/67 – the sentence was later remitted to six months' detention.

34. *Birmingham Mail*, 2 January 1915, TNA, WO 86/63.

35. *Birmingham Mail*, 24 December 1914.

36. *Birmingham Daily Post*, 3 November 1914,

37. *Dundee Courier*, 8 December 1914.

38. *Dundee People's Journal*, 22 March 1915.

39. *Illustrated Police News*, 31 October 1918, *West Sussex Gazette*, 6 March 1919, TNA, WO 364, Piece 645.

40. *Birmingham Daily Post*, 3 November 1914.

41. Woodbury, 'Causes for Military Desertion'.

42. Hansard, HC deb, 15 December 1919, Vol. 123, c161-162.

43. The incident is recollected in the diaries of his friend James Campbell, Liddle Collection, LIDDLE/WW1/GS/0262 and Army Service Records of Andrew Hardie at TNA, WO 363. Hardie was merely reprimanded for his mistake.

44. Richard van Emden (ed.), *Last Man Standing – The Memoirs of a Seaforth Highlander During the Great War* (Barnsley: Pen & Sword, 2012, Kindle edn), Chapter Four – The King's Commission, para 14.

45. K.W. Mitchison, *Gentlemen and Officers – The Impact and Experience of War on a Territorial Regiment 1914–1918* (London: Imperial War Museum, 1995). See Peter Simkins, *Kitchener's Army – The Raising of Britain's New Army 1914–1916* (Manchester: Manchester University Press, 1988) for further examples.

46. *Northampton Chronicle and Echo*, 4 January 1915.

47. *Sheffield Daily Telegraph*, 2 January 1917.

48. *Sheffield Independent*, 17 May 1915.

49. *Sheffield Evening Telegraph*, 2 June 1915, TNA, WO 86/65.

50. *Western Daily Press*, 29 June 1917.

51. *Western Mail*, 20 May 1916.

52. *Sheffield Daily Telegraph*, 16 September 1914.
53. *Dundee Evening Telegraph*, 31 August 1915.
54. Guy Chapman, *A Passionate Prodigality: Fragments of an Autobiography* (2nd edn, London: MacGibbon & Kee, 1965), p. 84.
55. Moran, *The Anatomy of Courage*, p. 55.
56. John Baynes, *Morale – A Study of Men and Courage: The Second Scottish Rifles at the Battle of Neuve Chapelle, 1915* (London: Leo Cooper, 1987).
57. See Richard van Emden, *Boy Soldiers of the Great War* (London: Bloomsbury, 2012, rev. edn) for an examination of this phenomenon.
58. *Shepton Mallet Journal*, 20 August 1915.
59. *Northampton Chronicle and Echo,* 12 October 1915.
60. *Burnley News*, 26 December 1914.
61. TNA, WO 363, Army Service Records of Joseph Onslow.
62. *Aberdeen Evening Express*, 4 July 1917, TNA, WO 363, Army Service Records of A.J. Mewse.
63. See TNA, MEPO 2/1743, TNA, HO 45/10891/3356508.
64. See Alison S. Fell, *Women as Veterans in Britain and France After the First World War* (Cambridge: Cambridge University Press, 2018) for more on the status of the WAAC.
65. *Sheffield Daily Telegraph*, 23 February 1918.
66. *Hull Daily Mail*, 11 May 1918 and TNA, WO 398/197/28, WAAC Service Records of Mary Jane Savage.
67. *Women's Dreadnought*, 21 December 1918.
68. *Leeds Mercury*, 9 December 1918.
69. *Manchester Evening News*, 9 February 1915.
70. *Coventry Evening Telegraph*, 1 October 1915.
71. *Beverley and East Riding Recorder*, 14 October 1916.
72. *Manchester Evening News*, 10 September 1914.
73. *Manchester Evening News*, 18 September 1916.
74. *Norwood News*, 16 February 1917, TNA, WO 363, Army Service Record of Thomas Weeden.
75. *Chester Chronicle*, 28 October 1916, TNA, WO 97, Pension Index Card, *Lancashire Evening Post*, 25 May 1921.
76. *Derry Journal*, 3 July 1918.
77. *Liverpool Echo*, 18 July 1916, *Dover Express*, 29 October 1915, 4 August 1916, TNA, WO 363, Army Service Records of William Mason.
78. *Nottingham Journal*, 10 June 1916, *Globe*, 3 March 1916, *Manchester Evening News*, 9 June 1916, *Birmingham Daily Post*, 10 June 1916,

Manchester Guardian, Dundee Evening Telegraph, 15 June 1916, *Hendon &
Finchley Times*, 16 June 1916.

79. *Pall Mall Gazette*, 7 March 1917, *Hull Daily Mail*, 31 March 1917.
80. See Lois S. Bibbings, *Telling Tales About Men – Conceptions of Conscientious
    Objectors to Military Service* (Manchester: Manchester University Press,
    2011) and Cyril Pearce, *Communities of Resistance: Patterns of Dissent in
    Britain, 1914–1919* (London: Francis Boutle, 2020).
81. F.P. Crozier, *The Men I Killed* (London: Michael Joscph, 1938; Kindle
    edn, London: Lume Books, 2016), pp. 32 and 97.
82. Max Plowman, *A Subaltern on the Somme* (London: Dent, 1927, Kindle edn).
83. Moran, *The Anatomy of Courage*, p. 189.
84. Hansard, HC deb, 15 December 1919, Vol. 123, cols 168–9.
85. *Manchester Evening News*, 29 March 1915.
86. *Leeds Mercury*, 20 September 1916.
87. *Birmingham Mail*, 24 December 1914.
88. *Manchester Courier and Lancashire General Advertiser*, 6 October 1915.
89. TNA, WO 364, British Army Pension Records of Thomas Alfred Jones.
90. See Carruthers' service records at LAC Canadian Expeditionary Force
    records, RG 150 [Online] [Accessed 9 August 2020], available at https://
    www.bac-lac.gc.ca/eng/discover/military-heritage/first-world-war/
    personnel-records/Pages/personnel-records.aspx.
91. *John Bull*, 9 February 1918.
92. *John Bull*, 22 June 1918.
93. F.A. Voigt, *Combed Out* (London: Swarthmore Press, 1920), p. 8.

Chapter 4: Arrested in Britain, Shot at Dawn

1. Hansard, HC deb, 19 February 1925, Vol. 180, c8.
2. Hansard, HC deb, 17 February 1925, Vol. 180, c33.
3. Julian Putkowski and Julian Sykes, *Shot at Dawn – Executions in World
   War One by Authority of the British Army Act* (London: Leo Cooper, 1993,
   5th imp.).
4. TNA, WO 93/49. This does not accord with the breakdown of the
   fourteen prepared by the Judge Advocate General in February 1925,
   but an investigation of each individual case file gives the numbers I have
   outlined.
5. This total includes civilians under army discipline like the Chinese
   Labour Corps, *SMEBEGW*, pp. 648 and 649.

6. See Crozier, *The Men I Killed* (Kindle edn), p. 30, Anthony Babington, *For the Sake of Example – Capital Courts Martial 1914–1918* (London: Paladin Books, 1985).

7. Gerard Oram, *Worthless Men – Race, Eugenics and the Death Penalty in the British Army during the First World War* (London: Frances Boutle, 1998), p. 27.

8. See for example the recollections of Philip Brocklesby, Liddle Collection, LIDDLE/WW1/GS/0201.

9. Chapman, *A Passionate Prodigality*.

10. Babington, *For the Sake of Example*.

11. See TNA, WO 93/49 and also A.P. Herbert, *The Secret Battle* (London: Methuen, 1919). It is worth pointing out that this is not an attitude specific to this time and place – the majority of people arrested in England and Wales for criminal offences forgo their right to free legal advice at the police station.

12. TNA, WO 71/653, Arthur Briggs.

13. *MML*, p. 50.

14. TNA, WO 71/405, J. Duncan.

15. TNA, WO71/459, J.E. Bolton.

16. TNA, WO 71/474, James Swaine.

17. Stephen Graham, *A Private in the Guards* (London: Heinemann, 1919), pp. 154–5.

18. TNA, WO 71/459, J.E. Bolton.

19. Huntly Gordon, *The Unreturning Army* (London: Bantam Books, 2015), pp. 136 and 148.

20. Both the quotation from Sir John French and the statistics are from an interview with Major General Sir Wyndham Childs that appeared in newspapers nationwide on 28 November 1918.

21. Brocklesby, Liddle Collection, LIDDLE/WW1/GS/0201.

22. *Ibid.*

23. This statistic only pertains to soldiers, *SMEBEGW*, p. 649.

24. TNA, WO 71/459, J.E. Bolton, WO 71/409, William Jones. Though serving under the name William Jones, there is evidence to suggest that this was an alias and the man's real name was Morgan Morgans – see Soldiers' Effects Records, 1901–60, National Army Museum, Chelsea, London, England.

25. TNA, WO 71/668, Daniel Gibson.

26. Of sixty-seven death penalty cases selected at random by the Judge Advocate General in a review in February 1925, twenty-four soldiers were arrested at Channel ports, TNA, WO 93/49.

27. The loss of travel papers was not infrequently cited by deserters as an excuse when they appeared in the civilian courts. Army officials present always gave the excuse short shrift claiming that men could easily obtain new tickets.

28. TNA, WO 71/432, Peter Sands.

29. Oram, *Worthless Men*, p. 59.

30. Babington, *For the Sake of Example*, p. 24.

31. TNA, WO 71/421, William Turpie.

32. *Western Mail*, 13 March 1915. Private Llewellyn would eventually receive eighty-four days' detention for the two months he was missing.

33. All figures aggregated from *SMEBEGW*, pp. 642–72.

34. TNA, WO 71/459, J.E. Bolton, TNA, WO 71/ 463, William Watts, WO 71/421, William Turpie.

35. TNA, WO 71/477, Griffith Lewis and John Jennings.

36. Graham, *A Private in the Guards*, p. 129.

37. TNA, WO 71/463, William Watts, WO 71/668, Daniel Gibson, WO 71/653, Arthur Briggs.

38. Graham, *A Private in the Guards*, p. 154.

39. TNA, WO 71/554, William Anderson, WO 71/539, John Lewis.

40. *Folkestone Express, Sandgate, Shorncliffe & Hythe Advertiser*, 9 December 1916.

41. TNA, WO 71/539, John Lewis.

42. Previous accounts of the story of these two seem to believe that both were home runners and were arrested together in Barking but an examination of the files now available shows this to be untrue – TNA, WO 71/539 and WO 71/554 in addition to Anderson's service record under WO 363 and newspaper reports of the time reveal the full story.

43. TNA, WO 71/421, WIliam Turpie.

44. Both quotes from TNA, WO 71/480, George Hunter.

45. TNA, WO 71/458, Charles Bladen.

46. TNA, WO 71/463, William Watts.

47. See Ben Shephard, *A War of Nerves* (London: Jonathan Cape, 2000) for a comprehensive examination of this subject.

48. Southborough Committee.

49. Moran, *The Anatomy of Courage*, p. 184.

50. *Taunton Courier, and Western Advertiser*, 20 February 1918.
51. *Burnley Express*, 13 August 1919.
52. *Yorkshire Evening Post*, 24 October 1919.
53. *Western Times*, 24 December 1915.
54. *Dover Express*, 11 January 1918.
55. Duckers, *Handed Over*, p. 51.
56. *Police Gazette*, 2 May 1916.
57. See Robert Graves' description of the punishment of Private Probert for failing to volunteer for overseas service, Graves, *Goodbye to All That*, pp. 77–8.
58. Mitchison, *Gentlemen and Officers*.
59. Army Service Records of Charles Ship, TNA, WO 363.
60. *Pall Mall Gazette*, 26 February 1917, *West London Observer*, 2 March 1917.
61. TNA, WO 213/16 .
62. *The National Roll of the Great War* (London: Nat. Pub. Co., 1920) [Online] [Accessed 23 November 2020], available at http://www.ancestry.co.uk.
63. A.B. Godefroy, *For Freedom and Honour? The Story of the 25 Canadian Volunteers Executed in the Great War* (Nepean, Ontario: CEF Books, 1998), p. 39.
64. For a full account of the Shot at Dawn campaign, see Janet Booth and James White, *He Was No Coward – the Harry Farr Story* (2017).
65. TNA, CAB 23-37-24.
66. Moran, *The Anatomy of Courage*, pp. 187–8.

Chapter 5: Safe Harbour

1. *Manchester Evening News*, 13 October 1915 amongst many other reports mentioning James Veevers.
2. Roberts, *The Classic Slum*, pp. 189–90.
3. *Liverpool Echo*, 19 November 1915.
4. *Birmingham Daily Post*, 14 December 1915.
5. *Gloucester Journal*, 16 February 1918.
6. *Sheffield Evening Telegraph*, 23 December 1915.
7. *The Justice of the Peace*, 17 February 1917.
8. Ken Weller, *Don't Be A Soldier – The Radical Anti-war Movement in North London 1914–1918* (London: London History Workshop, 1985).
9. Roberts, *The Classic Slum*, p. 100.

10. Woodbury, 'Causes for Military Desertion'.
11. Mary S. Allen OBE, *The Pioneer Policewoman* (London: Chatto & Windus, 1925), p. 35.
12. *Montrose, Arbroath and Brechin Review* and *Forfar and Kincardineshire Advertiser*, 12 February 1915.
13. *History of the Provost Branch at Home during the war. 'E' Area, Northern Command, HQ Sheffield*, Per John Maclaren, Liddle Collection LIDDLE/WW1/GA/POM/4.
14. *SMEBEGW*, pp. 77–85.
15. *Edinburgh Evening News*, 31 August 1915.
16. *Manchester Courier and Lancashire General Advertiser*, 29 September 1915.
17. *Manchester Evening News*, 19 October 1915.
18. *Portadown News*, 13 November 1915.
19. *Sheffield Evening Telegraph*, 23 December 1915.
20. TNA, WO 32/11664.
21. *The Justice of the Peace*, issues of 4 and 18 September 1915, 5 and 19 August 1916, 3 March and 21 April 1917.
22. Justices of the Peace Act 1361.
23. *The Justice of the Peace*, 17 February 1917.
24. *The Justice of the Peace*, 30 June 1917 edn, for example.
25. *Portadown News*, 29 January 1916.
26. *Leeds Mercury*, 21 April 1915.
27. *Sunderland Daily Echo & Shipping Gazette*, 29 July 1916.
28. *Belfast Newsletter*, 24 July 1915.
29. *Dundee People's Journal*, 31 July 1915.
30. *Whitstable Times and Hearn Bay Herald*, 15 December 1917.
31. LAC, Court Martial Records, RG150 – Ministry of the Overseas Military Forces of Canada, Series 8, File 649-N-4728, Microfilm Reel Number T-8673, Finding Aid Number 150-5 & Canadian Service Records [Online] [Accessed 10 October 2019], available at https://www.bac-lac.gc.ca/eng/discover/military-heritage/first-world-war/personnel-records/Pages/personnel-records.aspx.
32. *Manchester Evening News*, 22 November 1915.
33. Various papers, 3 June 1915.
34. *Sunderland Echo & Shipping News*, 26 October 1917.
35. *Hartlepool Northern Daily Mail*, 26 November 1915.
36. *Newcastle Journal*, 15 December 1917.
37. *Essex Newsman*, 3 February 1917.
38. *North Devon Journal*, 11 July 1918.

39. IWM Sound Archive, Clara Christina Thorpe, 9924.
40. *Kilkenny Moderator*, 1 March 1919.
41. *John Bull*, 26 February 1916.
42. *Birmingham Daily Post*, 20 October 1914.
43. Evidence given by Sir Charles Harris on 22 April 1920 before the Public Accounts Committee, *First, second, third and fourth reports from the Committee of Public Accounts, together with the proceedings of the committee, minutes of evidence and appendices* (1920), p. 100.
44. *Judicial Statistics England and Wales 1917 Part 1 – Criminal Statistics. Statistics Relating to Criminal Proceedings, Police, Coroners, Prisons, Reformatory and Industrial Schools, and Criminal Lunatics, for the Year 1917* (1919), p. 15.
45. *Manchester Courier and Lancashire General Advertiser*, 29 September 1915.
46. *Belfast Newsletter*, 22 and 23 July 1915.
47. *Liverpool Echo*, 10 November 1915.
48. *Yorkshire Evening Post*, 7 September 1916.
49. *Gloucester Journal*, 27 January 1917.
50. *Globe*, 30 August 1915.
51. *Framlingham Weekly News*, 17 March 1917.
52. *Aberdeen Evening Express*, 7 March 1918.
53. *Daily Record*, 7 January 1918 and various other papers.
54. *Leeds Mercury*, 21 April 1915.

Chapter 6: Alternative Employment

1. Weller, *Don't Be a Soldier*.
2. *Police Gazette*, 11 January 1916. For the 9 January 1917 edition, 1,245 men were listed as deserters, 217 of them noted as labourers.
3. 'The War and Hop Picking', *Birmingham Daily Post*, 15 September 1914.
4. *Whitstable Times and Herne Bay Herald*, 5 September 1914, Army Service Records of Stephen Burnett and William Vincent, TNA, WO 363 .
5. Plowman, *Subaltern on the Somme*, 'Court Martial', paragraphs 6 and 7.
6. Clark, *Echoes of the Great War*, p. 211.
7. Thompson, *The Making of the English Working Class*, p. 394.
8. TNA, WO 364/2116.
9. *Shipbuilding, munitions and transport areas. Copy of 'report and statistics of bad time kept in shipbuilding, munitions and transport areas'* (1916), Vol. 55, paper 220, p. 17.
10. *Hartlepool Daily Mail*, 26 November 1915.
11. *Yarmouth Independent*, 27 April 1918.
12. *Liverpool Daily Post*, 6 September 1917.

13. Ninety deserters were identified as miners in both the 11 January 1916 and 9 January 1917 editions of the *Police Gazette.*

14. TNA, WO 86/65, Judge Advocate General's Office: District Courts Martial Registers, Home and Abroad, Register of Charges: Home and Abroad (1915), *Newcastle Evening Chronicle*, 5 July 1915.

15. *Sheffield Daily Telegraph*, 26 August 1917.

16. *Liverpool Echo*, 22 March 1915.

17. *Illustrated Police News*, 21 June 1917.

18. Harry McShane and Joan Smith, *No Mean Fighter* (London: Pluto Press, 1978), pp. 69–70.

19. *Sheffield Daily Telegraph*, 19 March 1918. Piddock blamed his crimes on shell shock suffered with the Worcester Regiment.

20. *Defence of the Realm Manual* (London: HMSO, 1918).

21. *Oxfordshire Weekly News*, 17 October 1917, TNA, WO 363.

22. *Liverpool Daily Post*, 27 September 1916.

23. *Leeds Mercury*, 2 September 1918.

24. *People*, 25 August 1918.

25. *The Times*, 29 August 1918.

26. Guards regiments had always been prolific in this area. Joe Ackerley in his memoir *My Father and Myself* (London: Penguin Books, 1971) wrote that whilst he was sexually attracted to Guards, his own father had almost certainly engaged in homosexual prostitution during his Guards career, enjoying the patronage of a wealthy benefactor for years.

27. Joanna Bourke (ed.), *The Misfit Soldier – Edward Casey's War Story 1914–1918* (Cork: Cork University Press, 1999) – the original memoir is at the Imperial War Musuem, 80/40/01 under the name of John William Roworth.

28. *MML*, p. 97.

29. *SMEBEGW*, pp. 651–4.

30. *The Times*, 24 April 1917.

31. *Birmingham Daily Post* 24 April 1917.

32. TNA, WO 92/3 and WO 339/8867.

33. See Matt Houlbrook, 'Soldier Heroes and Rent Boys', *Journal of British Studies*, Vol. 42, No. 3 (2003). Working class men generally were seen as being exploited, a key theme of both the Dublin Castle Scandal and also the Cleveland Street Scandal of 1889. See Jeffrey Weeks, 'Inverts, Perverts and Mary-Annes: Male Prostitution and the Regulation of Homosexuality in England in the Nineteenth and Early Twentieth Centuries', in Martin

P. Duberman, Martha Vicinus and George Chauncey (eds), *Hidden from History: Reclaiming the Gay & Lesbian Past* (London: Penguin Books, 1989).

34. *Dundee Evening Telegraph*, 27 August 1918.
35. *The Times*, 28 August 1918, *People*, 1 September 1918 and 3 November 1918
36. *Pall Mall Gazette*, 6 September 1918. For a full account of the Billing Case see Philip Hoare, *Wilde's Last Stand: Scandal, Decadence and Conspiracy During the Great War* (London: Duckworth Books, 2011).

Chapter 7: Scamps in Khaki

1. *MML*, p. 61.
2. *Judicial Statistics, England and Wales, 1914. Part I. – Criminal Statistics. Statistics Relating to Criminal Proceedings, Police, Coroners, Prisons, Reformatory and Industrial Schools, and Criminal Lunatics, for the Year 1914* (1916), Volume Page: LXXXII.347, Volume: 82, 1914–16.
3. Robert Holmes *My Police Court Friends With the Colours* (Edinburgh and London: William Blackwood & Sons, 1915).
4. *Report of the Commissioners of Prisons and the Directors of Convict Prisons, with Appendices for the Year Ended 31st March, 1915* (1916), Volume Page: XXXIII.1, Volume: 33, 1914–16.
5. Denis Winter, *Death's Men – Soldiers of the Great War* (London: Penguin Books, 1979), p. 35. TNA, WO 97 series for Herbert Warrant.
6. *The Justice of the Peace*, 18 March 1916.
7. George Orwell, *The Road to Wigan Pier* (London: Victor Gollancz, 1937).
8. Coppard, *With a Machine Gun to Cambrai*, p. 7.
9. Dr Herman Mannheim, *Social Aspects of Crime in England Between the Wars* (London: George Allen & Unwin Ltd, 1940).
10. *Police Gazette*, 16 September and 27 October 1916, *Western Gazette*, 27 October 1916.
11. *Cambridge Independent Press*, 2 April 1915.
12. *People*, 6 September 1914.
13. *Belfast News Letter*, 23 January 1915.
14. *Manchester Guardian*, 13 April 1915.
15. *South Wales Gazette*, 11 June 1915.
16. *Yarmouth Independent*, 10 October 1914.
17. *Manchester Evening News*, 31 August 1915.
18. *Edinburgh Evening News*, 6 August 1915.

19. *Leeds Mercury*, 22 June 1915. Fred Norman would carry out similar offences in November 1915.
20. *Western Mail*, 15 April 1916
21. *Western Gazette*, 31 May 1918.
22. *Globe*, 28 January 1918.
23. *Nottingham Journal*, 19 October 1915.
24. *John Bull*, 29 January 1916.
25. TNA, WO 32/5476.
26. *Dublin Daily Express*, 7 July 1917.
27. *Hull Daily Mail*, 5 September 1917, *Aberdeen Evening Express*, 5 September 1917, *Manchester Guardian*, 5 September 1917, TNA, WO 329; Ref: 765, *Exeter & Plymouth Gazette*, 4 February 1927.
28. *Daily Mirror*, 29 January 1918, *Portsmouth Evening News*, 29 December 1920, TNA, WO86/80 & 86/68, 12 February 1916.
29. Babington, *For the Sake of Example*, p. 143.
30. *Edinburgh Evening News*, 30 October 1914.
31. *Sheffield Evening Telegraph*, 18 February 1915.
32. *Todmorden Advertiser and Hebden Bridge Newsletter*, 15 October 1915.
33. *Sunderland Daily Echo and Shipping Gazette*, 5 February 1915.
34. *Scotsman*, 9 April 1915.
35. *Manchester Evening News*, 15 December 1914.
36. See, for example, the diary of N.A. Turner-Smith, Liddle Collection, LIDDLE/WW1/GS/1640, and Cloete, *A Victorian Son*, p. 201.
37. *Globe*, 12 September 1915, *Police Gazette*, 8 February 1918.
38. *Luton Times and Advertiser*, 14 January 1916.
39. *Nottingham Journal*, 30 August 1915, *Manchester Courier and Lancashire General Advertiser*, 8 September 1915, *Illustrated Police News*, 14 February 1918, *Police Gazette*, 26 February 1918.
40. *Globe*, 23 June 1915.
41. *Sheffield Daily Telegraph*, 14 January 1914, N.A. Turner-Smith, Liddle Collection, LIDDLE/WW1/GS/1640, TNA WO 339/43203.
42. *Daily Record*, 3 March 1915.
43. *Sunday Post*, 12 September 1915, *Birmingham Daily Gazette*, 13 September 1915.
44. *Manchester Evening News*, 18 August and 18 November 1915.
45. *Pall Mall Gazette*, 28 April 1919.
46. TNA, PCOM 8/338, CRIM 1/15016, WO 364/2082.
47. *Liverpool Echo*, 19 April 1917.

48. *Pall Mall Gazette*, 27 November 1917.
49. *Yorkshire Evening Post*, 17 August 1918, 21 August 1918, *Leeds Mercury*, 23 August 1918, *Birmingham Daily Post* and others, 30 December 1918.

Chapter 8: Conscription – The Net Tightens

1. Major General Sir W.G. Macpherson, *History of the Great War Based on Official Documents, Medical Services General History Vol. 1* (London: HMSO, 1921), p. 126.
2. *Report on Recruiting by the Earl of Derby, K.G., Director General of Recruiting* (1916), pp. 5–7.
3. David Lloyd George, *War Memoirs of David Lloyd George* (London: Odhams Press, 1938), p. 438.
4. Army Council Instruction 336 of 1916, TNA, WO 106/371.
5. *Police Gazette*, 2 May 1916, pp. 14–22.
6. Army Council Instruction 467 of 1916, TNA, WO/106/371.
7. Army Council Instruction 752 of 1916, TNA, WO/106/371
8. *The Justice of the Peace*, 3 October 1914.
9. Military Service Act 1916 (session 2), Ch. 15.
10. *John Bull*, 15 January and 12 February 1916.
11. See Pearce, *Communities of Resistance*.
12. Weller, *Don't Be A Soldier*.
13. TNA, MH 47/3/1, p. 12.
14. *Yorkshire Evening Post & Leeds Intelligencer*, 21 February 1916, *Leeds Mercury*, 14 March 1916.
15. TNA, CAB 23/4/31.
16. *Manchester Guardian*, 15 February 1917.
17. TNA, MH 47/3/1, p. 12.
18. TNA, CAB 23/4/31.
19. This was a scheme introduced to help the army solve the problem of punishing men who continually refused to follow orders on the grounds of conscientious objection. If, after interview with the Central Tribunal, the man was felt to hold genuine beliefs he would be offered work of national importance and removed from the direct control of the army.
20. *SMEBEGW*, p. 673.
21. Pearce, *Communities of Resistance*.
22. *Ibid.* and Sheila Rowbotham, *Friends of Alice Wheeldon* (London: Pluto Press, 2015.).
23. *Sheffield Daily Telegraph*, 28 September 1918

24. *Surrey Advertiser*, 10 February 1917.
25. McShane and Smith, *No Mean Fighter*, pp. 69–70.
26. M.I. Lipman, *Memoirs of a Socialist Business Man* (London: Lipman Trust, 1980).
27. *Yorkshire Post & Leeds Intelligencer*, 24 July 1918.
28. TNA, MH 47/3/1.
29. 29 June 1916 as reported in TNA, MH 47/3/1.
30. *Leeds Mercury*, 31 May 1918, *Liverpool Daily Post*, 2 August 1918.
31. *Yorkshire Post & Leeds Intelligencer*, 18 May 1918.
32. *People*, 6 May 1917.
33. TNA, CAB 23/4/31.
34. Cyril Pearce, *Comrades in Conscience: The Story of an English Community's Opposition to the Great War* (London: Francis Boutle, 2001).
35. TNA, WO 106/371.
36. *Yorkshire Post & Leeds Intelligencer*, 5 September 1916.
37. *John Bull*, 23 September 1916.
38. Weller, *Don't Be a Soldier*, p. 50.
39. *Luton Reporter*, 27 August 1918.
40. *Yorkshire Post & Leeds Intelligencer*, 5 September 1916, *Yorkshire Evening Post*, 8 September 1916.
41. *Birmingham Mail*, 30 March 1917.
42. TNA KV 1/2,7/1.
43. *The Times*, 9 July 1917.
44. Macpherson, *Medical Services*, p. 128.
45. *The Times*, 31 May 1917, *Globe*, 19 October 1917, *Westminster Gazette*, 26 October 1917, *Birmingham Mail*, 31 October 1917.
46. *Manchester Evening News*, 23 June 1917.
47. Macpherson, *Medical Services*, p. 118.
48. *Ibid.*, p. 119.
49. See Hetherington, *British Widows of the First World War*, for examples.
50. TNA, WO 363, Army Service Records of William Henry Wadsworth and Sydney Addleman.
51. TNA, WO 363, Army Service Records of Gustavus Streeton.
52. *John Bull*, 6 January 1917.
53. *John Bull*, 17 March 1917.
54. *Leeds Mercury*, 14 September 1916.
55. *Leeds Mercury*, 3 October 1916.
56. TNA, NATS 1/934.

57. *Yorkshire Evening Post*, 18 September 1916.
58. Clark, *Echoes of the Great War*, pp. 60–1.
59. *John Bull*, 18 November 1916.
60. *Burnley News*, 28 July 1917.
61. *Yorkshire Evening Post*, 25 July 1917, *Craven Herald*, 27 July 1917.
62. *Craven Herald*, 3 August 1917.
63. *Craven Herald*, 13 July 1917.
64. *Craven Herald*, 5 October 1917.
65. *Craven Herald*, 12 October 1917, *Leeds Mercury*, 29 October 1917.
66. *Burnley News*, 24 August 1918.
67. Willey may have had mixed feelings about taking on such cases: his own son had been killed on the Somme in July 1916. Nevertheless, Willey's professionalism saw him represent a number of applicants for exemptions and also those charged with assisting deserters.
68. *Yorkshire Evening Post*, 5 September 1918. Though the man is not named in the newspaper reports, it is noteworthy that Cowling had a grocer's shop called Emmott's into the 1930s.
69. *Leeds Mercury*, 30 December 1918.
70. *Beverley & East Riding Recorder*, 9 September 1916.
71. All figures and the quote are from *Manchester Guardian*, 19 August 1918.
72. *Manchester Guardian*, 31 August 1918.
73. *Manchester Guardian*, 27 August 1918.
74. McPherson, Hansard, HC deb, 25 May 1917, Vol. 94, cc.2639-2640.
75. Hansard, HC deb, 11 June 1917, Vol. 94 cc581-3 and HC deb, 13 June 1917, Vol. *94 c935*.
76. *Yorkshire Evening Post*, 7 May 1918.
77. NATS 1/1029.
78. *SMEBEGW*, pp. 83–5.
79. *Ibid.*, p. 367.

Chapter 9: Irish Issues

1. *Liverpool Echo*, 8 November 1915.
2. *Dundee People's Journal*, 13 November 1915.
3. Some newspapers inflated the numbers of Irishmen seeking to board the *Saxonia*. Scottish titles seeming to be particularly prone to this, the *Dundee People's Journal* and the *Daily Record* turning the 600 into 900 whilst the 200 *California* emigrants were now 400.

4. Hansard, HC deb, 4 November, 1915, Vol. 75, c811.

5. TNA, CAB 37-137-11, memorandum dated 9 November 1915.

6. A point made by William O'Malley, MP for Galway and Connemara, in the subsequent discussions in Parliament about the *Saxonia* incident – see *Dublin Daily Express*, 11 November 1915.

7. *Liverpool Daily Post*, 8 November 1915.

8. Thomas P. Dooley, *Irishmen or English Soldiers? The Times and World of a Southern Catholic Irish Man (1876-1916) Enlisting in the British Army During the First World War* (Liverpool: Liverpool University Press, 1995), p. 40.

9. A number of sources described the vocal opposition to the rebels as consisting largely of 'separation women' – see Keith Jeffery, *Ireland and the Great War* (Cambridge: Cambridge University Press, 2000). See also Charles Townshend, *Easter 1916 – The Irish Rebellion* (London: Allen Lane, 2005).

10. Bourke (ed.), *The Misfit Soldier*.

11. Dooley, *Irishmen or English Soldiers?*.

12. Peter Karsten, 'Irish Soldiers in the British Army, 1792–1922: Suborned or Subordinate?', *Journal of Social History*, Vol. 17, No. 1 (Autumn 1983), pp. 31–64.

13. *Dublin Daily Express*, 16 May 1916.

14. TNA, WO 213/8.

15. *Northern Whig*, 22 January 1916.

16. TNA, CO 904/214/080.

17. *Derry Journal*, 12 September 1919.

18. *Waterford Standard*, 13 February 1918, [Online] [Accessed 28 October 2019], available at https://www.bureauofmilitaryhistory.ie., witness statement of James Fraher 1232.

19. *Belfast Newsletter, Northern Whig*, 21 February 1918.

20. www.bureauofmilitaryhistory.ie, statement of Alf Monahan 298 [Accessed 29 October 2019].

21. TNA, WO 339/64747.

22. *Derry Journal*, 5 November 1915.

23. *Belfast Newsletter*, 31 May 1917.

24. *Dublin Daily Express, Irish Independent*, 25 November 1916.

25. *Dublin Daily Express*, 28 July 1915 and *Ballymena Weekly Telegraph*, 31 July 1915.

26. *Derry Journal*, 25 February 1918 and 4 March 1918, *Northern Whig*, 18 January 1918, TNA, WO 86/81, www.bureauofmilitaryhistory.ie, statement of Patrick Breslin 1448 [Accessed 29 October 2019].

27. Arthur Horner, *Incorrigible Rebel* (London: MacGibbon & Kee, 1960).

28. *Belfast Newsletter*, 30 March 1916, *Larne Times*, 1 April 1916. Israel Sanofski and Jack Yaffin were the other casualties capable of verification, Moses Harris also died – see records at http://www.cwgc.org [Accessed 23 November 2020].

29. *Pall Mall Gazette*, 21 September 1918.

30. TNA, NATS 1/935.

31. TNA, NATS 1/958.

32. *Freeman's Journal*, 9 September 1916.

33. Commons sitting of Monday, 14 August 1916 reported in *The Times*, 15 August 1916.

34. *Londonderry Sentinel*, 24 August 1916, *Derry Journal*, 1 September 1916.

35. *Londonderry Sentinel*, 19 September 1916.

36. *Northampton Mercury*, 15 September 1916.

37. *Weekly Freeman's Journal*, 28 October 1916.

38. *The Times*, 15 May 1916.

39. *John Bull*, 22 September 1917.

40. *Linlithgowshire Gazette*, 10 November 1916.

41. *Motherwell Times*, 18 August 1916, Hansard, HC deb, Vol. 85 cc1397-1399, 14 August 1916.

42. *Irish Independent*, 1 September 1916.

43. Letter of 19 October 1916 to Inspector Underwood of Scotland Yard – TNA, HO 144/1456/313106.

44. *Liverpool Echo*, 28 November 1920.

45. *Dublin Evening Telegraph*, 9 September 1920.

46. *Liverpool Echo*, 2 November 1916, Service Records, TNA, WO 364, piece 2005.

47. See Adrian Gregory, '"You might as well recruit Germans": British public opinion and the decision to conscript the Irish in 1918', in Adrian Gregory and Senie Paseta (eds), *Ireland the Great War – 'A War to Unite Us All?'* (Manchester: Manchester University Press, 2002).

48. *Yorkshire Evening Post*, 7 May 1918.

49. *John Bull*, 25 January 1919.

50. TNA, NATS 1/909.

Chapter 10: Wild Colonial Boys

1. *SMEBEGW*, pp. 758—9 and 771.
2. Sandra Gywn, *Tapestry of War – a Private View of Canadians in the Great War* (Toronto: HarperCollins, 1992), p. 86, also Duguid, *Official History of the Canadian Forces*, Vol. 1, Part 1, pp. 49–50.
3. See Joy Parr, *Labouring Children – British Immigrant Apprentices to Canada 1869–1924* (London: Croom Helm, 1980).
4. Duguid, *Official History of the Canadian Forces*, Vol. 1, Part 1, p. 73.
5. *Western Daily Press*, 28 November 1914.
6. LAC, Canadian Expeditionary Force Personnel Files, RG150 [Online] [Accessed 10 October 2019], available at https://www.bac-lac.gc.ca/eng/discover/military-heritage/first-world-war/personnel-records/Pages/personnel-records.aspx.
7. Duguid, *Official History of the Canadian Forces*, Vol. 1, Part 1, p. 134.
8. *Gloucestershire Echo*, 6 November 1914.
9. Colonel G.W.L. Nicholson, *Official History of the Canadian Army in the First World War, Canadian Expeditionary Force 1914–1919* (Ottowa: Roger Duhamel, Queen's Printer and Controller of Stationery, 1962), p. 36.
10. *Gloucestershire Chronicle*, 14 November 1914.
11. *The Times*, 28 November 1914 and 2 December 1914.
12. Gwyn, p115
13. See Nicholson, *Official History of the Canadian Army*, p. 36.
14. Duguid, *Official History of the Canadian Forces*, Vol. 1, Part 2, p. 136.
15. TNA, WO 32/11401.
16. Nicholson, *Official History of the Canadian Army*, p. 38.
17. Duguid, *Official History of the Canadian Forces*, Vol. 1, Part 2, pp. 141–3.
18. LAC, CEF Personnel Files, Reference: RG 150, [Online] [Accessed 20 October 2019], available at https://www.bac-lac.gc.ca/eng/discover/military-heritage/first-world-war/personnel-records/Pages/personel-records.aspx.
19. Duguid, *Official History of the Canadian Forces*, Vol. 1, Part 1, p. 132.
20. David Campbell, 'Military Discipline, Punishment and Leadership in the First World War: the Case of the 2nd Canadian Division', in Craig Leslie Mantle (ed.), *The Apathetic and the Defiant – Case Studies of Canadian Mutiny and Disobedience 1812–1919* (Ottawa: Canadian Defence Academy Press, 2007).
21. LAC, RG150 – Ministry of the Overseas Military Forces of Canada, Series 8, File 649-B-39464, Microfilm Reel Number T-8661 &; CEF

Personnel Files Reference – RG 150; Volume: Box 754 – 34 [Online] [Accessed 21 October 2019], available at https://www.bac-lac.gc.ca/eng/discover/military-heritage/first-world-war/personnel-records/Pages/personel-records.aspx.

22. Christopher Pugsley, *On the Fringe of Hell – New Zealanders and Military Discipline in the First World War* (Auckland: Hodder & Stoughton, 1991), p. 28.

23. Figures quoted in unpublished thesis by Glen Wahlert, 'Provost: Friend or Foe?: The Development of an Australian Provost Service 1914–1945', MA, University of New South Wales, 1996.

24. Michael McKernan, *The Australian People and the Great War* (Melbourne: Thomas Nelson Australia, 1980), p. 117.

25. *John Bull*, 10 February 1917 – see also McKernan, *The Australian People and the Great War* and also E.M. Andrews, *The Anzac Illusion: Anglo-Australian Relations During World War I* (Cambridge: Cambridge University Press, 1993), p. 186.

26. Andrews, *The Anzac Illusion*, p. 105.

27. Figures quoted in Wahlert, 'Provost: Friend or Foe?' from Australian War Memorial (hereafter AWM), 25 1013/15.

28. Pugsley, *On the Fringe of Hell*, p. 153.

29. NAA B2455, Personnel Dossiers for First Australian Imperial Force Ex-Service Members, Crooks, T.R. [Online] [Accessed 3 March 2020], available at https://recordsearch.naa.gov.au.

30. Figures from General History of the AIF Detention Barracks, Lewes, AWM, 25 1013/14, quoted in Wahlert, 'Provost: Friend or Foe?'.

31. R. Blake (ed.), *The Private Papers of Douglas Haig* (London: Eyre & Spottiswoode, 1952), p. 291.

32. Christopher Pugsley, *The ANZAC Experience – New Zealand, Australia and Empire in the First World War* (Auckland: Reed Publishing, 2004).

33. Pugsley, *On the Fringe of Hell*, p. 138.

34. Peter Stanley, *Bad Characters – Sex, Crime, Mutiny, Murder and the Australian Imperial Force* (Miller's Point, New South Wales: Pier 9 Murdoch Books, 2010), p. 23.

35. Wahlert, 'Provost: Friend or Foe?', p. 16.

36. Pugsley, *The ANZAC Experience*.

37. See for example McKernan, *The Australian People and the Great War*, p. 116.

38. *Ibid.*, p. 129.

39. Arnold Rose discovered in his survey of US servicemen in Italy in 1943 that the fact a man was of Italian extraction was given as a specific reason for going absent. Arnold M. Rose, 'The Social Psychology of Desertion from Combat', *American Sociological Review*, Vol. 16, No. 5 (October 1951).

40. National Archives Australia (hereafter NAA), B2455, Personnel Dossiers for First Australian Imperial Force Ex-Service Members, Plant, Henry Homer [Online] [Accessed 3 March 2020], available at https://recordsearch.naa.gov.au. *Derbyshire Advertiser and Journal*, 18 January 1918.

41. Pugsley, *On the Fringe of Hell*, p. 153.

42. AWM, 25 1013/15, Annex D, quoted in Wahlert, 'Provost: Friend or Foe?'.

43. *The Times*, 6 February 1918, *Police Gazette*, 29 January 1918, NAA, B2455, Personnel Dossiers for First Australian Imperial Force Ex-Service Members, Kendall, Oscar F. [Online] [Accessed 3 March 2020], available at https://recordsearch.naa.gov.au.

44. NAA, B2455, Personnel Dossiers for First Australian Imperial Force Ex-Service Members, Davies, Ralph C. [Online] [Accessed 3 August 2020], available at https://recordsearch.naa.gov.au, 1911 UK Census from Ancestry.co.uk, *Diss Express*, 1 February 1918

45. *Yorkshire Post*, 18 May 1917.

46. *Londonderry Sentinel*, 7 July 1917.

47. NAA, B2455, Personnel Dossiers for First Australian Imperial Force Ex-Service Members, Hart, H.L. [Online] [Accessed 3 March 2020], available at https://recordsearch.naa.gov.au. *Police Gazette*, 7 September 1917, *Eastbourne Gazette*, 12 September 1917.

48. *Globe*, 23 and 30 September 1915, *Western Mail*, 1 October 1915.

49. LAC, RG150 – Ministry of the Overseas Military Forces of Canada, Series 8, File 649-B-2735, Microfilm Reel Number T-8652, Finding Aid Number 150-5 [Online] [Accessed 22 October 2019], available at https://www.bac-lac.gc.ca/eng/discover/military-heritage/first-world-war/personnel-records/Pages/personel-records.aspx.

50. LAC, RG150 – Ministry of the Overseas Military Forces of Canada, Series 8, File 857-8-4-18, Microfilm Reel Number T-8695, Finding Aid Number 150-5 [Online] [Accessed 22 October 2019], available at https://www.bac-lac.gc.ca/eng/discover/military-heritage/first-world-war/personnel-records/Pages/personel-records.aspx.

51. *Leeds Mercury*, 5 January 1918.

52. *Dundee Evening Telegraph*, 23 January 1917.
53. *Report of the Ministry Overseas Military Forces of Canada 1918* (Canada: Ministry of Overseas Forces of Canada, 1919), p. 502.
54. Allen, *The Pioneer Policewoman*, p. 94.
55. *Dover Express*, 23 July 1915.
56. Louie Stride, *Memoirs of a Street Urchin* (Bath: Bath University Press, 1984).
57. *Bath Chronicle and Weekly Gazette*, 16 August 1919.
58. *Surrey Advertiser*, 19 October 1918.
59. *Surrey Advertiser*, 16 April 1917. See Hetherington, *British Widows of the First World War* for more on Aileen Queenie Passmore and the forfeiture of pensions generally, Hutton's service records, LAC, CEF Personnel Records, RG 150 – Accession 1992-93/166, Box 4670 – 48, Court Martial Records RG150 – Ministry of the Overseas Military Forces of Canada, Series 8, File 649-L-23158, Microfilm Reel Number T-8676, Finding Aid Number 150-5 [Online] [Accessed 22 October 2019], available at https://www.bac-lac.gc.ca/eng/discover/military-heritage/first-world-war/personnel-records/Pages/personnel-records.aspx.
60. *Aberdeen Press and Journal*, 28 May 1919, LAC, Ottawa, Ontario, Canada, CEF Personnel Files; Reference: RG 150; Volume: Box 5961–55, Court Martial Proceedings (1916) T8672 0 649 – M- 1740 [Online] [Accessed 22 October 2019], available at https://www.bac-lac.gc.ca/eng/discover/military-heritage/first-world-war/personnel-records/Pages/personel-records.aspx.
61. TNA, RG 48/275, Letter dated 3 May 1918 to General Register Office.
62. *Judicial Statistics for England & Wales 1919, Part 1 – Criminal Statistics. Statistics Relating to Criminal Proceedings, Police, Coroners, Prisons, Reformatory and Industrial Schools, and Criminal Lunatics, for the Year 1919* (1921).
63. NAA, B2455, Personnel Dossiers for First Australian Imperial Force Ex-Service Members, Thomas, R. [Online] [Accessed 3 August 2020], available at https://recordsearch.naa.gov.au.
64. Fred Pitt's service records are at LAC CEF, RG 150 – Accession 1992-93/166, Box 7854 – 50 and Court Martial Records – RG150 – Ministry of the Overseas Military Forces of Canada, Series 8, File 649-P-27, Microfilm Reel Number T-8676, Finding Aid Number 150-5 and RG150 [Online] [Accessed 10 February 2019], available at https://www.bac-lac.gc.ca/eng/discover/military-heritage/first-world-war/personnel-records/Pages/personel-records.aspx, while the Imperial Order of the Daughters of the Empire citation is from www.gatheringourheroes.ca [Accessed 12 April 2019].

65. *The Times*, 9 October 1917.
66. *Chelsea News and General Advertiser*, 6 September 1918.
67. Allen, *The Pioneer Policewoman*, p. 94.
68. See for example, *The Times*, 24 February 1917.
69. TNA, MEPO 21/10108.
70. LAC, RG150 – Ministry of the Overseas Military Forces of Canada, Series 8, File 602-23-228, Microfilm Reel Number T-8694, Finding Aid Number 150-5 & Service Records RG 150 – Accession 1992-93/166, Box 10254–40 [Online] [Accessed 22 October 2019], available at https://www.bac-lac.gc.ca/eng/discover/military-heritage/first-world-war/personnel-records/Pages/personnel-records.aspx.
71. Hansard, HC deb, 11 June 1917, Vol. 94, cc581-3.
72. *Pall Mall Gazette*, 21 September 1918, *Sunday Mirror*, 13 October 1918 and 27 October 1918, *Globe*, 26 October 1918.
73. *SMEBEGW*, p. 29.
74. Figures from Nicholson, *Official History of the Canadian Army*, p. 532.
75. TNA, CAB 23-8-23, Cabinet Meeting of 14 November 1918.
76. Stanley, *Bad Characters*, pp. 115–16.
77. Pugsley, *On the Fringe of Hell*, p. 289.
78. *Sydney Morning Herald*, 2 December 1919.
79. *Birmingham Daily Gazette*, 11 December 1918 and NAA, B2455, Personnel Dossiers for First Australian Imperial Force Ex-Service Members, Ernest F. Buck [Online] [Accessed 3 August 2020], available at https://recordsearch.naa.gov.au.
80. *Western Times*, 16 January 1918 and NAA, B2455, NAA, B2455, Personnel Dossiers for First Australian Imperial Force Ex-Service Members, Sharp, E. and Maguire, T. [Online] [Accessed 3 August 2020], available at https://recordsearch.naa.gov.au.
81. *The Times*, 21 March 1918, *Gloucestershire Echo*, 6 March 1918, LAC, CEF 150 [Online] [Accessed 9 February 2019], available at https://www.bac-lac.gc.ca/eng/discover/military-heritage/first-world-war/personnel-records/Pages/personnel-records.aspx, TNA, CRIM 1/17411.
82. *Dundee Evening Telegraph*, 11 February 1920, 5 May 1920, 3 June 1920, *Falkirk Herald*, 8 May 1920.
83. *Dundee Courier*, 27 May 1920, NAA, B2455, NAA, B2455, Personnel Dossiers for First Australian Imperial Force Ex-Service Members, Fraser, A.J. [Online] [Accessed 3 August 2020], available at https://recordsearch.naa.gov.au.

Chapter 11: After the War – Amnesties and Bad Army Characters

1. *Shields Daily News*, 19 December 1918.
2. *SMEBEGW*, p. 385.
3. Horner, *Incorrigible Rebel*, pp. 34–5.
4. Andrew Rothstein, *The Soldiers' Strikes of 1919* (London: Macmillan Press Ltd, 1980).
5. *SMEBEGW*, p. 385.
6. TNA, WO 106/329. See *SMEBEGW*, p. 85.
7. Recorded by the Northern Command, York in TNA, AIR 1/553.
8. Ministry of Labour, *Eighteenth Abstract of Labour Statistics of the United Kingdom* (1926).
9. Aaron Smith, Liddle Collection, LIDDLE/WW1/GS/1490.
10. Anthony Carew, *The Lower Deck of the Royal Navy 1900–1939 – The Invergordon Mutiny in Perspective* (Manchester: Manchester University Press, 1981).
11. See *Daily Herald*, 28 November 1919 for a sample of letters from the marines involved.
12. Arthur Marwick, *The Deluge – British Society and the First World War* (London: Macmillan, 1965), p. 271.
13. TNA, WO32/5480.
14. Letter of 3 June 1919, TNA, WO 32/5476.
15. This article appeared in newspapers all over the country on 28 November 1918.
16. *John Bull*, 29 May 1920.
17. Hansard, HC deb, 15 April 1920, Vol. 127, c1987.
18. TNA, WO 32/5476, Memo of 19 November 1918.
19. TNA, WO 363, Army Service Records of James Emmott.
20. TNA, WO 32/5480, AWM, 27/363. This was not the whole truth, as a wholesale review of all sentences imposed on Australian offenders by courts martial was taking place from July 1919 onwards and an amnesty had been put in motion for all who had committed military offences only. The men may have been returned to Australia under armed guard, but the vast majority would be released and discharged from the army once they arrived there.
21. TNA, WO 32/5480.
22. *SMEBEGW*, p. 654.
23. *Report of the Commissioners of Prisons and the Directors of Convict Prisons for the Year 1918–1919* (1919).

24. TNA, CAB 23/37/24.
25. Hansard, HC deb, 22 March 1920, Vol. 127, c177-179.
26. It is worth noting that a similar amnesty was granted by Queen Elizabeth II when she was crowned in 1953.
27. TNA, CAB 23-9-24 – 26 February 1919.
28. Lord Cave – Secretary of State for Home Affairs – C.O. memo of 16 November 1918 in TNA, CAB 24/70/18.
29. *Yorkshire Evening Post*, 10 March 1919.
30. *Manchester Guardian*, 29 September 1919.
31. *John Bull*, 31 May 1919.
32. *Dundee Courier, Birmingham Gazette, Yorkshire Post & Leeds Intelligencer, Daily Herald*, 10 May 1919. A writer from the *Daily Herald* had some soldiers' letters taken from his house by the police, only to have them all returned the next day.
33. *SMEBEGW*, pp. 83–5.
34. *Daily Herald*, 29 November 1919.
35. Army Act, Section 158(1), quoted in *MML*, p. 35.
36. TNA, HO 45/24698, *The Times*, 13 May 1920.
37. TNA, WO 363, Service Records of George Vincent Hearne.
38. See Hansard, HC deb, 14 November 1918, Vol. 110, c75, *Yorkshire Evening Post*, 6 February 1919.
39. *Yorkshire Evening Post*, 30 April 1919, *Leeds Mercury*, 1 January 1920.
40. *John Bull*, 9 October 1920.
41. Section 9 Representation of the People Act 1918.
42. TNA, T 268/12 is Frank Nixon's personnel file covering the war years. His brother's conscientious objector stance is not mentioned.
43. *Yorkshire Evening Post*, 7 April 1919.
44. *The Times*, 15 April 1919.
45. *Dundee People's Journal*, 19 April 1919.
46. *Manchester Guardian*, 24 April 1919.
47. *Daily Herald*, 26 June 1919.
48. *Wicklow Newsletter and County Advertiser*, 14 December 1918, TNA, WO 86/ 86. Judge Advocate General's Office: District Courts Martial Registers, Home and Abroad
49. Hansard, HC deb, 30 June 1920, Vol. 131, c446.
50. *The Times*, 15 May 1919.
51. *Northampton Mercury*, 29 August 1919.
52. *Manchester Guardian*, 13 October 1919.

53. *Northern Whig*, 10 April 1919.
54. *Dundee Evening Telegraph*, 14 April 1920.
55. *John Bull*, 3 January 1920.
56. *Nottingham Journal*, 9 January 1920.
57. TNA, PIN 15/145, Letter from H.J. Greedy on behalf of the Army Council, 29 November 1921.
58. Frank Lennard Walters, Liddle Collection, LIDDLE/WW1/GS/1681.
59. TNA, WO 86/ 89, Judge Advocate General's Office: District Courts Martial Registers, Home and Abroad, WO 213/23, Judge Advocate General's Office: Field General Courts Martial and Military Courts, Registers.
60. *Western Daily Press*, 4 August 1920.
61. TNA, HO 45/10808/311118.
62. *Derby Daily Telegraph* and many others, 8 November 1921.
63. *Aberdeen Press & Journal*, 31 October 1921.
64. TNA, ADM 188, Registers of Services 1853–1924, *Lancashire Evening Post*, *Hull Daily Mail*, 31 October 1921, *Aberdeen Press & Journal*, 2 November 1921, *Rutland Daily Herald* (Vermont), 29 December 1921.
65. TNA, PIN 15/145.
66. The procedure had begun with aliens in Britain to prevent them from being arrested unnecessarily once hostilities were officially over and was thereafter extended to deserters.
67. TNA, PIN 15/145.
68. TNA, WO 329, Piece 1630, Durham Light Infantry.
69. Army Council Instruction 75 of 1921.
70. Letter of 28 July 1920, TNA, PIN 15/145.
71. TNA, WO 363, Army Service Records of John Robert Vokes.

Conclusion

1. Bourke (ed.), *The Misfit Soldier*.
2. Michael Martin, Liddle Collection, LIDDLE/WW1/TR/05/21
3. Winter, *Death's Men*, p. 230.
4. David Silbey, *The British Working Class and Enthusiasm for War, 1914–16* (London: Frank Cass, 2004).
5. Coppard, *With a Machine Gun to Cambrai*, p. 15.
6. John Keegan, *The Face of Battle* (London: Cape, 1976), p. 325.

Bibliography

Books

Ackerley, Joe, *My Father and Myself* (London: Penguin Books, 1971)

Allen, Mary S., OBE, *The Pioneer Policewoman* (London: Chatto & Windus, 1925)

Andrews, E.M., *The Anzac Illusion: Anglo-Australian Relations During World War I* (Cambridge: Cambridge University Press, 1993)

Babington, Anthony, *For the Sake of Example – Capital Courts Martial 1914–1918* (London: Paladin, 1985)

Barnett, Corelli, *Britain and Her Army 1509–1970: A Military, Political and Social Survey* (London: Allen Lane, 1970)

Baynes, John, *Morale – A Study of Men and Courage: The Second Scottish Rifles at the Battle of Neuve Chapelle, 1915* (London: Leo Cooper, 1987)

Beckett, Ian and Keith Simpson (eds), *A Nation in Arms: A Social Study of the British Army in the First World War* (Manchester: Manchester University Press, 1985)

Bet-el, Ilana R., *Conscripts – Forgotten Men of the Great War* (Stroud: The History Press, 1999)

Bibbings, Lois S., *Telling Tales About Men – Conceptions of Conscientious Objectors to Military Service* (Manchester: Manchester University Press, 2011)

Blake, R. (ed.), *The Private Papers of Douglas Haig* (London: Eyre & Spottiswoode, 1952)

Blatchford, Robert, *My Life in the Army* (London: Clarion Press, 1910)

Booth, Janet and James White, *He Was No Coward – the Harry Farr Story* (self-published, 2017)

Boulton, David, *Objection Overruled* (London: MacGibbon & Kee, 1967)

Bourke, Joanna, *Dismembering the Male – Men's Bodies, Britain and the Great War* (London: Reaktion Books, 1996)

Bourke, Joanna (ed.), *The Misfit Soldier – Edward Casey's War Story 1914–1918* (Cork: Cork University Press, 1999)

Braybon, Gail (ed.), *Evidence, History and the Great War – Historians and the Impact of 1914–18* (Oxford: Berghahn Books, 2003)

Brophy, John and Eric Partridge, *The Long Trail – Soldiers' Songs & Slang 1914–18* (London: Sphere Books, 1969)

Bush, Julia, *Behind the Lines – East London Labour 1914–1919* (London: Merlin Press, 1984)

Carew, Anthony, *The Lower Deck of the Royal Navy 1900–1939 – the Invergordon Mutiny in Perspective* (Manchester: Manchester University Press, 1981)

Chapman, Guy, *A Passionate Prodigality: Fragments of an Autobiography* (2nd edn, London: MacGibbon & Kee, 1965)

Clark, Andrew, *Echoes of the Great War: The Diary of the Reverend Andrew Clark 1914–1919* (Oxford: Oxford University Press, 1985)

Cloete, Stuart, *A Victorian Son: An Autobiography* (London: Collins, 1972)

Coppard, George, *With a Machine Gun to Cambrai* (London: HMSO, 1969)

Corns, Cathryn and John Hughes-Wilson, *Blindfold and Alone – British Military Executions in the Great War* (London: Cassell, 2001)

Crozier, F.P., *The Men I Killed* (London: Michael Joseph, 1938; Kindle edn, Lume Books, 2016)

Dallas, Gloden and Douglas Gill, *The Unknown Army – Mutinies in the British Army in World War 1* (London: Verso, 1985)

Dooley, Thomas P., *Irishmen or English Soldiers? The Times and World of a Southern Catholic Irish Man (1876–1916) Enlisting in the British Army During the First World War* (Liverpool: Liverpool University Press, 1995)

Duberman, Martin P., Martha Vicinus and George Chauncey (eds), *Hidden from History: Reclaiming the Gay & Lesbian Past* (London: Penguin Books, 1989)

Duckers, J. Scott, *Handed Over – the Prison Experiences of Mr J. Scott Duckers, Solicitor, of Chancery Lane, under the Military Service Act* (London: C.W. Daniel Ltd, 1917)

Duffett, Rachel, *The Stomach for Fighting: Food and the Soldiers of the Great War* (Manchester: Manchester University Press, 2012)

Duguid, Colonel A.F., *Official History of the Canadian Forces in the Great War 1914–1919 – From the Outbreak of War to the Formation of the Canadian Corps, August 1914 to September 1915, Vol. 1, Part 1* (Ottowa: King's Printer, 1938)

Ebenezer, Lynn, *Fron-goch and the Birth of the IRA* (Llanwrst: Gwasg Carreg Gwalch, 2006)

Emsley, Clive, *Soldier, Sailor, Beggarman, Thief – Crime and the British Armed Services Since 1914* (Oxford: Oxford University Press, 2013)

Farwell, Byron, *For Queen and Country – a Social History of the Victorian and Edwardian Army* (London: Allen Lane, 1981)

Feilding, Rowland, *War Letters to a Wife* (London: Medici Society, 1929)

Fell, Alison S., *Women as Veterans in Britain and France After the First World War* (Cambridge: Cambridge University Press, 2018)

Godefroy, A.B., *For Freedom and Honour? The Story of the 25 Canadian Volunteers Executed in the Great War* (Nepean, Ontario: CEF Books, 1998)

Gordon, Huntly, *The Unreturning Army* (London: Bantam Books, 2015)

Graham, Stephen, *A Private in the Guards* (London: Heinemann, 1919)

Graves, Robert. *Goodbye to All That* (1929; London: Penguin Books, 1960edn)

Gregory, Adrian and Senie Paseta (eds), *Ireland the Great War – 'A War to Unite Us All?'* (Manchester: Manchester University Press, 2002)

Gywn, Sandra, *Tapestry of War – A Private View of Canadians in the Great War* (Toronto: HarperCollins, 1992)

Hannam-Clark, T., *Some Experiences of a Court-Martial Officer* (Gloucester: Crypt House Press, 1932)

Herbert, A.P., *The Secret Battle* (London: Methuen, 1919)

Hetherington, Andrea, *British Widows of the First World War – The Forgotten Legion* (Barnsley: Pen & Sword, 2018)

Hoare, Philip, *Wilde's Last Stand: Scandal, Decadence and Conspiracy During the Great War* (London: Duckworth Books, 2011)

Holmes, Robert, *My Police Court Friends With the Colours* (Edinburgh and London: William Blackwood & Sons, 1915)

Hopkinson, Michael (ed.), *Frank Henderson's Easter Rising – Recollections of a Dublin Volunteer* (Cork: Cork University Press, 1998)

Horner, Arthur, *Incorrigible Rebel* (London: MacGibbon & Kee, 1960)

Jeffery, Keith, *Ireland and the Great War* (Cambridge: Cambridge University Press, 2000)

Keegan, John, *The Face of Battle* (London: Cape, 1976)

Lipman, M.I., *Memoirs of a Socialist Businessman* (London: Lipman Trust, 1980)

Lloyd George, David, *War Memoirs of Lloyd George* (London: Odhams Press, 1938)

Lock, Joan, *The British Policewoman – Her Story* (London: Robert Hale, 1979)

McKernan Michael, *The Australian People and the Great War* (Melbourne: Thomas Nelson Australia, 1980)

McShane, Harry and Joan Smith, *No Mean Fighter* (London: Pluto Press, 1978)

Mannheim, Dr Herman, *Social Aspects of Crime in England Between the Wars* (London: George Allen & Unwin Ltd, 1940)

Mantle, Craig Leslie (ed.), *The Apathetic and the Defiant – Case Studies of Canadian Mutiny and Disobedience 1812–1919* (Ottawa: Canadian Defence Academy Press, 2007)

Martin, Bernard, *Poor Bloody Infantry – A Subaltern on the Western Front 1916–17* (London: John Murray, 1987)

Marwick, Arthur, *The Deluge – British Society and the First World War* (London: Macmillan, 1965)

Meacham, Standish, *A Life Apart – The English Working Class 1890–1914* (London: Thames & Hudson, 1977)

Messenger, Charles, *Call to Arms – The British Army 1914–1918* (London: Cassell, 2006)

Mitchison, K.W., *Gentlemen and Officers – The Impact and Experience of War on a Territorial Regiment 1914–1918* (London: Imperial War Museum, 1995)

Moore, William, *The Thin Yellow Line* (London: Leo Cooper, 1974)

Moran, Lord, *The Anatomy of Courage* (London: Constable, 1945)

Morton, Desmond and J.L. Granatstein, *Marching to Armageddon: Canadians and the Great War 1914–1919* (Toronto: Lester and Orpen Derrys Ltd, 1989)

Nicholson, Colonel G.W.L., *Official History of the Canadian Army in the First World War, Canadian Expeditionary Force 1914–1919* (Ottawa: Roger Duhamel, Queen's Printer and Controller of Stationery, 1962)

Nicholson, W.N., *Behind the Lines: An Account of Administrative Staffwork in the British Army, 1914–18* (London: Jonathan Cape, 1939)

Oram, Gerard, *Worthless Men – Race, Eugenics and the Death Penalty in the British Army during the First World War* (London: Frances Boutle, 1998)

Orwell, George, *The Road to Wigan Pier* (London: Victor Gollancz, 1937)

Pankhurst, E. Sylvia, *The Home Front* (London: Cresset, 1932)

Parr, Joy, *Labouring Children – British Immigrant Apprentices to Canada 1869–1924* (London: Croom Helm, 1980)

Pearce, Cyril, *Comrades in Conscience: The Story of an English Community's Opposition to the Great War* (London: Francis Boutle, 2001)

Pearce, Cyril, *Communities of Resistance: Patterns of Dissent in Britain, 1914–1919* (London: Francis Boutle, 2020)

Pearson, Geoffrey, *Hooligan – A History of Respectable Fears* (London: Macmillan, 1983)

Plowman, Max, *A Subaltern on the Somme* (London: Dent, 1927, Kindle edn)

Pugsley, Christopher, *On the Fringe of Hell – New Zealanders and Military Discipline in the First World War* (Auckland: Hodder & Stoughton, 1991)

Pugsley, Christopher, *The ANZAC Experience – New Zealand, Australia and Empire in the First World War* (Auckland: Reed Publishing, 2004)

Putkowski, Julian, *British Army Mutineers 1914–1922* (London: Francis Boutle, 1998)

Putkowski, Julian and Julian Sykes, *Shot at Dawn – Executions in World War One by Authority of the British Army Act* (London: Leo Cooper, 1993, 5th imp.)

Read, Daphne (ed.), *The Great War and Canadian Society* (Toronto: New Hogtown Press, 1978)

Reid, Fiona, *Broken Men: Shell Shock, Treatment and Recovery in Britain 1914–1930* (London: Continuum, 2010)

Richards, Frank, *Old Soldiers Never Die* (London: Faber & Faber, 1964 edn)

Roberts, Maria, *Absolutely Unfit to Remain: Gay Sex and the Army in the First World War* (London: FeedaRead.com Publishing, 2016)

Roberts, Robert, *The Classic Slum – Salford Life in the First Quarter of the Century* (London: Penguin Books, 1973)

Robinson, Field Marshall Sir William, *From Private to Field Marshall* (London: Constable, 1921)

Rothstein, Andrew, *The Soldiers' Strikes of 1919* (London: Macmillan Press Ltd, 1980)

Rowbotham, Sheila, *Friends of Alice Wheeldon* (London: Pluto Press, 2015)

Scott, W.R. and J. Cunnison, *The Industries of the Clyde Valley During the War* (Oxford: The Clarendon Press, 1924)

Sellwood, A.V., *Police Strike – 1919* (London: W.H. Allen, 1978)

Senior, Michael, *The Soldier's Peace: Demobilizing the British Army 1919* (Barnsley: Pen & Sword, 2018)

Shephard, Ben, *A War of Nerves* (London: Jonathan Cape, 2000)

Silbey, David, *The British Working Class and Enthusiasm for War, 1914–16* (London: Frank Cass, 2004)

Simkins, Peter, *Kitchener's Army – The Raising of Britain's New Army 1914–1916* (Manchester: Manchester University Press, 1988)

Skelley, Alan Ramsay, *The Victorian Army at Home* (London: Croom Helm, 1977)

Spencer, John C., *Crime and the Services* (London: Routledge & Kegan Paul Ltd, 1954)

Stanley, Peter, *Bad Characters – Sex, Crime, Mutiny, Murder and the Australian Imperial Force* (Miller's Point, New South Wales: Pier 9, Murdoch Books, 2010)

Stride, Louie, *Memoirs of a Street Urchin* (Bath: Bath University Press, 1984)

Jonathan Swan, *Law & War: Magistrates in the Great War* (Barnsley: Pen & Sword, 2017)

Thomas, Alan, *A Life Apart* (London: Victor Gollancz, 1968)

Thompson, E.P., *The Making of the English Working Class* (London: Pelican Books, 1986 edn)

Thurtle, Ernest, *Military Discipline and Democracy* (London: C.W. Daniel, 1920)

Townshend, Charles, *Easter 1916 – The Irish Rebellion* (London: Allen Lane, 2005)

Van Emden, Richard, *Boy Soldiers of the Great War* (London: Bloomsbury, 2012 edn)

Van Emden, Richard (ed.), *Last Man Standing – The Memoirs of a Seaforth Highlander During the Great War* (Barnsley: Pen & Sword 2012, Kindle edn)

Voigt, F.A., *Combed Out* (London: Swarthmore Press, 1920)

Watcyn-Williams, Morgan, *From Khaki to Cloth* (Cardiff: Western Mail & Echo Ltd, 1949)

Weller, Ken, *Don't Be A Soldier – The Radical Anti-war Movement in North London 1914–1918* (London: London History Workshop, 1985)

Wilson, Patrick (ed.), *So Far From Home* (Australia: Kangaroo Press, 2002)

Winter, Denis, *Death's Men: Soldiers of the Great War* (London: Penguin Books, 1979)

Wright, Ian, *Ring Out the Thousand Wars of Old – The Forest of Dean World War One Conscientious Objectors* (Bristol: Bristol Radical History Group, 2017)

Official Publications

Army. Report on Recruiting by the Earl of Derby, K.G., Director General of Recruiting (1916)

Army. Report of the War Office Committee of Enquiry into 'Shell Shock' (1922)

Coal Mining Organisation Committee. Report of the Departmental Committee Appointed to Inquire into the Conditions Prevailing in the Coal Mining Industry Due to the War. Part 1 – Report (1916)

Defence of the Realm Manual (London: HMSO, 1918)

First, second, third and fourth reports from the Committee of Public Accounts, together with the proceedings of the committee, minutes of evidence and appendices (1920)

General Annual Report on the British Army for the year ending 30th September 1898 (1899)

General Annual Report on the British Army for the year ending 30th September 1913 (1914)

Judicial Statistics, England and Wales, 1914. Part I – Criminal Statistics. Statistics Relating to Criminal Proceedings, Police, Coroners, Prisons, Reformatory and Industrial Schools, and Criminal Lunatics, for the Year 1914 (1916)

Judicial Statistics England and Wales 1917 Part 1 – Criminal Statistics. Statistics Relating to Criminal Proceedings, Police, Coroners, Prisons, Reformatory and Industrial Schools, and Criminal Lunatics, for the Year 1917 (1919)

Judicial Statistics for England & Wales 1919, Part 1 – Criminal Statistics. Statistics Relating to Criminal Proceedings, Police, Coroners, Prisons, Reformatory and Industrial Schools, and Criminal Lunatics, for the Year 1919 (1921)

Macpherson, Major General Sir W.G., *History of the Great War Based on Official Documents, Medical Services General History Vol. 1* (London: HMSO, 1921)

Manual of Military Law, 6th edn, 1914 (London: The War Office, 1914)

Ministry of Labour. Eighteenth Abstract of Labour Statistics of the United Kingdom (1926)

Mitchell, Major T.J. and Miss G.M. Smith, *Medical Services – Casualties and Medical Statistics of the Great War* (London: HMSO, 1931)

Report of the Commissioners of Prisons and the Directors of Convict Prisons, with Appendices for the Year Ended 31st March, 1915 (1916)

Report of the Commissioners of Prisons and the Directors of Convict Prisons for the Year 1918–1919 with appendices (1919)

Report of the Ministry Overseas Military Forces of Canada 1918 (Canada: Ministry of Overseas Forces of Canada, 1919)

Shipbuilding, munitions and transport areas. Copy of 'report and statistics of bad time kept in shipbuilding, munitions and transport areas' (1916)

Statistics of the Military Effort of the British Empire during the Great War 1914–1920 (London: HMSO, 1922)

Articles

Grady, Dr Kate, 'Disciplinary Offences at the Court Martial' [2016], *Crim L.R.*, Issue 10

Houlbrook, Matt, 'Soldier Heroes and Rent Boys', *Journal of British Studies*, Vol. 42, No. 3 (2003)

Karsten, Peter, 'Irish Soldiers in the British Army, 1792–1922: Suborned or Subordinate?', *Journal of Social History*, Vol. 17, No. 1 (Autumn 1983)

Penton, J.C., 'Lessons from the Army for Penal Reformers', *Howard Journal of Criminal Justice*, Vol. 7, Issue 2, July 1947

Rose, Arnold M., 'The Social Psychology of Desertion from Combat', *American Sociological Review*, Vol. 16, No. 5 (October 1951)

Woodbury, E.N., 'Causes for Military Desertion – A Study in Criminal Motives', *Journal of Criminal Law and Criminology*, Vol. 12, Issue 2, Article 7, 1921

Thesis

Wahlert, Glen, 'Provost: Friend or Foe?: The Development of an Australian Provost Service 1914–1945', MA, University of New South Wales, 1996

Libraries and Archives

British Library, Boston Spa
Leeds Central Library
The Liddle Collection, University of Leeds
The National Archives, Kew

Websites and Online Resources

www.ancestry.co.uk
www.bac-lac.gc.ca – Library & Archives Canada
www.britishnewspaperarchive.co.uk
www.bureauofmilitaryhistory.ie
www.hansard.parliament.uk
www.iwm.org.uk – IWM Sound Archive
www.longlongtrail.co.uk
www.naa.gov.au – National Archives Australia

Index